ENGINEERING YOUR YOUR START-UP

A Guide for the Hi-Tech Entrepreneur

Michael L. Baird

Professional Publications, Inc.
Belmont, CA 94002

Engineering Your Start-Up

Printed in the United States of America

ISBN: 0-912045-48-5

Professional Publications, Inc.
1250 Fifth Avenue, Belmont, CA 94002
(415) 593-9119

Current printing of this edition (last number): 6 5 4 3 2

This book is dedicated
to the memory of
David H. Bowen
(September 19, 1946–May 14, 1992),
publisher of *Software Success*
and the consummate software entrepreneur.

Contents

List of Figures xi
List of Tables xiii
List of Sidebars xv
Foreword xvii
Preface xix
Acknowledgments xxi
Introduction xxiii

■ **Part 1 THE GENESIS**

   1 **Start-Up Opportunities for High-Tech
       Entrepreneurs** 3

      Opportunities for Start-Ups Abound 3
      The Lure of Freedom 5
      The Professional Engineer 5
      The Recent College Graduate 5
      From Technology to Product to Marketing 7
      Is It Time to Create Your Own Job? 7
      Issues to Consider 8
      Small Business: Not Synonymous with
         Start-Up Business 9
      Take Risks! 12

   2 **The Technology-Oriented Professional
       as Company Founder** 19

      Founder's Roles and Responsibilities 19
      Offices 20
      Founder Career Paths 22
      Entrepreneur's Profile 23
      What is Next? 24

   3 **Life in Your Start-Up** 25

      Success and Failure: Statistics 25
      Vacation and Time Off 27
      Working Hours 28
      Divorce 30
      Holding Your Business Together 30

Professional Publications, Inc. ▪ Belmont, CA

Personal Planning Process 30
Allocation of Effort 31

■ **Part 2 GETTING DOWN TO BUSINESS**

4 **Market- versus Technology-Focused Approach
   to Growing a Business** 35
Delivering Benefits to Customers 35
Technology and Markets 35
Rapid Time to Market 40

5 **When High-Growth Business is Desirable
   and Necessary** 43
Why Grow? 43
The Self-Employed 44
Grow a Commanding Position in a Defensible
   Market Segment 44
Attract Customers in Expanding Markets 45
Develop a Product Family 45
Achieve Critical Mass and Economy of Scale 45
Diversify to Diminish Business Risks 46
Create Career Opportunities 47
Create Future Start-Up Opportunities 47
Create Market Value, Attract Investments,
   and Cash Out 47

6 Start-Up Financing Terminology and Stages 49

■ **Part 3 DUE DILIGENCE**

7 **Elements of a Successful Start-Up** 65
Success Ingredients 65
Leadership and Business Basics 66

8 **Create Your Management Team and
   Board of Directors** 69
Management 69
The Entrepreneurial Team 76
Board of Directors 77
Advisory Board 81
Mentors 81

Professional Publications, Inc. ■ Belmont, CA

9 Evaluate Markets and Target Customers 83

Traditional Business Model 83
Customers and Markets 84

10 Define Your Product or Service 91

Overview 91
Choosing the Right Product 92
Finding Good Product Ideas 92
Marketing and Competitive Analysis Considerations 94
Exceptional Product Attributes 98
Producing Your Product 99

11 Write Your Business Plan 107

Form versus Content 107
Types of Business Plans 107
Getting Started 108
Find a Team and Write a Plan, or Write a Plan and
     Find a Team? 109
When to Write the Plan 109
How Long Should It Take to Write Your Plan? 110
Essential Tools 111
Good Business Planning 111
Business Plan Basics 111
Plan Emphasis 112
New Venture Business Plan Outlines 113
Institutional Venture Partners' Suggested Business
     Plan Contents 114
A Personal Favorite 115
Adding or Highlighting Sections 118
Classic Problems 119
Use Standard Ratios 120
Looking Like an Amateur 120
Financial Pro Forma Documents to Generate
     and Master 122
Working Backward 124
Get Good Data 124
Do Not Ignore Your Own Data 124
Balance Sheet 125
Profit and Loss (P&L) Statement 125

Revenue versus Income 127
Sources and Uses of Cash (and Cash Flow) 128
Break-Even Analysis 131
Investor's Hurdle Rate of Return on Investment 132
Exit Strategy 139
Private Placement Memorandum 139

12   Funding Issues 155

Investment Criteria 155
Cheap Start-Ups are Finished 156
Looking for Seed Cash 156
How Much Money? 157
Seed, Start-Up, and Subsequent Funding Rounds 158
The Nightmare: Running Out of Money 158
Where to Get Money 158
Shopping versus Selling Your Business Plan 169

■ Part 4   MAKING IT PAY

13   Remuneration Practices for Your Start-Up 181

Salaries 181
Equity Ownership: Stock and Stock Options 184
Other Compensation 185
Employment Contracts 185

14   Stock Ownership, Grant, and Award Practices for Your Start-Up 187

Risk-Reward Scale 188
Corporations 190
Partnerships 190
Limited Liability Companies (LLCs) 191
Incorporate with a First-Class Lawyer 191
Ownership Interest Over Time 192
How Many Shares Should You Grant? 192
Common and Preferred Stock 194
Authorized and Outstanding Shares 194
Acquiring Stock 195
Founder's Stock 195
Restricted Stock Grants 196
Future Tax Liability on Restricted Shares 199

Section 83(b) Election 199
Transferable Shares 200
Venture Capital Ratchets 202
Punitive Financing 207
When and How Often to Grant Stock 208

15 Stock Option and Stock Option Grant Practices for Your Start-Up 211

Stock Option Grants versus Stock Grants 211
When to Grant Stock Options 212
How Often to Grant Stock Options 212
On How Many Shares Do You Grant Options? 213
Two Kinds of Stock Options 215
Nonqualified Stock Options (NQSOs) 217
Option Vesting and Exercise Schedules 218
Exercising Options 218
The Future of Stock Options 218
A Comparison of Tax and Accounting Effects on
ISOs and NQSOs 219

16 Other Equity and Wealth-Building Vehicles 225

Unrelated Stock Purchase 225
Tax-Free Exchange of Intellectual Property for Stock 227
Investment Through the Provision of Real Property 227
Warrants and Stock Purchase Plans 228

17 Valuing Your Equity Position 233

Terminology 234
Valuation at Launch 235
Valuation at Capitalization 236
The Effect of Founder's Cash on Company Valuation 236
Future Value of the Start-Up as a Multiple of Sales 237
Future Value of a Company by
Miscellaneous Multiples 237
Future Value of the Start-Up as a Function of Sales,
Profit Margin, and Price-Earnings Ratio 238
What Percentage of the Company Value is Yours? 239
Alpha Partners Capitalization Model 240
Von Gehr & Tan Model 240

Q.E.D.'s Valuation Methods 242
Valuation Benchmarks from VentureOne Study 247

18 Other Compensation and Start-Up Employment
    Considerations 249

Entrepreneurs Need Insurance 249
Insurances—Individual or Group? 249
Medical Insurance 250
Retirement Plans 251
Employment Contract 252
Emotional Distress Compensation 253
Golden Handcuffs—When and How to Stay 254
Golden Parachutes—When and How to Leave 254
Summary 255

■ Part 5 DOING IT

19 Making the Start-Up Decision 259

Mortgage the House? 259
Leaving a Current Employer 260
Intellectual Property Protection (IPP) 261
Be Prepared for a Lawsuit 264
Stay Fit 264
What if Your Start-Up Fails? 264

20 Some Final Comments 271

Professional Resources 275
References and Suggested Readings 277
Index 283

List of Figures

Figure 1-1   Rates of Return for 200 Venture Capital-Backed
Ventures from 1973–1983 4

Figure 1-2   Reasons Cited for Starting One's Own Business 6

Figure 1-3   The Income Substitution–Wealth Creation Spectrum 10

Figure 1-4   Forms of New Engineering-Related Businesses 11

Figure 3-1   Annual Time Off for Small-Business Owners 27

Figure 3-2   Anticipated Weekly Time Commitments of CEOs 29

Figure 3-3   Effort Allocated by Founders During First Six Months ... 31

Figure 4-1   Market- and Customer-Driven Technology-Fueled
Business Machine 36

Figure 4-2   Subjective Plot of Potential Risk and Reward 39

Figure 4-3   The Time-Value of Money 40

Figure 6-1   Stages of a Company's Growth 51

Figure 6-2   Twelve Years of IPOs 52

Figure 7-1   Five Controllable Ingredients for Start-Up Success 66

Figure 8-1   Management Completeness-Experience Grid 70

Figure 8-2   Team Size and Product Status in Business
Plan Reception 71

Figure 9-1   Competitive Forces in Your Marketplace 86

Figure 9-2   Marketing Strategy 87

Figure 10-1   Cost versus Perceived Differentiation Model 94

Figure 10-2   Positioning of a Software Product 95

Figure 10-3   Sample Statement of Requirements Outline 100

Figure 10-4   Sample Functional Specification Outline 101

Figure 10-5   Performance Specifications 102

Figure 10-6   Product Design and Development Methodology 103

Figure 11-1   Operational Stages of Company Growth 108

Figure 11-2   Start-Up Scenario 110

Figure 11-3   Productivity for the Top 200 Electronics Companies 122

Figure 11-4   Balance Sheet 126

Figure 11-5   Profit and Loss (Income) Statement 127

Figure 11-6   Plot of Profit and Loss (Income) Statement 128

Figure 11-7   Sources and Uses of Cash Statement 130

Figure 11-8   Simple Cash Flow Statement 131

Figure 11-9   Cash Flow Projection Chart 132

Figure 11-10   Break-Even Analysis Chart: Realistic Case 133

Figure 11-11   Business Plan Toolkit Screen 146

Figure 12-1   Primary Sources for Seed Capital for
               High-Tech Companies 159

Figure 12-2   Angels versus Venture Capital Support 161

Figure 12-3   Computer-Related Seed Deals Closed 165

Figure 12-4   Venture Capital Funding Cycle 167

Figure 14-1   Start-Up Risk-Reward Scale 190

Figure 14-2   Business Ownership Interest Over Time 192

Figure 14-3   83(b) Election Form Letter 201

Figure 14-4   Consequences of Antidilution Ratchet 204

Figure 17-1   Deal Size and Pre-Money Valuation versus
               Stage of Company Development 248

List of Tables

Table 4-1   Market Positioning 36

Table 7-1   Entrepreneurial Success Through Classical
           Management Functions 67

Table 8-1   The Entrepreneurial Team 76

Table 11-1   Operating Expenses for Software Companies
           as a Percent of Revenue 123

Table 11-2   Break-Even Analysis Table 133

Table 11-3   IRR for Given Cash Flow 138

Table 12-1   Summary of Exemptions to Registration
           with the SEC 162

Table 12-2   Recent Reductions in Venture Capital Disbursements 166

Table 14-1   Stock and Stock Options 189

Table 15-1   Tax Effect on Company 219

Table 15-2   Tax Effect on Employee 221

Table 17-1   Popular Methods of Valuation 238

Table 17-2   Alpha Partners Capitalization Model 241

Table 17-3   Valuation Assessment Table by Von Gehr & Tan 242

Table 17-4   First Chicago Method for Valuation 245

Table 17-5   Popularity of Principal Valuation Methods 246

Table 17-6   Equity Relinquished versus Source of Capital 247

List of Sidebars

Resources Available to Start-Up Entrepreneurs 13

Symantec Corporation:
    Responding to a Changing Market Need 42

Financials for Engineers—A Crash Course 54

Trials and Tribulations in the Financing of One
    Start-Up Company 58

Business Plan Writing Aids and Financial Planning Aids 141

One Venture Capitalist's Perspective on Plan Emphasis 150

A Strong-Management Strong-Market Business Plan 152

Software Success—Who Gets Funding How and Where? 176

Playing on Employee Desire for Stock Grants 209

Exploiting Employee Desire for Stock Options 223

Founder Retains Control Through Foresight 231

Digital Vision, Inc., and Contrex, Inc.:
    Schlumberger Ltd.'s Buyout of One of the Author's Start-Ups 266

Professional Publications, Inc. ▪ Belmont, CA

Foreword

Entrepreneurship is the call of the 1990s. This is particularly the case in high technology, where our society continues to place more feverish demands on American ingenuity for improvement and innovation in the products and services that surround our lives. Everyone looks to create the fastest chip, the lightest laptop, and the most powerful software. There is no limit to the technological advances realized with every new product introduced, which is exactly the reason why there has never been a better time to consider an entrepreneurial venture.

It is hard to escape the image of entrepreneurial success in today's media-conscious environment. Multibillionaire founder Bill Gates of Microsoft has appeared repeatedly on the covers of business magazines. Entrepreneur Ross Perot reaches out to be the president of the United States. Successful entrepreneurs are ubiquitous at a time when loyalty to *Fortune* 500 companies continues to diminish amid the trend of layoffs and reorganization. When you consider that the overwhelming majority of new jobs created this decade will come from start-up companies, a high-tech business venture seems a reasonable, if not downright admirable, proposition.

As the president and chief executive officer of Silicon Valley Bank, I have met with thousands of ambitious entrepreneurs from every walk of life. I am very proud to have provided guidance and assistance to many of these individuals, many of whose companies are now quite successful. What do these successful individuals all have in common with each other?

You will not find it surprising when I tell you that these individuals all share the same trait: motivation. Not motivation for wealth, money, or power, though. Rather, the more successful people are those who desperately want and seek out autonomy and challenge. They want to use their drive, skills, and hard work to turn an idea or a dream into a company. Start-up entrepreneurs have a special passion for life and view each new workday as a new challenge. Of course, I know my generalities cannot assimilate life in a high-tech start-up, but I believe *Engineering Your Start-Up* delivers the important information and sage advice those of you considering a high-tech venture need in order to make informed decisions on how to proceed.

Many entrepreneurs who want to start a venture do not know where to begin or what to expect. In this book, classic formulas for success are laid out in no-nonsense terms. Life in a start-up is described vividly, and real-world anecdotes detail both failures and successes. Valuable advice is presented for creating wealth using founder's stock and stock options, which are topics not always familiar to technically oriented entrepreneurs. While the book specifically addresses the high-tech entrepreneur, those considering employment at a start-up will find it helpful in understanding the dynamics involved in working in that environment.

In the investment community, we see higher quality start-ups today than in the 1980s. Competition for venture funding is intense and global. Successful companies plan from day one to attract syndicates of investors who will carry the company from the concept stage through an initial public offering or acquisition by a larger, usually public, company. Many start-ups establish early strategic partnering relationships with customers, suppliers, and governments worldwide. Those companies that are well planned, are created by strong teams, and offer proprietary technology that plays into growing and targeted markets can obtain funding. With funding comes an excellent chance for success. This book will arm you with the knowledge necessary to create such a company.

Life in a start-up is one of the most exciting things you can experience, and I encourage you to explore your options. Do your homework, find your place in life, and live your entrepreneurial dream.

Roger V. Smith
President and CEO of Silicon Valley Bank
August 1992

Preface

"Whatever advice you give, be short."
— Cicero, *Ad Atticum IX*

I first thought of writing this book in 1985, just one week after the president and I decided that our high-tech venture capital-backed start-up must file for Chapter 11 bankruptcy. Although that pending disaster actually turned into a successful corporate acquisition of our company, it did prompt me to seriously reconsider my commitment to entrepreneurship. Today I remain involved exclusively in start-ups, and because so many people have asked for my advice over the years, I committed to put it into writing.

I wrote this book based upon enjoyable and profitable experiences at several start-ups in various stages of incubation: one as the founding president, three as the engineering vice president, one as the marketing vice president, and a number more as a consultant. I hope that you too will benefit financially and obtain enjoyment from creating your new business.

In preparing this book, I have made a special attempt to verify all information, especially as it pertains to the subjects of law, securities, taxes, and investments. However, these laws change frequently and vary state by state (especially securities laws). Therefore, on these important investment, legal, and tax matters, follow this book's advice by seeking expert counsel. You must be prepared to assume full responsibility for the outcome of your decisions.

As we proceed, I will reference a number of books and articles (listed in References and Suggested Readings) that you might want to acquire, read, and keep for reference. It is not practical for me to repeat their more detailed expert opinions and writings that you may need later.

One thing is certain: With your common sense and this book as a guide, you can determine the risks and rewards of starting your new venture. This book tells you which questions to ask and what information you need to obtain to make an informed decision.

Professional Publications, Inc. ■ Belmont, CA

I can guarantee you that starting your own business is going to be the greatest thrill of your life. Creating value for your customers, creating jobs for your employees, contributing to your own success, and giving yourself and your family complete psychological and financial independence will make all the work worthwhile.

Read and enjoy!

Michael L. Baird
August 1992

Professional Publications, Inc. ▪ Belmont, CA

Acknowledgments

*"When life deals us blows that we can't overlook,
some suffer in silence and some write a book."*
— E. B. de Vito, *Wall Street Journal*, July 7, 1987

Completing this book was a wonderfully satisfying affair, and I have lots of people to thank for helping to make it happen. I especially want to acknowledge the gift of precious time and the many contributions made by the following reviewers: Janet Brewer, attorney-at-law with the Law Offices of Janet L. Brewer in Palo Alto, CA; Kenneth R. Allen, attorney-at-law with Townsend and Townsend in Palo Alto, CA; Janet G. Effland, vice president of the venture capital firm Alan Patricof Associates, Inc., in Menlo Park, CA; Anthony C. Bonora, senior vice president of research and development at Asyst Technologies in Milpitas, CA; the late David H. Bowen, publisher of *Software Success* in San Jose, CA; William J. Wall, vice president of finance and administration and CFO of Resumix, Inc., in Santa Clara, CA; Dr. David K. Lam, founder of Lam Research Corporation and president and CEO of Expert Edge Corporation in Palo Alto, CA; Ed Zschau, former U.S. congressman and chairman and CEO of Censtor in San Jose, CA; Dr. Phillip B. Nelson, industrial psychologist with the Institute for Exceptional Performance in San Francisco, CA; and Dr. Jeanne Gilkey of the University of Phoenix in San Jose, CA.

In addition, the following individuals provided advice or resource materials: Bruce W. Jenett, attorney-at-law with Fenwick & West, Palo Alto, CA; Dr. Jim Plummer, president of Q.E.D. Research and venture capital consultant in Palo Alto, CA; C. Gordon Bell of Los Altos, CA, formerly of Digital Equipment Corporation and author of *High-Tech Ventures*; Mary Cole; and Kathy Janoff.

My wife Heidi grammar-checked the manuscript. My terrific kids, Robby and Sandy, missed way too many bike rides with their dad.

Jason Standifer, acquisitions editor at Professional Publications, helped me step-by-step through the arduous process of giving birth to and marketing a book. Wendy Nelson, marketing and acquisitions manager, suggested numerous improvements. Lisa Rominger, production manager, and Jessica Whitney, copy editor, orchestrated production of this book. Also, Mary Christensson was the permissions editor, Lynelle Dodge created the text design and produced the illustrations, Paula Goldstein designed the cover, Sylvia Osias typeset the book, and Kurt Stephan proofread text and illustrations.

Introduction

The fact that start-up companies have been generating new jobs while large established companies have been laying people off has caused a great deal of media attention to be focused on start-ups. At the same time, starting your own business has been glamorized by a steady stream of articles and books about successful entrepreneurs.

The good news is that all of this exposure has made it socially acceptable for people to quit their big company jobs and start their own enterprises. The bad news is that much of the available information for new companies glosses over or completely ignores the monumental effort required to successfully launch an organization. Over the years, numerous entrepreneurs have told me about the discouragement and hard work they faced in launching their companies.

Starting a company is a very difficult process, but much of the discouragement results from unrealistic expectations. When I left Amdahl Corporation to launch my first software company, my boss at the time told me, "Dave, you think this is going to be a sprint, but it's really a marathon." He was the first of many wonderful people who extended a helping hand and showed me the lay of the land.

Starting a company in Silicon Valley enabled me to meet other entrepreneurs who were futher along in their ventures. Some had started dozens of businesses, while others were just beginning their second year. No matter what stage of the game they were at, I learned something from everyone I talked to.

While reading *Engineering Your Start-Up*, I thought back to my early days as an entrepreneur and gleaned new insights into issues I had wrestled with time and time again. Mike Baird reached out and helped me, and, in turn, I shared some of my experiences with Mike, which are included in this book.

If you are considering initiating your own start-up from a large-company environment, I strongly urge you to read this book from cover to cover. Then, reread it every few months and refer back to it with questions as they come up in your business.

Professional Publications, Inc. ▪ Belmont, CA

If you have already started your own business, much of what you read here will confirm what you already know, but you may gain deeper insight into why things are the way they are.

Everyone who reads this book will feel a sense of camaraderie as they read about other people who have embarked on this journey.

Good luck to you all as your businesses grow and evolve!

David H. Bowen

Professional Publications, Inc. ▪ Belmont, CA

1

THE GENESIS

Part One of *Engineering Your Start-Up* discusses opportunities for the entrepreneurial engineer, clarifies your new role as the CEO and founder of your own business, and describes life in your new start-up. If you have not given much thought to how starting your own business might impact your life, then these chapters should be especially beneficial.

■ ■ ■ ■ ■

1

Start-Up Opportunities for High-Tech Entrepreneurs

*"Software opportunities continue to provide the best
paths for engineers wanting to start their own companies."*
— David H. Bowen

Opportunities for Start-Ups Abound

While the number of start-ups may be down from its highest levels, the number that will succeed is not. Although it is true that less venture capital is available these days, those companies good enough to get it are more likely to do well.

As Figure 1-1 suggests, venture capital-backed companies have made money for some, but not all, start-up entrepreneurs. While a venture fund's investors have the safety of diversification, your shot must be on target. Your gain will roughly mirror that of your investors' return in your start-up. So you see, you have roughly a one-third chance of losing money, a one-third chance of breaking even, and a one-third chance of becoming substantially wealthy.

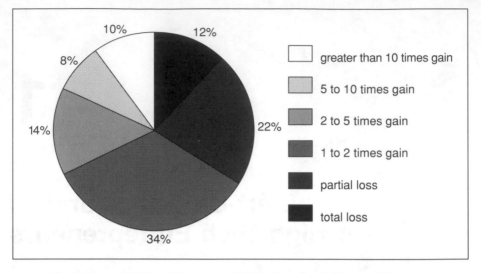

Figure 1-1   Rates of Return for 200 Venture Capital-Backed Ventures
from 1973–1983
Source: TTG Research and J. Trudel, *High Tech with Low Risk: Venturing Safely Into the 90s*

This book teaches you how to launch and finance your successful start-up. There remain numerous areas of opportunity for engineering-related start-up companies, some of which involve markets far larger than those of the 1980s. These new technologies will continue to drive out the old. For example, personal computers are increasingly becoming connected in networks and supplanting what minicomputers and mainframes used to do. That requires new hardware and software tools that you could develop. Hardware and software for pen-based computers are hot, as is software for Windows™-based applications. Medical electronics and biotechnology also continue to cross new horizons, and wireless communication is emerging as an important growth area.

However, as you will come to appreciate, your business success will depend on much more than simply developing an exciting new technology. But that is what you are best at—developing new technology. While others may be expert in marketing, finance, and other aspects of business, they will lack your knowledge of key enabling technology. So who will be the winner? You are betting that you can learn how to plan and build a successful technology-based business faster and better than a nontechnical businessperson can learn how to exploit technological know-how. To discover whether that is a good bet, read on. The winner is usually a person who is most determined to win, and it seems that you have a good head start.

The Lure of Freedom

Autonomy clearly ranks first on the list of reasons why individuals start their own companies, followed by the desire for income and wealth. Figure 1-2, adapted from studies of new firms in Minnesota conducted by Paul D. Reynolds, professor of business administration at Marquette University, illustrates some of the major reasons cited by entrepreneurs for wanting to start their own businesses.

The Professional Engineer

There are over 5 million professional engineers and scientists in the United States. These well-educated, hardworking men and women represent some of the best and brightest talent in our country. Their contributions to the profits of business and industry represent billions of dollars each year. Yet many of these individuals will work extremely long hours, often for minimal satisfaction, security, and financial reward.

One MIT study indicates that about half of these professionals have seriously considered starting their own businesses. Another study by Execunet determined that 60% of corporate executives would start their own business if they could. Sixty percent also would prefer working for a smaller company if they changed jobs. Your dreams are not alone, and this book is the answer. It will teach you how to launch your own successful business and accumulate significant wealth in the process.

In the remainder of this book I often use *engineers* as a generic term that applies to many other technology-oriented professionals. For example, if you are a research scientist wanting to start a business, you will need to become more applied and less theoretical. To be successful, entrepreneurial engineers must become business planners and marketers as well.

The Recent College Graduate

About 200,000 engineering and science college students graduate each year. Many of them dream of starting their own businesses, but are especially frustrated by lack of experience. Nevertheless, this may be the best time to start your own business. Think about it—you have unequaled energy, enthusiasm, fresh knowledge, and university contacts, all of which will diminish over time. Many people at this point in life think that they can do anything, and often they are right! Family burden is frequently less of a problem for a fresh graduate also. What are the risks of taking a plunge?

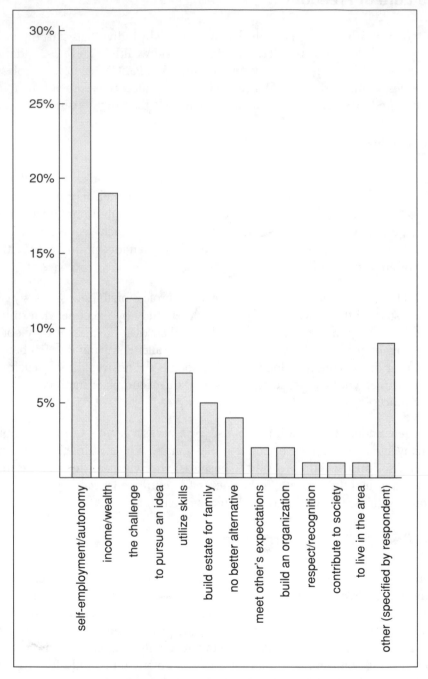

Figure 1-2   Reasons Cited for Starting One's Own Business

From Technology to Product to Marketing

Whether you are a practicing engineer or a recent college graduate, if you have an interest in starting your own business there are many opportunities for you to explore. Dreaming about it is not enough. You need to plan a course of action to launch your successful technology-based business.

- Identify appropriate products to develop based on your technological skills. (As will be discussed in this book, while your products will be technology-based, your business must be market- and customer-driven and technology fueled.)

- Determine how to develop and produce those products.

- Take your products to market rapidly and successfully.

Is It Time to Create Your Own Job?

With a couple of tenuous exceptions such as IBM or Hewlett-Packard, there really is no such thing as job security, even in a *Fortune* 500 company. IBM, for example, is making it tougher for those seeking lifetime employment through their implementation of a new policy requiring a substantial percentage of employees to be rated "unsatisfactory" in performance reviews—forcing many to leave.

Since the mid-1980s, as corporations have responded to global competition and technological change by merging and consolidating, downsizing and delayering, 2 million middle-management positions have been permanently eliminated. American corporations have unilaterally repealed the unwritten law that once bound them to their managers, and have been jettisoning them in carload lots.

The U.S. Bureau of Labor Statistics assistant commissioner Martin Ziegler says that statistical revisions will add 650,000 more jobs lost in the 1991 recession to bring the total number to more than 1.4 million. Furthermore, 700,000 more jobs will be lost in 1992 if corporations keep slashing payrolls at their current pace, says Dan Lacey, editor of *Workplace Trends*. Could your job be one of these?

According to the Bureau of Labor Statistics, early in 1992, the official unemployment rate was around 7.1%, representing 8.9 million Americans. Estimates of true unemployment, however (factoring in the 6.3 to 6.7 million workers holding part-time jobs because that is all they can find and the 1.1 million discouraged workers who are no longer being counted), ranged around 10.4%. In 1991, one in every five American workers was unemployed at some point (25 million people, almost 20% of the workforce) according to the Conference Board, a business research center in New York. One in every four U.S. households in early 1992 included someone who was unemployed in 1991.

David Bowen, publisher of *Software Success*, points out that the real problem for a middle-aged middle manager is holding his or her job for another 20 to 30 years:

> Middle managers are defined as making over $40,000 per year. About one million middle managers lost their jobs in 1991. Since there is about a ten percent chance of losing your job every year, over 30 years, there is only about a four percent chance of holding your job! $(0.90)^{30} = 4.24\%$. And, middle managers who change companies every five to ten years will end up without good retirement plans since they never stayed put.

Issues to Consider

Quitting your job and starting a company is stressful and full of uncertainty. If you are a typical reader, you have been employed for several years in a large, stable company. If you are seriously considering leaving a position that has the appearance of security and a good salary (although with limited financial upside) for the excitement of the fast lane in a start-up, you need to consider for more than a moment what this means to you and your family. There are many important issues, and you need facts to satisfy your concerns. I have listed some major questions that you need to ponder as you read the remainder of this book.

- What are your life goals?

- What are you getting into, and is this really what you want to do? Are you prepared for very hard work, or are you more of a "quality-of-life" person?

- Will your business have a chance to succeed financially? Are you willing to bet your chances for success with one or two other key employees?

- What is your quality of life now, and how would it change?

- Can you separate the excitement and glamour of a start-up from its reality?

- Are you prepared to be consumed by your business? It will never let up and you will never escape it during its formative years.

- What can a start-up do to you physically and mentally? Are you strong and healthy enough to pull off a start-up?

- What are the time demands of a start-up? Do you like to recreate on weekends, or will you work? How much time do you want or need with your family?

- Are you ready for extensive travel and "give it all you have" performances for customers and investors?

- Does establishing and maintaining a reputation in, for example, the research community mean a lot to your personal development? Is going to technical conferences important? Will a start-up afford such luxuries?

- Will you escape that *Fortune* 500 feeling of being a wage slave even if you launch a start-up? Are there other types of captivity that will trap you?

- Realistically, what is the chance to become independently wealthy?

- Can you survive without a paycheck for three to nine months, either while your start-up is getting funded or after your start-up crashes and burns?

- What are the alternatives if you stay? Is there something better between a start-up and your current employer?

- Have you considered the possibility of a start-up ruining a stable marriage?

- Do you thrive on continuous change (not always improvement) or despise it?

- How old are you? When is the best time to move?

- Last, and perhaps most important, is your spouse and family. Will they be fully supportive and excited as well? If not, the additional stress makes your odds much worse. Will you have their support? Their support is critical, since they will share with you the inevitable financial and time sacrifices.

Small Business: Not Synonymous with Start-Up Business

The words *small business* and *start-up* at first may seem synonymous. Clearly not all small businesses are start-ups (check out the VCR rental store on the corner), but most start-ups do begin small. Your start-up is the result of setting in motion a new company, and to what size and at what rate your company grows is critical to your financial success. Though there is some debate concerning what constitutes a small business, for the purposes of this book it is defined as an independently owned and operated company with fewer than 20 employees. A company expanding at a rate of more than 10% a year is considered fast-growing.

Your start-up business, if it survives, is destined to become either an income substitution business or a wealth-building business, as illustrated in Figure 1-3, depending mostly on how fast and large it grows.

People who simply do not want to work for someone else can easily start up a small income substitution business, such as a one-man lawn mowing service. Joe may even earn as much mowing lawns as he did working for Mr. Bemis, and this may make Joe happy. This kind of small business is called an *income substitution business*.

A *consultancy* is a business formed by an individual to provide services and is generally limited to creating an income stream. A *proprietorship* is a business formed by an individual or related family members and also is generally limited to income substitution. You will often find unemployed engineers holding themselves out as consultants.

If your small business does not have high growth as an objective, and it is not team-driven, it most likely will not become the wealth-building vehicle you need for financial success and independence (see Figure 1-4). The successful wealth-building start-up business for engineers, for which this book was written, was characterized by the charter of the bygone Silicon Valley Entrepreneurs Club, which assisted entrepreneurs in

> creating and managing team-driven and high-growth companies. Such companies commonly have annual sales goals of from $10–$100 million or more over a period of three to five years.

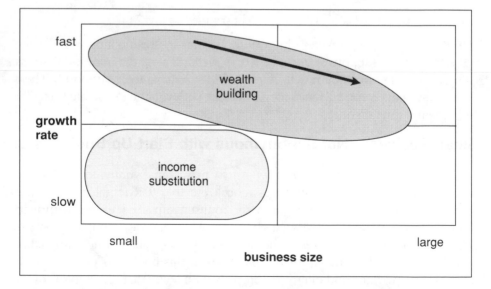

Figure 1-3   The Income Substitution–Wealth Creation Spectrum

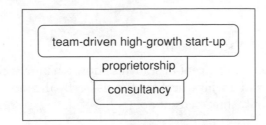

Figure 1-4   Forms of New Engineering-Related Businesses

If Joe has the makings of a true entrepreneur, there is nothing to prevent him from growing a very profitable lawn mowing organization that could create great wealth for him. There may be a need for a nationally recognized quality lawn care franchise, for example.

Robert Ronstadt, publisher of *Ronstadt's Financials*, a software package for financial planning, similarly categorizes ventures into three categories:

Type of Venture	Sales Range	Employees
lifestyle	0 to $1 million	0 to 4
smaller high-profit	$1 million to $20 million	5 to 50
high-growth	over $20 million	over 50

Individuals who want independence and autonomy start lifestyle ventures. These people do not want the aggravation that growing a business entails, and they prefer to conduct their business lives much like their personal lives. There is nothing wrong with wanting to conduct a lifestyle venture, but if that is really your objective, do not try to act like a venture-backed start-up.

Smaller, high-profit ventures allow the entrepreneur not to relinquish equity or ownership control. This can be a challenge to an engineer who may not have access to the financing that a high-growth business requires. This book will be useful for smaller, high-profit business venture planning.

Successful high-growth ventures usually lead to nationally and internationally known businesses. Significant outside funding is required to grow this kind of venture. The engineer aspiring to create a high-growth business will be seeking to maximize the market value of the company, and in the process will create significant wealth for himself or herself, the venture's investors, and many of the company's employees.

Take Risks!

One study from UCLA suggested that

> in kindergarten, 25 percent of students show a natural need for high achievement and a willingness to take risks. By the time they get to high school, only three percent do.

If you really do have that entrepreneurial craving, do not hang on to a job you do not love—jump on the start-up bandwagon, take some calculated risks, and enjoy the rest of your life.

It would be great to retire at 40, if that is what you want to do, but I only know of four ways to such financial independence, and only the last one is truly satisfying and in your control:

- You might marry it.

- You might inherit it.

- You could steal it.

- You could earn it in your start-up.

If risk-taking is not part of your personality, however, you may want to seriously consider keeping your *Fortune* 500 job for as long as possible. Bowen, advisor to many would-be entrepreneurs, says, "I talk to many 'big company employees' who think they want to take risks, but they don't have a clue what risk really is." Look into yourself and try to see what is inside. What is right for you?

Resources Available to Start-Up Entrepreneurs

Accounting Firms

Many of the top accounting and consulting firms along with many banks and law firms publish excellent, free booklets on venture capital, securing financing, private placements, writing business plans, growing a business, business valuations, doing business overseas, going public, etc. By simply making a few phone calls from the Yellow Pages you will have more quality reference material than you will ever need. Some good places to start are:

Coopers & Lybrand

(Ask for *Charting a Course for Corporate Venture Capital* and *Valuation Services.*) Coopers & Lybrand is known for its expertise in business advice. High-tech clients include Atmel Corp., Genus Inc., Cisco Systems Inc., Triad Systems, and California Biotechnology Inc. Coopers & Lybrand would be an excellent choice for the engineering- or technology-based start-up entrepreneur. Contact Alan L. Earhart, Coopers & Lybrand, Ten Almaden Blvd., Suite 1600, San Jose, CA 95113. Phone (408) 295-1020. Additional offices: Boston, Paul Joubert (617) 574-5000; Los Angeles area, Melanie McCaffery (714) 251-7200; San Francisco, Cynthia Feldman (415) 957-3000.

Price Waterhouse

(Ask for *Taking Your Company Public* and *Expanding Into Exports.*) High-tech clients include Applied Materials, Hewlett-Packard, Biogen Inc., Connor Peripherals, and Borland International. Contact Benjamin Brussell, Price Waterhouse, 555 California Street, San Francisco, CA 94104. Phone (415) 393-8500. Additional offices: San Jose, Michael Patterson (408) 282-1200; Boston, Patrick M. Gray (617) 439-4390; San Diego, Thomas E. Darcy (619) 231-1200.

KPMG Peat Marwick

(Ask for *Business Planning* from KPMG's Private Business Advisory Services.) High-tech clients include National Semiconductor, Phillips, Motorola, Siemens, and Sequel. Contact Samuel J. Paisley, KPMG Peat Marwick, 1755 Embarcadero Road, Palo Alto, CA 94303. Phone (415) 493-5005.

Ernst & Young

(Ask for the *Ernst & Young Business Plan Guide, Outline for a Business Plan*, or buy Daniel Garner and Robert Conway's related book, the *Ernst & Young Guide to Raising Capital*.) High-tech clients include Apple Computer, Sun Microsystems, Intel, Tandem Computers, and Genentech. Ernst & Young is the acknowledged leader in professional services for high-technology companies. Contact Roger Dunbar, Ernst & Young, 55 Almaden Blvd., San Jose, CA 95115. Phone (408) 947-5500. Additional offices: Palo Alto, Dave Ward (415) 496-1600; Palo Alto, Ken Lee (415) 858-0505; San Francisco, Mark Pickup (415) 951-3331; Walnut Creek, Mark Pickup (510) 977-2907.

Arthur Andersen & Co.

(Ask for *An Entrepreneur's Guide to Starting a Business, The Life Cycle of a High Technology Company: A Guide for Success, An Entrepreneur's Guide to Developing a Business Plan, An Entrepreneur's Guide to Going Public, Compensation and Strategies for Corporate Directors, Effective Executive Compensation—A Competitive Advantage, Employee Stock Ownership Plans: An Executive Overview*, and *Executive Compensation Strategies*.) Arthur Andersen is the largest accounting firm in the U.S. High-tech clients include Cadence Design Systems Inc., WYSE Technology Inc., Oracle Corp., Amdahl Corp., and Acuson Corp. For Silicon Valley residents, contact Mark Vorsatz, Managing Partner, Arthur Andersen, 333 West San Carlos Street, Suite 1500, San Jose, CA 95110. Phone (408) 998-2112. Additional offices: San Francisco, Thomas B. Kelly (415) 546-8200; Oakland, Marvin A. Friedman (510) 238-1320.

Deloitte & Touche

High-tech clients include Atari, Microsoft, Syntex Corporation, Rockwell International, and 3Com. Deloitte & Touche specializes in providing services to high-technology growth companies. In Silicon Valley, contact Mark A. Evans, Deloitte & Touche, 60 South Market Street, Suite 800, San Jose, CA 95113. Phone (408) 998-4000. Additional offices: Boston, David Elsbree (617) 261-8000; Los Angeles, Alan Frank (213) 688-0800; Costa Mesa, John Moulton (714) 436-7100.

Grant Thornton

High-tech clients include Televideo Computer Systems, Western Microwave, Scorpion Technologies, DocuGraphix, and DSP Technology. Contact Gary J. Gemoll, Grant Thornton, 150 Almaden Blvd., Suite 600, San

Jose, CA 95113. Phone (408) 275-9000. Additional offices: San Francisco, Gary J. Gemoll (415) 986-3900; Los Angeles, Richard A. Stewart (213) 627-1717; Boston, Sanford R. Edlein (617) 723-7900.

Small Business Administration Assistance Programs

The Small Business Administration (SBA) sponsors three major assistance programs for entrepreneurs.

Service Corps of Retired Executives (SCORE)

SCORE is an outstanding organization consisting of more than 12,000 retired and active executives in over 735 chapters and offices across the country. These individuals, having successfully completed their own active business careers, are very willing to provide free advice to start-up entrepreneurs. Use them to your full advantage. SCORE is one of the best-kept secrets and most underutilized organizations around. Look up either SBA or SCORE in your phone book to find a contact.

Small Business Development Centers

SBDCs offer start-ups and growing companies a variety of free services. SBDC's individual state headquarters are usually located in the business school of a university. Sub-centers are located throughout each state. Some centers serve all clients in a region, and others offer specialized expertise to the whole state.

Small Business Institutes

SBIs serve only existing businesses and consist of teams of business school seniors along with graduate students and their professors. These teams will conduct a management audit and provide a confidential case report of your existing business for about $200, and might include a full marketing plan or a focus on one specific area of concern.

Small Business Administration Publications

SBA is an excellent source of more than 50 free and low-cost introductory pamphlets and manuals covering many aspects of starting a small business. Ask for the latest *Directory of Publications*, which is free from any SBA office (see your local phone book), or by calling (800) U-ASK-SBA, which will connect you to the SBA's Office of Public Communications. Or, you could write to Small Business Administration, Office of Public Communications, 409 Third Street SW, Washington, DC 20416. While the

SBA is geared toward the small business, its resources are well worth utilizing during your early growth years.

Incubators

To assist start-ups, many cities offer incubation facilities, which consist of communal office space at reduced rates and a host of business services. To find the incubator closest to you, contact the National Business Incubation Association, 1 President Street, Athens, OH 45701. Phone (614) 593-4331, fax (614) 593-1996. Dinah Adkins is the executive director representing 620 members.

The *Wall Street Journal* (August 9, 1991) reported that the number of incubators has grown to about 450 from 50 in seven years, and they house an estimated 7,500 nascent companies.

Center for Entrepreneurial Management

Joseph R. Mancuso, who has written extensively on business, runs the Center for Entrepreneurial Management, a nonprofit organization consisting of about 3,000 members. Dues of $96 give you the opportunity to network with other entrepreneurs and also a subscription to *Success*. Write to Center for Entrepreneurial Management, 180 Varick Street, Penthouse, New York, NY 10014-4606. Phone (212) 633-0060.

American Management Association

The AMA's Growing Companies Program is directed toward small businesses. Many of the AMA books, self-study guides, audio- and video-tapes, seminars, and conferences are excellent, although not always cheap. Contact the American Management Association, 135 West 50th Street, New York, NY 10020. Phone (212) 586-8100. Individual membership fees are $160.

University Assistance

A couple of university programs can help you get a jump start, regardless of your location.

Massachusetts Institute of Technology
MIT's Enterprise Forum Inc. will analyze product ideas, business plans, or entire companies for about $200. Contact Paul E. Johnson, Director,

MIT Enterprise Forum Inc., Massachusetts Institute of Technology, 201 Vassar Street, Room W59-219, Cambridge, MA 02139. Phone (617) 253-8240, fax (617) 258-7264. Also operated by the MIT Enterprise Forum is the Venture Capital Network. This group can play the role of matchmaker, linking wealthy individual investors or "angels" with entrepreneurs needing start-up cash. See Chapter 12 for discussion on angels and on obtaining funding for your start-up. A fee is charged to both investors and entrepreneurs for a subscription to the network. They also can provide the names of many affiliated organizations. For more information write to the Venture Capital Network, c/o the above address, or call (617) 253-7163.

James Madison University

The Center for Entrepreneurship at James Madison University, an SBA Small Business Development Center, provides a national service called Innovation Evaluation Program. For $100 they will test the feasibility and patent potential of a new idea or product using a computer model. Contact Roger Ford, Director, Center for Entrepreneurship, James Madison University, College of Business Building, Harrisonburg, VA 22807. Phone (703) 568-3227.

2

The Technology-Oriented
Professional as Company Founder

*"At a start-up, life suddenly seems unfair. A deadline
is a deadline. Employees don't have several layers of
management to buffer them from the outside world."*
— T. J. Rodgers, 1986, Cypress Semiconductor

To achieve a successful start-up, portray yourself as your business' founder and
chief executive officer. You will see a picture of excitement, opportunity, and
challenge. Let us look more closely.

Founder's Roles and Responsibilities

As founder of your own company, your business role initially spans the entire
spectrum. Until you have the financial resources to add a competent staff in
which you have great confidence, you are responsible for everything from managing the business and developing your ideas to selling the final product. Your
duties will include everything from signing checks to emptying trash cans, and
you must attend to all the administrative details of starting and maintaining a
business. There are also legal issues in incorporating and licensing the business.
Insurance, taxes, rents, utilities, bank accounts, and letterhead and business

cards will all need to be taken care of during the first week. These things, however, can be fun to work on and might even be delegated to others.

Some much tougher problems represent your first real challenges—managing the five elements of a successful start-up:

1. creating your management team and board of directors
2. evaluating markets and targeting customers
3. defining and developing your product
4. writing your business plan
5. raising funds

Unless you start your company with a seasoned management team, you are the boss, and the burden of each of these elements falls on you. That is why you probably will give yourself the titles of *chief executive officer* and *president*.

Offices

You need to be familiar with the key offices of a corporation and with the roles and responsibilities of those holding such positions. In California, the secretary of state would require you to complete a statement by domestic stock corporations designating your company's

> CEO (i.e., president), secretary, and CFO (i.e., treasurer). The corpo-
> ration must have these three offices in accordance with corporations
> code. Any [or all] of the offices may be held by the same person unless
> the articles [of incorporation] or bylaws provide otherwise.

Chairman of the Board

The *chairman of the board* is the member of the corporation's board of directors who presides over its meetings and who is the highest ranking officer in the corporation. The chairman may or may not have the most actual executive authority in a firm. In some corporations, the position of chairman is either a prestigious reward for a past president or an honorary position for a prominent person, a major stockholder, or a family member. It may carry little or no real power in terms of policy or operating decision-making. In a start-up, the position of chairman of the board is usually initially held by the founder, at least until a sophisticated investor helps fund the company and requests to occupy that position.

Chief Executive Officer

The title of *chief executive officer* (CEO) is reserved for the principal executive. The CEO is the officer of the firm who is principally responsible for the activities of the company. The CEO designation is usually an additional title held by the chairman of the board, the president, or another senior officer (such as a vice chairman or an executive vice president). In most seed-stage and start-up companies, the founder is both the president and the CEO. (Chapter 6 covers the distinctions between seed, start-up, and the various other stages of new companies.)

President

After the chairman of the board, the *president* is the highest-ranking officer in a corporation (unless the president also holds the CEO title, in which case the president and CEO can have more actual executive authority than the chairman). The president is appointed by the board of directors and usually reports directly to the board. In smaller companies the president is usually the CEO, and exercises authority over all other officers in matters of day-to-day management and policy decision-making.

Chief Operating Officer

In larger corporations the CEO title is frequently held by the chairman of the board. This leaves the president or an executive vice president as the *chief operating officer* (COO), responsible for personnel and administration on a daily basis. The COO reports to the CEO and may or may not be on the board of directors. (COOs who are presidents typically serve as board members, while COOs who are executive vice presidents usually do not.) The COO title is also often used in recognition that an operations person has taken on increased responsibility from the president or CEO.

Chief Technical Officer

The title of *chief technical officer* (CTO) is a curious one. It is widely used in Silicon Valley to recognize key individuals upon whom a company is clearly dependent for technical contributions. If you are an engineer with an idea for a product and want to exploit that product in a business start-up, you do not necessarily have to be the CEO and president. Do you really want to manage? If not, maybe you would rather be the CTO. The remainder of this book explores the ramifications of taking on operations management responsibility and your preference should be clearly established by the time you get to the last chapter.

Vice President of Engineering/Research and Development

The position of vice president of engineering is not one to be underestimated. It involves a substantial challenge, and your company's success will depend upon this person's ability to deliver your product on specification, on budget, and on time.

For the vice president of research and development, schedule pressures are not as severe. This person is responsible for developing the technology needed for future generations of your company's products. Most start-ups cannot afford both a vice president of engineering and a vice president of research and development, in which case one person must serve both roles. The company's long-term future rests on this person, and whoever holds this position should be confident in his or her ability to produce future products.

Would you be happy starting your own company, but not holding the top slot? This is a very important question for you to consider. If you want to be successful but have little management experience, it makes a lot of sense to start up with other experienced management. Together, you may all make a lot more money than any one person could alone. We will talk more about management teams later, but plant this option in your mind. Who do you want to be in your new company; what role do you want to play? What will make you happy, while allowing you to meet your financial objectives?

Founder Career Paths

The fact that you are reading this book implies that starting your own business is obviously an idea at the top of your list. However, while you might be determined to start your own business and hold the positions of president and CEO, you may also have a preplanned career path that eventually puts you back into a technical position where you would be most comfortable and happy. This might also make other key employees and your investors quite happy. Investors might even insist that you make such a transition as a condition for continuing to fund the business, especially if they are later unhappy with your performance. One perfectly reasonable career path would lead you initially to start and run your company as president and CEO, and later to assume the position of vice president of engineering or vice president of research and development.

A typical scenario for an engineer founding a high-growth, technology-based company involves first launching that company by holding the president and CEO titles. Later, bringing in professional management and funding may provide the opportunity to move into the vice president of engineering or vice president of research and development role, where one might be most productive and comfortable. The title of chief technical officer would be appropriate in such a situation. Many founding engineers get forced back into those roles either as a condition for obtaining initial or additional venture capital funding, or as a result of poor operating performance. If you want to be the CEO and president, and are up to the task, by all means go for it. However, if you lack the experience or disposition, why not plan to hold a position you would really enjoy?

Professional Publications, Inc. ▪ Belmont, CA

Michael S. Malone's book, *Going Public*, which describes the successful Initial Public Offering (IPO) of MIPS Computer Systems, Inc., quotes the founders as saying,

> One of the things we did right was to recognize that we weren't going to be management. We could help in technology or any place else we were needed, but we were not businessmen. We had seen the stories of big egos that invent something wonderful and then think they can be CEO—and they can't, and it crashes the company. None of us aspired to run the company and that's why we've got this marvelous management team in place.

Learn from others' successes!

Entrepreneur's Profile

Edward B. Roberts' recent book, *Entrepreneurs in High Technology*, contains the most comprehensive study to date of personality traits of the engineer creating a start-up. Many of the characteristics listed below are loosely based on Roberts' scientific observations. If you can associate with many of these statements, then you know this book was written for you, as these are the characteristic influences on becoming a technical entrepreneur.

- I have a long-felt, strong desire to start my own business.

- I had a self-employed father.

- I have a minimum of a four-year undergraduate degree, or a master of science degree in some technical field.

- I think I can do a better job than others in delivering a service or in producing a product. I am willing to work hard for something that is important to me.

- I am very independent and have a continuing need to meet and overcome challenges.

- I have only moderate needs for group achievement and power, and a low need for affiliation. (There is a psychological theory that says everyone holds two of three needs more closely than the third: achievement, power, or affiliation. For example, if you value affiliation with associates and achievement of group results, it is unlikely that you can lead from a position of real power. As an analogy, you cannot maximize both revenue and profits—something has to give.)

- I have at least a decade of work experience.

- I have published more papers and obtained more patents than my associates. I am highly productive.

- In my work, I carry out applied development work, not research.

- In my career, I have already risen to managerial levels.

- I have only modest concern for financial rewards (at the time of start-up).

- I am more extroverted than my technical associates at work, but relative to the rest of the world, I still look more like an introverted inventor than a businessperson.

- In my current place of work, I feel challenged and find satisfaction.

- Although I am an engineer, I tend to buy more books on business than on technology.

- I read the business section of the newspaper nearly every day.

Having these characteristics does not necessarily mean you will be a successful entrepreneur. A strong orientation toward marketing is necessary and is emphasized throughout this book.

What is Next?

The following chapters further describe life in your start-up, and emphasize the importance of teams, high-growth, and a customer- and market-focused versus technology-focused strategy. Studying unfamiliar business and financing terms and visualizing approaches to solving start-up problems will prepare you to create a management team, identify customers and markets, define products and services, write business plans, and obtain funding. Essential wealth-building tools and strategies are extensively described, educating you about unfamiliar yet essential practices involving stock grants, stock options, and other instruments.

3

Life in Your Start-Up

"Few people do business well who do nothing else."
— The Earl of Chesterfield

In this chapter we present some statistics and observations that candidly lay the facts on the line: what are your chances of being successful and happy in a start-up? Some individuals thrive in the excitement of the fast lane. Others encounter an inability to cope with the overload, stress, and constant change start-ups can entail.

Success and Failure: Statistics

What will happen if you launch a start-up—how will your life differ? First, do not assume you will even be able to get started. Optimistically, perhaps only 10–30% of start-ups that seriously look for venture capital actually get funded. Realistically, the number might even be much lower. Any one venture capital firm will typically fund only a fraction (0.6%) of the hundreds or thousands of business plans it receives in any given year. Even should you get the business started, do not take personal success for granted.

- It has been estimated that less than half of the entrepreneurs who start companies surviving five years or more actually remain with their start-up.

- If your company is funded, becomes successful, and goes public, you will earn about $6.5 million within five years.

- Only 10% of venture capital-funded start-ups go public.

- Sixty percent of venture capital-funded high-tech companies go bankrupt.

- Founders of typical high-tech companies own less than 4% of the company after the initial public offering, far less than 10 years ago.

According to Drew Field's book *Take Your Company Public*, in the past few years there have been roughly 700,000 new incorporations each year. However, there have been fewer than 300 initial public offerings—that is only a 0.04% success rate for going public. Keep in mind, however, that this is a distorted figure since it includes all sorts of small businesses.

Michael S. Malone's book, *Going Public*, states that in Silicon Valley, "of the ten thousand or more companies that have been founded in the last three decades, no more than a hundred have gone public." That translates into about a 1% rate for engineering-related start-ups that also successfully complete an IPO.

Edward B. Roberts' *Entrepreneurs in High Technology* also provides a great deal of valuable data.

- The actual failure rate of high-technology companies founded by MIT associates is only 15–30% over the first five years.

- Having a Ph.D. degree leads to more failures than for those with master's degrees, except in certain fields such as biotechnology.

- It may be harder to completely fail than imagined. Only about 20% of the large number of MIT spin-off firms ever are liquidated or go bankrupt. When the press mentions that about 80% of all businesses fail, remember that many of these are small businesses such as gas stations and used car lots.

The so-called living dead make up the majority of the surviving start-up endeavors. These companies do not fail in that they go bankrupt or go out of business, but they do not really succeed either. While some may provide an interesting and stable living for their employees, many others provide low salaries, no capital gains on the company's stock, no retirement funds, and no vacations. These employees might have been better off staying with their former companies. It is important to know when to bail out of a living dead situation.

Vacation and Time Off

More than likely, you will be totally consumed by your start-up business for the first few years. It will be with you every hour of every day. It will seem at times that there is no end to it. The old saying "it ain't over 'til it's over" aptly applies. Any scheduled break, weekly recreation time, or short vacation will provide only a brief respite from the pressures of your business. Bill Gates, founder of Microsoft Corporation, took only two three-day vacations during the first years of his start-up. Even later, he took one week of vacation a year. Do not plan on taking two- or three-week vacations during your first few start-up years either.

The 1991 MasterCard BusinessCard Small Business Survey study of small businesses showed that 22% of their owners took no vacation, as detailed in Figure 3-1. A *small business* was defined here as a firm with at least one employee but less than 100 employees. According to the U.S. Small Business Administration (1988), there are slightly fewer than 4 million such firms in the U.S.

It is well known that small-business owners find vacations hard to take. They fear customers will evaporate. They are reluctant to trust someone else to fill in, and they will convince themselves they are indispensable.

As a start-up entrepreneur you will feel many of these same pressures. You have only so much money and time to complete your product, produce sales, and generate revenues. Will you take two weeks off to recharge during your concept development, seed, or start-up phases? Probably not. You may very well go three to ten years without taking a real vacation. Even if you do get a few days

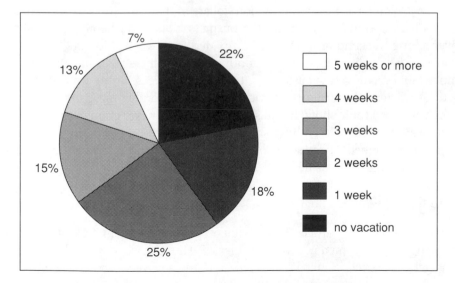

Figure 3-1   Annual Time Off for Small-Business Owners

Professional Publications, Inc. ▪ Belmont, CA

off now and then, you will likely find that you need or want to be in constant communication with those in the office.

It is difficult to imagine the CEO today who does not have a cellular phone in his or her car, and who is not in constant touch with the organization, its customers, and its investors. Home facsimile machines and portable computers with modems for accessing electronic mail (ubiquitous today) truly make getting away from work impossible. The fact that you will probably take your computer with you on a family vacation could also have an impact on your family. They may wonder why you even came along if you have to work so hard.

However, it is possible to remain very calm and relaxed as you start a venture, acting on the notion that it is good for the business to get away and recharge yourself at regular intervals. In this way you may do well enough, but you most likely will not maximize the growth and valuation of your business. Putting recreation ahead of business is a quality of life issue, a priority only you can establish. Just be aware that there will be many internal pressures within yourself, along with external pressures that you cannot always ignore.

For example, are you really going to skip that next board meeting where you need to ask for some more funding? Is it a good idea to turn down the invitation to attend your lead VC's annual CEO meeting? Should you send someone else to talk to that critical customer who is considering taking his business elsewhere? As a start-up entrepreneur, you are an integral part of your new company, and you will find that you need to be available to handle such situations.

Perhaps if you have one or two million dollars in the bank, are still on plan, and have no exceptional problems in the business, you might be able to go skiing over a long weekend or head off to Club Med for a week. More likely, though, you will be coming up with yet another new business plan and looking for more money, cultivating customers, finding employees, lining up distributors, setting up manufacturing or service operations, conducting a press tour, or preparing for a trade show. It will seem that there is never enough time. But for a dedicated, intelligent, enthusiastic person, the stressful period in a start-up is greatly outweighed by the sense of accomplishment and fulfillment of creating your own successful business.

Working Hours

A 1991 *Inc.* magazine article showed that 66% of the founder CEOs of the fastest growing *Inc.* 500 companies worked at least 70 hours a week while the company was getting started. Only 13% were still doing so five years later. Figure 3-2 details the results of the *Inc.* 500 study. The only founders who managed 40 hour

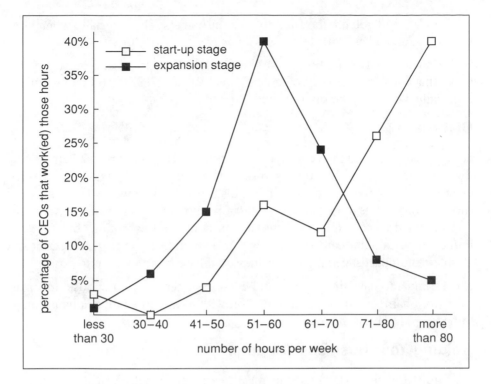

Figure 3-2   Anticipated Weekly Time Commitments of CEOs

or less workweeks were presumed to have been involved in other businesses at the time of start-up.

As one drives past the many high-technology business parks housing start-up companies in Silicon Valley, it is not unusual to see cars in the parking lots on Saturdays and Sundays. Workweeks of six or seven days are more common than the standard five-day workweek.

Evidence suggests that start-up entrepreneurs typically work well over 10 to 12 hours a day, six to seven days per week. That is almost double the number of hours put in by the typical *Fortune* 500 employee. In fact, in your start-up, you might work even more than this, considering that every night you will bring something home. If nothing else, you will have problems to ponder, or work-related reading. Gates of Microsoft, for example, found himself regularly working 65 hours a week, even after his company went public. More than once start-up entrepreneurs in the hard-driving, high-technology Silicon Valley may find themselves working around the clock to meet an important deadline. It is not unusual to find sleeping bags tucked away in a cabinet for those nights when it is too late and you are too tired to make it home safely, especially when you have to be up and at it in a few hours anyway.

If you already work long hours like this for someone else, then you will be in good shape for starting your own company. Working hard can be rewarding, especially if it is for your own business.

Divorce

Start-up entrepreneurs have a high divorce rate. They may prefer being with their businesses more than their spouses. The pressure and stress of a start-up can tarnish any relationship with time. This is not to say, however, that start-ups cause divorces. It is more likely that start-up entrepreneurs typically have more reasons for divorce. Roberts' observations reinforce this notion, but he also found empirical data hard to come by. You should, however, think seriously about what impact starting your business will have on those around you.

It is essential to have the support and encouragement of your spouse during a start-up. Sharing your vision and mission with a supportive loved one is going to be very important to you.

Holding Your Business Together

William H. Davidow, a famous Silicon Valley venture capitalist and author, states, "There has to be something that holds a company together beyond making money...the glue is that your people better love what they're doing, better be committed to the mission, [and] better believe in winning." While Davidow was addressing the problem of managing MIPS Computer Systems, Inc., after going public, his words apply to every phase of your start-up. This is your leadership challenge: to impart this same love, commitment, and belief to your team! Chapter 8 will discuss further the importance of building such a team, and how to make it happen.

Personal Planning Process

When considering whether (and if so, how) to continue with your venture, you will want to examine the personal side of starting your own business. You need satisfying answers to questions that might not come out during the traditional business plan writing process described in Chapter 11.

First, you should clearly establish an alignment of the compelling interests of yourself and your founding team. What are the personal driving forces behind your wanting to start this venture? Do you each share a common vision of the company's mission? What product will be built? Who will be the customers? How fast and how large will the business grow? Apple Computer, for example, set out to create an insanely great product. All the founders believed that, and their success followed. However, you need to do more than simply recognize the need for establishing this common vision and alignment of interests. The remainder of this book should guide you toward achieving that goal.

Second, you need to objectively assess the motivation and expectations of the founding team.

Do not jump into the business plan writing mode until you have thought out the preceding questions.

Allocation of Effort

Roberts measured the allocation of effort in technology start-ups by engineer-founders during their first six months of business. He found that less than one-third of their time at work was spent in engineering, as shown in Figure 3-3.

The lesson here is that, while you may be successful, you may not always spend your time doing what you thought you would be doing. The following chapters discuss how you can make your business successful, rewarding, and fun.

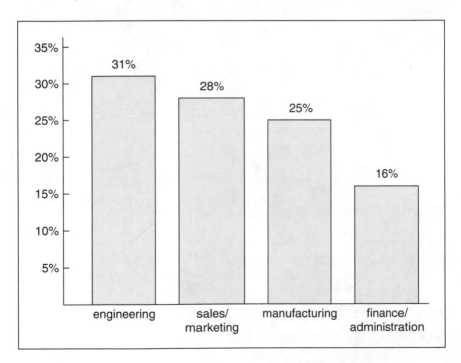

Figure 3-3   Effort Allocated by Founders During First Six Months

2

GETTING DOWN TO BUSINESS

Part Two of this book deals with some important concepts that can make or break your start-up endeavors. As an engineer, you especially must develop a keen appreciation for the essential role of marketing as a focus for growing your business. You must realize that growth will be essential for your success, and you should learn the basic finance-related terminology you will encounter as you launch your start-up.

4

Market- versus Technology-Focused Approach to Growing a Business

"Marketing is essentially viewing the enterprise from the viewpoint of the customer, and there is very little difference between it and the management of the enterprise as a whole."

— Peter F. Drucker

Delivering Benefits to Customers

If your technology enables you to quickly develop a unique product that customers will purchase, satisfying a vital market need and leading to rapid profitability, then you are on the right track. However, engineers are especially apt to neglect the essence of a successful business, which is delivering benefits to customers. Delivering benefits is not the same as selling technology.

As Figure 4-1 depicts, the elements of a successful business include, among other concerns, technology and markets.

Technology and Markets

Technology is certainly an essential element of an engineering-related start-up. However, to focus your business on your technology alone is foolhardy. Understanding and exploiting markets is also an essential element of any start-up.

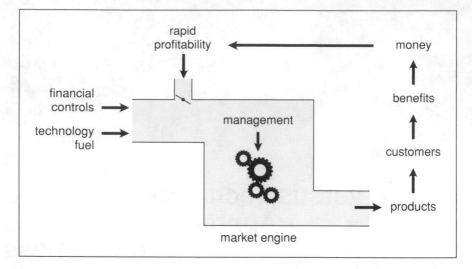

Figure 4-1   Market- and Customer-Driven Technology-Fueled Business Machine

Market Positioning

Where does your proposed product fall in Table 4-1?

Table 4-1   Market Positioning

new market	II marketing driven (new use for an existing product)	I missionary sales, technology push
existing market	III face entrenched competition	IV market-driven, technology-fueled, market pull
	existing product	new product

If your product falls in any quadrant other than quadrant IV you need to be careful. An examination of each quadrant follows.

In quadrant III, the *existing product/existing market* quadrant, you would be a new entrant in the marketplace. Although perhaps acceptable for an income substitution business, this is probably not a lucrative market position for a technology-oriented engineering start-up. Opening a new restaurant would fit into this category.

Quadrant II, the *existing product/new market* quadrant, represents an opportunity for a business with superior marketing and selling skills to create new demand for an existing product. Typically, engineering-related firms will not play in this position. An example is 3M, which found lucrative markets for tape-based products. 3M's Post-it™ brand self-stick removable notepad is an excellent example of marketing an existing technology (glue and paper) to a new market (almost everyone who works in an office).

Quadrant I, the *new product/new market* territory, is the classic yet very difficult path taken by pioneering, technology-driven entrepreneurs. These individuals take all the arrows in their backs, often only to have new market entrants quickly exploit their expensive ground-breaking efforts. Of course, there have been some big successes in this area, but there have also been some very big failures.

The first video games and home computers are examples of new products that played in new markets. The markets in these cases absorbed almost everything offered. However, early players often had a rough beginning. Texas Instruments, for instance, offered a home computer that was wonderful for playing games. But it had to be patient and dig deep into its pockets because it took a couple of years to get the FCC approval that finally made the new products attractive to the market. Other ventures (such as Trilogy's attempt to create wafer-scale integration electronics for computers) consumed hundreds of millions of investors' dollars before ultimately failing.

Quadrant IV, the *new product/existing market* quadrant, is the safest category. Here, you can leverage your engineering technology to produce an advanced, new product, delivering more benefits at lower cost to customers in a market that is not only receptive to but demanding your new development. Here you let the market pull you into deciding which product to develop. Do not push your technology onto a resisting market.

Technology Push

A business focus based on technology is often called a *technology push* because you are relying on your new technology to push customers into a new market.

Engineers, especially, are likely to have ideas for products never before imagined. Our discussion throughout this book on the importance of identifying customers and markets for your products emphasizes your need to have a commanding position in a protected market niche. You do not need a new product to do that. Instead, you can simply "do the common thing uncommonly well," says Paul Oreffice, chairman of Dow Chemical. A new concept is usually evident to the market, and it is difficult to develop any fresh idea in total secrecy. Also, unless you have an enforceable patent, you would not have a significant advantage over rivals entering into competition with you. A really new idea will place you in technology-push territory where you will be forced to do missionary sales, which require educating the market. This delays the profitability of your idea.

A good example of the difficulty of pushing brand-new technology into new markets to achieve business success is reflected in the experiences of Xerox Corporation. In many of Xerox's attempts to exploit new markets using the most advanced technology, other companies ultimately reaped the rewards when the markets were ready.

Market Pull

Many high-technology start-ups are finding that instead of pushing breakthrough hardware technology onto the market, they are better off by participating at the commodity level and distinguishing themselves through exceptional service and cost. Niche-oriented markets with ever-shortening product life cycles characterize the 1990s. Products must increasingly be designed for world markets. From inception, growth businesses will need to compete globally.

A viable business model is to recognize unique market opportunities that slightly stretch state-of-the-art technology, and then develop products based upon these identified market needs and your technological capability.

A business focus based on market need is often called *market pull* because you are relying on the market's desire for a specific benefit to be met through an expansion of state-of-the-art technology. In market pull, the customers are ready and you must deliver the technology. In technology push, on the other hand, the presence of customers is questionable even if you can deliver the technology.

Market- and Customer-Driven Technology-Fueled Strategy

The key to launching a successful technical start-up is to make maximum use of any proprietary technology you can develop while, at the same time, focusing on market opportunities. This is called a *market- and customer-driven technology-fueled* strategy. The term *market-driven technology-fueled* was first embraced and popularized by Measurex Corporation in the 1980s to guide its business.

New Markets

If, instead, you have a new technology focus, you may be forced to create new markets to sell your products. Creating a new market for a new product is a very difficult and expensive task. It will take extra money and extra time to reach a break-even point if you are creating both a new product and a new market. You must strive for rapid profitability.

Risk and Reward

Of course, the less market risk you entertain, the fewer rewards you might expect. For example, if in the early 1990s you chose to compete in the personal computer mass storage arena, you had several choices of products you could develop. As depicted in Figure 4-2, a low-risk, very low-reward strategy would point you toward an existing "me-too" stable product such as the 3.5-inch hard disk drive market. Clearly this market lags behind technology capability. A more moderate avenue would have you developing 2.5-inch hard disk drives for notebook and pen-based computers, but you would have lots of competition and the rewards would be tempered. A higher risk path with higher potential rewards would have you developing the smaller sub-two-inch drives, already in development, and clearly desired (pulled) by the market for even more portable and compact computers. Slightly more risky would be a pure market pull memory card substitute for rotating media storage devices. On the other hand, a technology push product approach would have you developing exotic memory substitutes like holographic memory modules.

After you have itemized your alternatives, make sure that:

1. your potential rewards exceed your risks
2. you maximize the spread between potential risk and reward
3. the market does not lag your technology capability
4. your technology is pulled by the market
5. you do not push your technology on the market

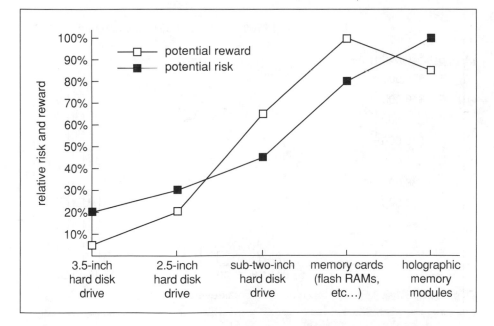

Figure 4-2   Subjective Plot of Potential Risk and Reward

In our example, the technology-focused holographic memory module approach might be most attractive to you as an engineer, but the current market clearly desires more down-to-earth products such as memory cards and smaller disk drives. Deal with your technology-related product ambitions in manageable risk stages. If you take on a risky product, make certain that you have the financial backing to complete it. The greatest mistake you can make is to start a business that you cannot finance. If you need to raise money to move on to the next stage of risk, make sure that you secure adequate financing. If you run out of money, you will lose all control of your business.

Rapid Time to Market

Rapid time to market and rapid profitability are commonly recognized as keys to start-up success. Time consumption, like cost, is quantifiable and therefore manageable. Today's new-generation companies recognize time as the fourth dimension of competitiveness and, as a result, develop new products rapidly, operate with flexible manufacturing and rapid-response systems, and place extraordinary emphasis on research, development, and innovation. Organizations are structured to produce quick responses rather than low costs and control. Figure 4-3 illustrates the mathematics of the time-value of money with a conceptual view of the different capital investments that would be required to achieve break-even in the years indicated.

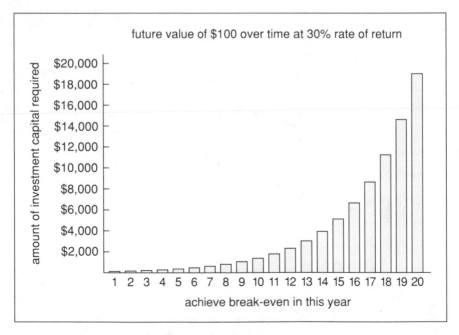

Figure 4-3   The Time-Value of Money

The figure depicts a typical venture capitalist desiring returns of 30% compounded annually. You can see that if you double your time to break even, you will exponentially increase the investment needed.

By becoming a time-based competitor, your start-up can get there first and develop a distinct competitive advantage over more technically sophisticated companies that attempt to push the market.

Symantec Corporation: Responding to a Changing Market Need

In the early 1980s, a large number of high-technology companies were launched in the area of artificial intelligence (AI). AI included robotics, computer vision, and natural language understanding. Each of these areas drew substantial investments but almost none returned any rewards. It was a classic case of technology push. The market in the 1980s for products derived from AI technologies was virtually nonexistent despite the millions of dollars poured into it.

Symantec Corporation originally intended to develop AI products that enabled a computer to understand natural language. Potential applications ranged from natural language translators for the military and tourists to typewriters to which one could speak. Unlike most AI start-ups, Symantec's new management finally realized that the market was not responding to its technology and shifted focus before it was too late. Today, Symantec is a leading public company in the personal computer utility software market. (You may recognize it not only for its well-known SAM software to ward off computer viruses, but also its acquisition of Norton Utilities.) Its new market has proven to be one of the highest margin niches venture capitalists could have invested in during the early 1990s.

Symantec was successful because it responded to market need. This is an interesting case because Symantec seemingly abandoned its technology base. On closer examination, however, it was obvious that its marketable technology consisted of exceptional state-of-the-art computer science and programming skills that could be applied to pressing market needs. Added to Symantec's technology fuel was its savvy market-driven strategy, which resulted in admirable success.

Professional Publications, Inc. ▪ Belmont, CA

5

When High-Growth Business is Desirable and Necessary

"A growing company in a growing market can survive
a lot more management blunders and bad luck than
a company in a stable market and still succeed."

— Gordon B. Baty

Why Grow?

Understanding the importance of growth in business is something one learns. Few engineers have had the required training in finance and economics to internalize the need for growth, and the need is not obvious through introspection. Thus, one of the most difficult concepts for entrepreneurs to understand is why their new businesses must grow. It follows that one of the most difficult conclusions for an engineer to accept is that growing a successful business involves much more than engineering and technology. Often the CEO of an engineering-related start-up will be engaged in almost everything except engineering and product development.

The primary purpose of this chapter is to explain why growth is not only desirable, but necessary, if you are to achieve even modest financial objectives.

The Self-Employed

If you are a self-employed engineer and want to create wealth, you must focus on growth. Many engineers become self-employed (consultants) and motivated by losing a job. If you find yourself in this position, you need to understand the limits of your success as a one-person business.

The 1990s revealed an increasing number of self-employed entrepreneurial individuals. About 8.97 million people (7.7% of all workers) were self-employed. This was the highest level of self-employment in 25 years. Few of these people quit their jobs voluntarily. You will want to do better than these individuals; the average income from a business owned by one person was only $12,352 when doctors and lawyers were excluded. As you launch your technology-based start-up, whether motivated by choice or by losing a job, you will need to look to growth for financial success. Since one-person businesses (which, by definition, cannot grow) do not yield significant incomes nor do they create vast wealth, the successful entrepreneur must look for growth opportunities.

Grow a Commanding Position in a Defensible Market Segment

According to William H. Davidow's *Marketing High Technology*, "Marketing must invent complete products and drive them to commanding positions in defensible market segments."

What this means in terms of growth is that your business must expand at least to the point where it can survive. A General Electric study showed that companies with a market share greater than 30% were almost always profitable, whereas companies with a market share of less than 15% almost always lost money. Since mathematically no more than six companies can have a greater than 15% market share, you must grow your business to one of a few commanding a 15–30% minimum market share. This does not mean you have to be a giant company to play in a giant market. Rather, you must identify segments of your market that you can dominate (that requires growth). Before you try to compete with General Motors or IBM, make sure you can garner a 15% minimum market share in a small, related, and well-protected market segment.

Joe Christenson, president of Pattern Processing Technologies, Inc., stated the case well for his company in a recent annual report.

> Despite a trend towards continuing consolidation in the late 1980s, the market is still fragmented with over 40 companies capturing a portion of the market. Our goal at PPT in the 1990s is to grow faster than the market and thus continue to increase our market share and successfully ride the trend toward consolidation.

Christenson clearly understands that growth is essential not only for extraordinary success, but also for mere survival.

Attract Customers in Expanding Markets

Although it is understood that customers want to be sure their vendors will still be around in a few years to provide them with parts, service, software upgrades, etc., it is frustrating for the start-up engineer to make a sales presentation and then hear the customer say, "The product is just right, but will you be there next year to service it?" After all, how are you supposed to launch your new business if customers want to purchase only from proven sources? This is one reason you need to identify an unfilled market need, and to provide a product with several times the performance-price advantages over competitive products.

Many start-up businesses find good customers in *Fortune* 500 companies. Individual customers in these companies often associate with a struggling entrepreneur, and will help you over many hurdles. In return you need to help these individuals do their jobs well by providing a product that delivers on its promises.

Develop a Product Family

A single product does not constitute a business. Therefore, you must strive to provide a family of products to meet market needs. You should grow to provide solutions to different customers with differing needs. For example, a successful software company will need to make its software available on a variety of hardware platforms and operating systems.

Because customers are most often drawn to brand names, your product's trade name will only gain national or international recognition with volume sales and extensive publicity. Marketing communications and public relations efforts need to be amortized over a large, growing product base.

Since your first product serves a finite part of the market, you must grow to reach new markets with new needs. If you have only that first product, once your market is saturated your business ceases to grow.

Achieve Critical Mass and Economy of Scale

All the supporting infrastructure of your business, including your plant and equipment, management salaries, inventory control systems, accounting systems, and all other fixed costs, need to be spread out over your product base. Without a growing product base, the single-product enterprise will soon be overburdened with fixed costs. Until your company revenues exceed some critical mass, your fixed costs will restrain profitability.

Growth also permits you to add staff with specialized experience to your business. Without a sufficient volume of activity, you and your managers will be forced to become jacks-of-all-trades: you may be doing many things, but no one thing is being done well or efficiently. Since your business must be efficient to be competitive and profitable, it follows that you will need an expanded staff including various divisions of expertise. To attract top employees to your business you must provide both opportunity and financial reward. These, too, come from growth.

Economy of scale applies to every successful business. Henry Ford was perhaps the most famous entrepreneur to understand and apply the concepts of economy of scale to achieve critical mass, as he introduced mass production and the moving production line, transforming the early twentieth century handcrafted automobile business into a modern industry.

The Boston Consulting Group's 1968 book *Perspectives on Experience* argued that the cost of doing business decreased 20–30% every time business (sales) doubled. Although the BCG recommended that "if market dominance cannot be achieved, then an orderly withdrawal from the business is best," you will not always have to completely dominate a market. Many markets can support a number of successful companies, particularly if the markets themselves are growing.

Diversify to Diminish Business Risks

Though it has been said that you can always win the game of business as long as you do not place all your bets on one product, one customer, one supplier, or one investor, some attempts are going to fail. By diversifying your business, however, by producing a family of products and selling to customers in different industries, you will increase your chances for success. It is wise, though, to make sure you have established yourself on solid ground (i.e., established a 30% market share) before you start diversifying.

Your company must grow in order to diversify. This is not to say you should not stick to what you know best, however. As your business grows and reaches customers with different economic buying cycles and different problems to be solved, you will decrease the risk that a single catastrophic event could end your business.

Start-ups are exciting and risky, and you can thrive on that precariousness to make the most of your personal, financial, and emotional investment, but you do not want to persist in that state of uncertainty forever. It may be an oversimplification, but most start-ups are destined to either die, join the the living dead (i.e., barely subsist), or grow to success. For example, if you stay small and maintain a one-customer, one-product kind of business, you will someday have a cash-flow crisis that will bankrupt your venture. If you grow just to the size where your business breaks even, you have created an income substitution business. Finally, if you grow and never stop, you can achieve great wealth and security.

If you have to be in a start-up to get your kicks, do not make it the same start-up for a decade! Grow to success, and then restart if you have to.

Create Career Opportunities

Great companies are run by great people. Great people are attracted to great companies. Getting, and then keeping, key employees is essential. Exceptional people need to grow, to learn, and to take on increasing responsibility. Only a growing company can provide such an attraction for the people you need. Almost everyone wants to be promoted to a better position, and those positions can only be created through growth.

Create Future Start-Up Opportunities

One of the best sources of a start-up idea is one's previous employer. If your company grows, it will create an abundance of new ideas. Not all of these ideas can or should be exploited by the core business, and many employees will someday leave to create new start-ups, based in part on exploiting these untouched opportunities. These start-up opportunities can be yours if you choose. Or, your company can beneficially invest in those ideas that need a start-up environment to flourish by providing initial funding in exchange for equity ownership (in new start-ups).

Create Market Value, Attract Investments, and Cash Out

You and your investors will someday want to exchange your stock certificates for cash. To do this, your company must be of sufficient size and profitability to either go public or be acquired by another (usually public) company. In either case the result is that you and your investors would then hold marketable securities. This is normal and desirable—and it requires that your company grow.

6

Start-Up Financing Terminology and Stages

> *"Money is the seed of money, and the first guinea is sometimes more difficult to acquire than the second million."*
> — Jean Jacques Rousseau, *A Discourse on Political Economy*

This book is concerned with the formation of your new company, which falls into the category of early stage financing—what is loosely called a *start-up*. Starting and developing your own successful high-growth company will take you through several major financing stages, known in investment circles as early-stage financing, expansion financing, and IPO/acquisition/buyout financing.

Each of these stages consists of key financing events. For example, in early-stage financing, there is a *seed* financing event that occurs when you first obtain funding to launch the business (or even just to explore a product idea or for research and development, long before there is a business), *start-up* financing, which is used for product development and initial marketing, and *first-stage* or *early-development* financing, which allows you to initiate manufacturing and sales. Many venture capitalists speak of seed financing events as comprising a separate investment stage because of the diversity and range of scope in these incubation deals.

The best way to characterize the stages of your company's growth is to speak the language of investors. Stanley E. Pratt's *Guide to Venture Capital Sources* and James L. Plummer's *Q.E.D. Report on Venture Capital Financial Analysis* converge on the investment community's various definitions. You must understand what these investment and company growth terms mean if you are to properly represent your situation to prospective investors, team members, and employees. Figure 6-1 is derived from Pratt's and Plummer's prose.

From Figure 6-1, it is evident that a start-up is a private company in a very early stage of maturation. It is thus interesting to note that the term *start-up* is often inappropriately used in reference to young public high-technology companies. Someone once said start-up is a state of mind. Perhaps some of these companies are able to retain the flair of start-ups, but most likely they would not have the risk, financial leverage, and reward opportunity, or the lack of infrastructure, instability, and uncertainty associated with a true start-up. Nor do they meet the start-up financing level description of "not having sold product" yet.

The term start-up as used by the layperson is often similarly misused by the first-time entrepreneur in his or her representations to investors. Be certain not to expose naïveté in these circumstances. Likewise, the term early development is often erroneously used to refer to a pre-start-up or pre-seed-level company. If you incorrectly represent your recently incorporated but yet uncapitalized company to an investor as one in early development when it is actually in pre-seed stage, you probably just lowered your valuation by about 50% in his or her eyes! Study Figure 6-1 closely before approaching investors for funds. You must speak the language to play the start-up game. There really is not that much to learn here, but it is essential that you learn a few key terms. This chapter has been kept short so that you can study and master this vernacular.

You should be conversant with expansion financing terms and business growth milestones. Postexpansion financing terminology helps you recognize the need and understand the alternatives for cashing out when you are finished with your start-up. You will hear your investors discussing their postexpansion financing exit strategies. They will need to return to themselves, their limited partners, or other funding sources their invested capital and gains at some point in time, usually within three to seven years. During weak IPO markets (e.g., during the late 1980s into 1990), investors found themselves taking a longer ride with their private start-up investments than in the past (e.g., during the mid-1980s). During a strong IPO market, such as that experienced in 1991 and early 1992, things turn around rapidly. However, no one can predict how long the latest hot IPO market window will last.

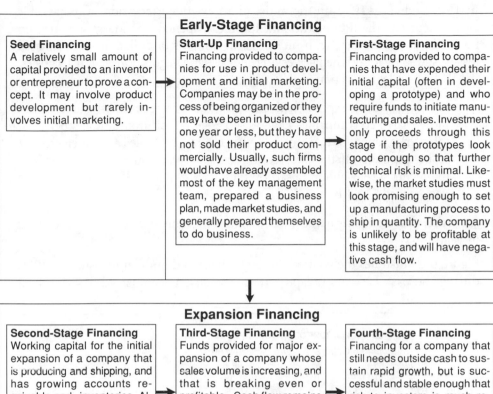

Early-Stage Financing

Seed Financing
A relatively small amount of capital provided to an inventor or entrepreneur to prove a concept. It may involve product development but rarely involves initial marketing.

Start-Up Financing
Financing provided to companies for use in product development and initial marketing. Companies may be in the process of being organized or they may have been in business for one year or less, but they have not sold their product commercially. Usually, such firms would have already assembled most of the key management team, prepared a business plan, made market studies, and generally prepared themselves to do business.

First-Stage Financing
Financing provided to companies that have expended their initial capital (often in developing a prototype) and who require funds to initiate manufacturing and sales. Investment only proceeds through this stage if the prototypes look good enough so that further technical risk is minimal. Likewise, the market studies must look promising enough to set up a manufacturing process to ship in quantity. The company is unlikely to be profitable at this stage, and will have negative cash flow.

Expansion Financing

Second-Stage Financing
Working capital for the initial expansion of a company that is producing and shipping, and has growing accounts receivable and inventories. Although the company has clearly made progress, it may not yet be showing profit, and cash flow may still be negative.

Third-Stage Financing
Funds provided for major expansion of a company whose sales volume is increasing, and that is breaking even or profitable. Cash flow remains a concern. These funds are used for further plant expansion, marketing, working capital, or development of an improved product.

Fourth-Stage Financing
Financing for a company that still needs outside cash to sustain rapid growth, but is successful and stable enough that risk to investors is much reduced. The cash-out point for venture capital investors is thought to be within a couple of years.

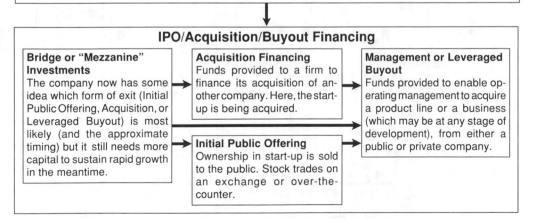

IPO/Acquisition/Buyout Financing

Bridge or "Mezzanine" Investments
The company now has some idea which form of exit (Initial Public Offering, Acquisition, or Leveraged Buyout) is most likely (and the approximate timing) but it still needs more capital to sustain rapid growth in the meantime.

Acquisition Financing
Funds provided to a firm to finance its acquisition of another company. Here, the start-up is being acquired.

Initial Public Offering
Ownership in start-up is sold to the public. Stock trades on an exchange or over-the-counter.

Management or Leveraged Buyout
Funds provided to enable operating management to acquire a product line or a business (which may be at any stage of development), from either a public or private company.

Figure 6-1 Stages of a Company's Growth

Professional Publications, Inc. ■ Belmont, CA

In 1991 and early 1992, in the midst of an extended recession, a remarkable event occurred: the IPO market unexpectedly opened up. Many start-ups on the verge of bankruptcy, with nil sales and millions of dollars in accumulated losses, suddenly found themselves on the IPO bandwagon. On March 19, 1992, the *Wall Street Journal* reported that

> IPOs continue to explode with sales headed for a record first quarter. More than 120 companies have raised $7.4 billion from initial stock sales since January 1. At this rate, first quarter IPO sales are expected to be a record. If the pace continues, this year could well shatter the record $18.3 billion raised by IPOs in 1986, as well as last year's near-record $16.4 billion.

All of this was happening in the midst of one of the longest and hardest recessions in years.

Figure 6-2 illustrates the volume (in total dollars and number of issues) of IPOs during the past 12 years (adapted from *Barron's*, December 23, 1991, "Wall

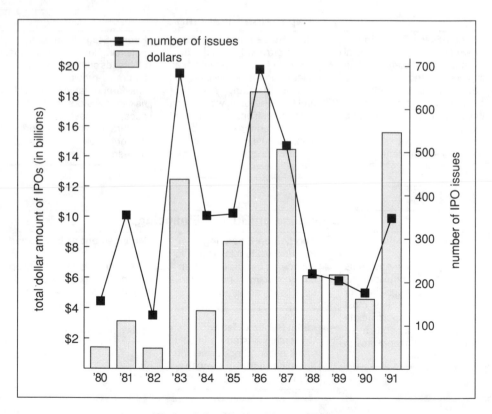

Figure 6-2   Twelve Years of IPOs

Professional Publications, Inc. ▪ Belmont, CA

Street's Baby Boomers: 1991 Rates as a Spectacular Year for IPOs," p. 35). The average deal size has increased over these years from about $10 million to $40 million, indicating that the more recent IPO underwritings were for stronger, larger, usually more mature companies. Many hot, high-ticket biotechnology deals helped escalate the total dollar volumes and the larger deal sizes seen in the past two years. The most common exit strategy today, however, is the acquisition of the start-up company by a larger corporation.

Financials for Engineers—A Crash Course

Measures of Financial Stability

Related to raising funds is maintaining the financial stability of your company once it is launched. As you build your business, you will want to institute financial controls to make sure that your business stays healthy and does not get into trouble, and you need to know when additional funds will be required. Because it is important that you be conversant and comfortable with financial concepts when selling your business plan, this section will explain some relevant indicators of financial health, insolvency, and bankruptcy.

Ratio Analysis

There are numerous key ratios that analysts use in evaluating a company's financial position. These ratios relate to:

- *balance sheet conditions:* asset evaluation, cash accounts, receivables risk, inventory risk, prepaid expenses, company investments, fixed asset analysis, intangibles such as goodwill, deferred charges, and estimated liabilities for future costs and losses

- *liquidity analysis:* cash adequacy, trend in current liabilities to total liabilities, current liabilities to stockholder's equity, current liabilities to revenue, financial flexibility, funds flow evaluation, and availability and cost of financing

- *solvency analysis:* long-term funds flow, financial solvency, unrecorded assets, unrecorded liabilities, and noncurrent liabilities

- *probability of business failure:* bankruptcy prediction

Others break ratios down into liquidity, profitability, and efficiency ratios.

Since your start-up will likely have almost no sales, no profits, few assets, little inventory, no retained earnings, etc., most of these traditional ratios are meaningless. The use of a few key ratios, however, might suffice for a quick "sanity check" of the possibility of going bankrupt, which is your main concern over the near term.

Glossary of Terms for Ratio Analysis

This section contains very brief and informal definitions of the basic terms needed to compute and understand our few key ratios. These terms are used in the ratio equations that follow.

- *accounts payable:* obligations to pay for goods or services that have been acquired on open account from suppliers

- *accounts receivable:* amounts due to the company on account from customers who have bought merchandise or received services

- *current assets:* total cash, securities, inventory, accounts receivable, etc., that can be converted into cash within one year

- *current liabilities:* total of all monies such as accounts payable and salaries payable owed by the company that will fall due within one year

- *net sales:* equals gross sales less sales returns and allowances, sales discounts, etc.

- *total assets:* equals current assets plus fixed assets

- *working capital:* a liquidity measure equal to current assets minus current liabilities. It is called working capital because it is the amount available to operate your business on a daily basis.

Key Liquidity Ratios

The *current ratio* measures your ability to meet short-term obligations.

$$\text{current ratio} = \frac{\text{current assets}}{\text{current liabilities}}$$

A good rule of thumb is that your current ratio should be greater than or equal to 2.0 (i.e., current assets should be at least twice current liabilities). If your current ratio is too low, you may not be able to pay your bills. Roberts reports that, of the high-technology companies he studied, a typical current ratio was 2.5. Companies in the electronics industry averaged 3.17.

The *quick ratio* is a variation of the current ratio; it is more of an acid test of your ability to meet short-term obligations. The quick ratio eliminates inventory that is less liquid, and some people further discount accounts receivable by 25% to better reflect liquidity.

$$\text{quick ratio} = \frac{\text{cash} + \text{accounts receivable}}{\text{current liabilities}}$$

A safe quick ratio would be at least 1.0.

The *turnover of cash ratio* measures the turnover of working capital to finance your sales. The ratio should be below 5 or 6. Make sure you have sufficient working capital to finance your level of sales.

$$\text{turnover of cash ratio} = \frac{\text{sales}}{\text{working capital}}$$

Key Efficiency Ratio

The *investment turnover ratio* measures your ability to generate sales in relation to your assets, which is especially important if your business requires a large investment in fixed assets.

$$\text{investment turnover ratio} = \frac{\text{net sales}}{\text{total assets}}$$

Altman's *Z*-Score Measure for Predicting Bankruptcy

One very interesting computation you can try is E. Altman's *Z*-score measure of predicting bankruptcy in the short run. Auditors are required to recognize and report on possible business failure. If a business does fail and the auditor has not mentioned problems concerning the continuity of the business, a liability suit could be instituted. Do not be surprised if Altman's formula shows your start-up to have a high probability of failure—many of the numerators in the equation will be zero. At least you know where you stand; start-ups are risky business!

$$
\begin{aligned}
Z_{score} = {} & \frac{\text{working capital} \times 1.2}{\text{total assets}} + \frac{\text{retained earnings} \times 1.4}{\text{total assets}} \\
& + \frac{\text{operating income} \times 3.3}{\text{total assets}} \\
& + \frac{\text{market value of common and preferred stock} \times 0.6}{\text{total liabilities}} \\
& + \frac{\text{sales} \times 1.0}{\text{total assets}}
\end{aligned}
$$

Z_{score}	probability of failure
1.8 or less	very high
1.81 to 2.7	high
2.8 to 2.9	possible
3.0 or higher	very low

Insolvency and Bankruptcy

Many start-up founders will someday find their ventures to be insolvent or (technically) bankrupt. You need to know what these terms mean.

Insolvency
Insolvency may refer to either equity insolvency or bankruptcy insolvency.

Equity insolvency means that the business is unable to pay its debts as they mature. It is common for a start-up business to be equity insolvent (unable to meet its daily debts), yet have assets that exceed in value its liabilities. Such a business would be said to be *illiquid*.

Bankruptcy insolvency means that the aggregate liabilities of the business exceed its assets.

Similarly, it is common for a business to be bankruptcy insolvent yet be able to survive and meet its current daily debts.

Insolvency, while not in itself proof that your business will fail, should be treated as a serious warning signal—one that can lead to bankruptcy.

Bankruptcy
Bankruptcy is a serious condition that can lead to the liquidation or reorganization of your company in order to satisfy creditor or stockholder claims.

Technical bankruptcy is the term used when a company has already committed an act of bankruptcy while insolvent, which would allow a creditor to file a court petition forcing the company into formal bankruptcy. There are six acts of bankruptcy, one as simple as giving preference to a creditor during insolvency.

In addition to periodically generating and analyzing formal cash management control documents, indicators, and ratios, you also will want to want to get a quick intuitive handle on your cash needs. To do this, examine how much you are spending each month, factor in any cash from sales that you might generate, and then compute how long you can last until you secure a new round of financing. Always keep your eye on that point where you could run out of money, and do your best never to let it happen.

Trials and Tribulations in the Financing of One Start-Up Company

This is both a happy and a sad story. It tells of one of the more interesting small start-ups in the high-technology field. PPT (originally incorporated as Pattern Processing Corporation), based on exciting technology in an exciting field, got a great start and was supported financially for a long time despite six years of continuous losses. Two of the three founders left the company before it became profitable. New management took over to turn the company around, and the original exotic technology was set aside for a more practical variety. Included in this case study are many numbers, valuations, and percentages to give a realistic example of equity ownership, dilution, and valuations that you might expect in your start-up.

Background

In the early 1980s Larry Werth, 34, decided to quit his job at Medtronic, Inc. (a high-tech medical products company in Minneapolis), in order to launch his start-up. A few years earlier Werth had done some graduate work on an interesting technical idea for robotic machine vision—giving eyes to computers to inspect industrial parts. This was exciting technology that was being eyed by venture capitalists across the country. Control Data Corporation provided a popular low-cost incubator facility for many Minneapolis start-ups in its modern downtown building. Werth rented 500 square feet in the Control Data incubator with the aid of a business assistance grant from the Small Business Association, who subsidized two-thirds of the first $10,000 of costs for business services provided to PPT by an affiliate of the Control Data Business Advisors Program.

High Technology

In the mid-1970s Werth was a research assistant in the electrical engineering department at the University of Minnesota. There he invented a statistical pattern classification machine vision algorithm that was motivated by neurophysiology studies. His business idea was to cast this algorithm into hardware, creating a unique, high-speed device to offer to the emerging machine vision market. An interesting twist was that he would not disclose the function of the algorithm to his potential customers or investors, promoting instead only its benefits when applied to solving certain problems. Werth gave little thought to the potential market for his invention. However, members of the investment community were soon stumbling over each other looking for deals in the new and exotic machine vision and robotics industry.

Seed Financing

Werth wrote a partial business plan while employed at Medtronic and told several investors the story of his invention and his passion to build a business around it. The business was incorporated December 9, 1981. For the next three months, while employed at Medtronic, Werth and company searched for capital and researched the availability of patent protection.

A few months later, two venture capital firms seeded the business with a total of $60,000 (enough to carry Werth's team for about six months) in exchange for 15.6% of the company. This valued PPT at $385,000 on a post-money basis. As soon as this seed capital was assured, Werth and his two cofounders quit their jobs at Medtronic.

Werth's start-up team consisted of himself, Mike Haider (a financial specialist who also led marketing), and Larry Paulson, a sharp hardware design engineer. Werth's lean team, representing the bare necessities, was quite attractive, containing leadership, marketing, and quality engineering. Commencing April 1, 1982, Werth, Paulson, and Haider began receiving $35,000 annual salaries.

Start-Up and IPO at the Same Time

Because a new securities law was generated that permitted the creation of quick, small intrastate public stock offerings, in early 1983, less than one year after start-up, Werth and his team were members of a publicly-traded corporation. Pattern Processing Technologies' IPO raised $300,000 in exchange for 44% of the stock, for a post-offering valuation of about $650,000.

Early Development Financing

PPT soon thereafter raised its total equity financing to $1.7 million.

Just before the IPO, Werth owned 129,600 shares (33.8%) at a cost of $800, Haider and Paulson each owned 97,200 shares (25.3%) at a cost of $600, and the two small venture firms owned 30,000 shares each (7.8%) with warrants to purchase an additional 40,000 shares each, for a total cost of $60,000. The founders' shares cost them about six-tenths of a cent per share (adjusted for splits and stock dividends).

Expansion Financing

PPT had raised over $10.5 million in private and public equity financing through 1991. Its stock price was published in the paper daily, and it did quite well from 1983 to 1987, rising from $1.00 to about $10.00. After six years of continued nonprofitability, from 1983 to 1989, however, the stock was reverse split in 1989 into one share for every 20. Shares sold for well over $2.00 in 1992, which is equivalent to about $0.10 adjusted for splits. PPT was not profitable until fiscal year 1990, and the founders' shares were substantially diluted in the meantime. Stockholders made money in late 1989 to 1991, as the stock rose from $0.50 to over $3.00 when the company finally made the transition to profitability on a quarterly annualized sales rate of $2.6 million. With just under 2 million shares outstanding on a fully diluted basis, this small company of 25 employees has a tidy market capitalization of about $5 million on sales of about $1.8 million. It is worth noting that the company has net operating loss (NOL) carryforwards for tax purposes of about $8 million. The value of this company for its NOL tax write-off potential alone would be worth about $4 million to an acquiring business in the 50% tax bracket.

Postscript

PPT no longer utilizes the original technology upon which the company was based, and is one of the last surviving companies in the machine vision business. In 1989, Werth moved on to pursue his pattern-recognition idea at Electro-Sensors, Inc., with the backing of a related investor group. Werth notes,

> There is still value in the idea of casting algorithms into hardware to realize high speed. My technology was important then and it contributed to helping PPT survive while most others in that business failed.

Werth is right, and you want to make sure that you have technology-fuel for your business. Werth came out of the experience whole—not rich, not impoverished. Werth suggests,

> Don't underestimate the slow pace at which industry makes purchases [of high-technology products]. Promotion alone won't change that fact.

This time he is doing his research and development first and focusing on a specific application (market need): computerized reading of paper forms filled out by hand.

In conclusion, if you too have a good idea, a little luck in finding funds, a willingness to leave your present job, and the passion and conviction to start your own business, the preceding story could be about you. Becoming more successful in your business than the PPT founding team, however, requires a more focused market- and customer-driven technology-fueled strategy.

You cannot go public as a start-up today unless you find yourself in an exceptional situation. You might, however, be able to go public in an active IPO market after your investors have invested several million dollars and if you have a new product with prospects for sales, even if you are toying with insolvency and have nil sales to date.

Finally, be cautious of inventing on company time and with company resources. If Werth's invention had been of any interest to Medtronic, he could have had a nasty intellectual property rights challenge on his hands.

3
DUE DILIGENCE

Part Three of this book really gets into the meat of things. Before you launch your business you need to thoroughly understand the basic ingredients of a successful start-up. Because these topics are so important, Chapter 7 is devoted solely to outlining them. You will need a very clear map of where you must travel if you ever expect to get to a satisfactory destination.

The process of investigating your start-up's success factors is called *due diligence*. Before investors put cash into a start-up, they exercise due diligence to try to discover everything that could impact their business investment. You must do likewise. Investigate and master all the success-contribution factors that will make or break your business: management team, board of directors, markets, customers, products, business plans, and fund-raising. These form the base upon which you will build your business.

David H. Bowen, publisher of *Software Success*, emphasizes,

> Investors look at between ten and one thousand possible investments for every one they make! Entrepreneurs make very real investments of their sweat and years of their life. Don't start a company just to do it. Ask yourself if you would invest as your alter ego. Don't start a company you wouldn't invest in.

7

Elements of a Successful Start-Up

"Conventional wisdom: Get a million-dollar idea, find some venture capital and go. Reality: Venture capital companies are not interested in ideas. Get some seed money, make sure your prototype and your company are 'debugged', and then go."

— Gordon B. Baty

Success Ingredients

This chapter gives a brief introduction to the following five chapters which comprise the meat of the book.

What is the first thing a company has to have to be in business? It may seem like a cliché, but not everyone knows the answer. You need a customer, which relates to the broader concept of a market to sell to. If no one purchases your product or service, you will soon go broke. This leads to the suggestion that your start-up should also have a product or service, or at least the technological base and firm plans to develop one. Obviously, you will need management talent, too, to run your business efficiently, and even the best management will fail without adequate financing. Finally, every company needs a business plan; otherwise you will not know what you and your competitors are doing, where you want to go, how you will get there, and when you have reached success.

These critical ingredients, being tightly connected, cannot be thoroughly examined out of context. Figure 7-1 illustrates the relative importance of each element for a typical start-up situation. As for other ingredients for success, such as luck and persistence, you are on your own.

Because it is so important for the entrepreneurial engineer to understand what makes a business successful, a separate chapter is devoted to each of the five principal start-up elements.

Leadership and Business Basics

Success derives from the disciplined administration of a written or unwritten plan for coordinating and leading the energies and resources of a variety of players toward a common vision and mission. The founding entrepreneur must provide this broad vision and mission, and demonstrate the leadership needed to grow the company. While each CEO will have a particular area of interest or expertise, such as selling or developing a product, he or she must be able to operate across the broad spectrum.

For the start-up entrepreneur, Steven Brandt's *Entrepreneuring: The Ten Commandments for Building a Growth Company* lists 10 important operational leadership style-related activities you must execute consistently and well. His 10 "commandments" are shown in the left-hand column of Table 7-1. The center column lists associated classical management functions and the right-hand column lists related points that are emphasized in this book. Understanding the relationships between these business basics will help you to develop your own effective leadership style.

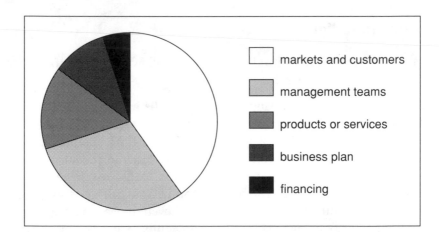

Figure 7-1   Five Controllable Ingredients for Start-Up Success

Professional Publications, Inc. ▪ Belmont, CA

Table 7-1 Entrepreneurial Success Through Classical Management Functions

Brandt's Commandments*	Classical Management Function	Emphasis for the Entrepreneur
1. Limit the number of primary participants to people who can consciously agree upon and directly contribute to that which the enterprise is to accomplish, for whom, and by when.	staffing	Launch your start-up with a complete, experienced, and compatible management team.
2. Define the business of the enterprise in terms of what is to be bought, precisely by whom (i.e., the customers), and why.	planning	Use a market- and customer-driven strategy to define your product.
3. Concentrate all available resources on accomplishing two or three specific operational objectives within a given period of time.	organizing directing controlling	A superb business plan calls for superb, focused execution.
4. Prepare and work from a written plan that delineates who in the total organization is to do what, by when.	planning	Write a solid business plan that the team believes in.
5. Employ key people with proven records of success at doing what needs to be done in a manner consistent with the desired value system of the enterprise.	staffing	Create a complete, experienced, and compatible management team.
6. Reward individual performance that exceeds agreed-upon standards.	staffing	Motivate with a fair remuneration plan, including equity participation.
7. Expand methodically from a profitable base toward a balanced business.	controlling	Pursue rapid profitability leading to high growth.
8. Project, monitor, and conserve cash and credit capability.	controlling	Never run out of money!

*Adapted from Steven C. Brandt, *Entrepreneuring: The Ten Commandments for Building a Growth Company*, New York: New American Library, 1982, with permission of the author.

Table 7-1   (continued)

Brandt's Commandments	Classical Management Function	Emphasis for the Entrepreneur
9. Maintain a detached point of view.	planning	Develop a market-driven strategy. Do not concentrate on your technology to the exclusion of other success factors.
10. Anticipate incessant change by periodically testing adopted business plans for their consistency with the realities of the world marketplace.	planning controlling	Develop and maintain an operational business plan after funding is obtained.

8

Create Your Management Team and Board of Directors

"There is something rarer than ability.
It is the ability to recognize ability."
— Elbert Hubbard

Management

An old cliché of real estate is that the three most important factors in selling a house are location, location, and location. Arthur Rock, a venture capitalist, was quoted as saying that, in starting a new company, the three most important factors are "people, people, and people." As is discussed throughout this book, there are several dimensions for success in selling your business, including people (management), markets and customers, products and technology, planning, and financing. This chapter focuses on the people (namely management teams), as well as your board of directors.

You will start your business somewhere in the management completeness-experience grid depicted in Figure 8-1. Will you start your business with a full or a partial management team? Will that team be experienced or inexperienced?

	inexperienced (0)	experienced (1)	very experienced (2)
complete team (2)	2	3	4
partial team (1)	1	2	3
no team (0)	0	1	2

Figure 8-1   Management Completeness-Experience Grid

The value of your management team in the eyes of investors will be directly related to the experience and completeness of your team. One simple metric is obtained by assigning zero, one, or two points each for completeness and experience. The sum then indicates the overall perceived capability of your start-up's management to investors and customers. Which companies in the grid would you want to invest in or buy a product from—the 1s, 2s, 3s, or 4s?

It has been established that in order to achieve high growth and to be successful in the long run, you will want to grow your business with a top-notch management team. There are many examples of successful start-ups founded by inexperienced management (Apple Computer, Inc., Sun Microsystems, etc.) who either turned out to be top-notch managers or had to be replaced. The key is to identify when and if one needs to bring in more experience. In particular, you will have to decide for yourself how important and practical it is for you to be or remain the CEO.

Though a good market is critical also, without an exceptional management team even the most ideal market cannot be fully exploited. This is evidenced in the fact that many business plans with no product and no technical team have attracted financing when written by a proven management team, and were targeted toward a growing market, which obviously had customers.

The size and commitment of your management team will have a lot to do with the reception your business plan receives in the investment community. Stanley R. Rich and David E. Gumpert's *Business Plans That Win* contains an evaluation system that captures the fact that the quality and completeness of the management team and product are important to investors. Figure 8-2, adapted from Rich and Gumpert, makes it obvious that investors prefer strong, complete management teams.

Management Status			most desirable
Level 4: All members on board and experienced.	5	6	7	8
Level 3: All members identified; some on board only after funding.	4	5	6	7
Level 2: Two founders; others not identified.	3	4	5	6
Level 1: Single entrepreneur.	2	3	4	5
	Level 1: Idea only; market assumed.	Level 2: Prototype operable but not develop- ed for produc- tion; market assumed.	Level 3: Product fully developed; few or no users; market assumed.	Level 4: Product fully developed; satisfied users; market established.

Product Status

Figure 8-2   Team Size and Product Status in Business Plan Reception

Venture capital investors would like to build their start-up portfolios based on 6s and 7s. Less probable are the companies that evaluate to 4s and 5s.

MIPS Computer, the subject of Malone's book, *Going Public—MIPS Computer and the Entrepreneurial Dream*, was known as the $100 million company with the $1 billion over-the-hill-gang management team. Largely because of its solid management team, MIPS was one of the first high-technology companies able to go public after the 1987 stock market crash.

Most start-ups are founded by people much like yourself. These founders have ambition, persistence, good ideas, and an ability to work with and motivate people. They may also have financial savvy. Often founders are persistent to a point of obsession. Unfortunately, though, some founders may retain all control, give poor direction, make business decisions for nonbusiness reasons, bring in ineffective relatives or friends, and be slow to correct operational problems.

Worst of all, they may not be capable of learning from the past, thus tending to repeat mistakes. Will your start-up team have perfect, proven management? Probably not initially. It is an imperfect world. How do you go about selecting quality team members?

A Kind of Marriage

The management team of a start-up will likely share more time and experiences, solve more problems, and ride rougher waters together than any other association of individuals. It really is a kind of marriage. Few secrets will or can be kept, and common interests and visions drive the survival of the relationship. Deep feelings from respect to hatred are likely to develop. Like marriages, many relationships will dissolve. It is vitally important that you choose the right team members at the beginning. Do not launch your start-up with any less due diligence than you would for a marriage!

If possible, consult or work part time with candidates before making any decisions. Get to know the people. Make sure they pass the chemistry test. If you like a good laugh now and then, but a candidate never cracks a smile, you two might not make a very happy team.

Team Members

Your core start-up team will probably consist of three members:

- team leader (presumably you, holding the CEO and president titles)
- vice president of marketing and sales
- vice president of engineering (perhaps also holding the chief technical officer [CTO] title)

Together, this team will drive the business and determine what product to develop and how to build and sell it.

Reasonably soon you will need to add, at least part time, a chief financial officer (CFO) for financial controls and a vice president of manufacturing if your product has significant manufacturing content (unlike software).

A glance at this list will emphasize that you, as CEO, will have far too many duties to manage the entire business and manage the engineering development activity also. Many start-up entrepreneurs cannot let go of the engineering roles with which they have been associated and in which they find their primary strengths. You will have to make the decision to

- be the CEO and leave the engineering to someone else
- let one of your team members take the CEO position
- possibly compromise the initial growth of your business by acting as both the CEO and the engineer

Many entrepreneurs might argue for the last option, pointing out many success stories. However, in almost all of these cases, initial growth was limited, impacting the rapid creation of wealth. Also, the businesses were eventually successful, usually because the entrepreneur was able to grow to assume the CEO role full time, successfully replacing his or her part-time engineering position with a full-time engineering manager, or the entrepreneur eventually relinquished the role of CEO, taking on the engineering management position full time.

Know Yourself

Before jumping ahead to build your winning team, you first need to get to know yourself. Dr. Philip B. Nelson of the Institute for Exceptional Performance is frequently called upon by top executive recruiting firms to measure the characteristics and competencies of candidates, compare that data with the desired position characteristics and competencies, and recommend individuals who would be compatible and synergistic in top-performing management teams. He utilizes a proprietary Position Suitability Profile System™ worksheet to plot the following characteristics and competencies:

- problem solving: thoroughness, practicality, analytical ability, creativity, broad perspective

- motivation: drive, determination, persistence, initiative, goal orientation

- work habits: self-discipline, responsibility, decisiveness, integrity, dependability

- organization/planning: planning, organization, setting priorities, punctuality, flexibility

- interpersonal characteristics: self-confidence, amiability, persuasiveness, stability, perceptiveness

- leadership characteristics: delegation, firmness, participation, recognition, example

Not every reader will have access to Dr. Nelson, but you can achieve similar self-analysis results with a little work.

- Get candid feedback from your peers on how you appear to them.

- Decide on the types of team members you will need to complement your skills, challenge you to do your best, and supplement your weaknesses.

- If you bring together team members with whom you are most comfortable, you may not end up with a well-balanced team. For example, if you are not a thorough person, but you feel most comfortable with similar people, who on your team will be thorough enough when you need it?

- Use a matrix to plot some of Nelson's characteristics, styles, and competencies of potential team members. Look for dangerous similarities or extreme incompatibilities with your personality.

A Winning Team

Now that you have a clearer view of your own strengths and weaknesses, you can visualize what characteristics and competencies in others will round out and complement your team. High-performing management teams must be compatible and synergistic. Each member must:

- challenge the others

- provide mutual inspiration

- get along and work well together

- be able to perform in contained chaos

- maintain control despite the extreme pressure

One profile of successful winning start-up presidents (recounted by Charles A. Skorina, an executive search consultant with Charles A. Skorina & Co.), provides a three-point checklist, useful not only for yourself but for your potential team members as well. Winners:

1. thrive on risk
2. are incurable optimists
3. have dogged persistence

Make sure both you and your team will thrive on the chaos often associated with a start-up. In all likelihood, at some point in time, key employees will leave, prototypes will fail, money will run out, or key customers will vanish. You must be able to stay the course, pursue the goal, and enjoy the game.

Successful Matches

Do more than just hope for smooth teamwork. If prolonged disputes or shouting matches occur in the frenzy of your start-up, it will be destructive of morale and performance. Look for good matches. Avoid the following incompatible differences in work habits and ethics, too many of which may signal danger in your proposed relationship.

- small company orientation vs. big company orientation
- open and generous vs. protective
- sense of humor vs. humorless
- high energy vs. low energy
- team player vs. individual player
- honest and direct vs. cagey and indirect
- sees glass half-full vs. sees glass half-empty
- treats others with respect vs. treats others as objects

If the values, goals, and objectives of you and a proposed partner do not mesh, then it would be wise not to join together in this start-up. Assuming you have identified no serious conflicts, teaming with otherwise qualified old friends may work well if you can establish a decision-making process that works smoothly.

Signing on Management Team Members

You do not simply interview people to select them for inclusion in your team. You need to develop trust and respect in a relationship, and you must share a common vision of what the business can and should be. It takes time to find and meet the right people, and this step in growing your business is critical.

If you select even one poor team member, your venture is highly likely to fail. A start-up generally does not have the luxury to make such a costly mistake. Besides, beyond creating wealth, you will want more than all else to make this an enjoyable adventure.

Make sure that you understand your candidates' backgrounds: where they have succeeded and failed, what they have learned, how they intend to help run this business differently, etc. Ask for references of past employers and coworkers, and speak with them regarding the personalities and work habits of the candidates.

If you think an unproven management candidate has potential, will that person be willing to step down to replace himself or herself with more professional management if need be as the business grows? Will your potential team members agree to move aside if proven to be less than effective? You must create a team with a balance between doing and managing that will result in action. As technically oriented and creative managers, you and your team members must, if you discover an inability to manage among yourselves, be the first to suggest hiring your own replacements. Ask people such questions directly, though, and you may be surprised at the variety of answers you will hear. Ask, and then listen carefully to the answers. Do not rely on the assumption that your management candidates must be good to have gotten where they are.

The Entrepreneurial Team

Bob Hansens, president of the Silicon Valley Entrepreneurs Club, artfully describes the entrepreneurial team members and their related roles. It may be useful for you to think of your start-up team in terms of his structure, which is slightly modified and transcribed in Table 8-1.

Table 8-1   The Entrepreneurial Team

Team Leaders	Achievement-Oriented Managers	Technology Team Leaders	Advisory Board (part time)
chairman of the board	chief operating officer (COO)	chief technical officer (CTO)	entrepreneurial team members
chief executive officer (CEO)	chief financial officer (CFO)	vice president of engineering	providers of professional services (law, accounting, etc.)
president	vice president of marketing	director of technology	providers of capital
	vice president of sales	chief scientist	industry experts and consultants
	vice president of manufacturing		university professors

As described in Chapter 2, one individual can hold multiple titles and positions. The CEO is the most important and, subsequently, potentially the weakest link in a start-up. As the CEO, you must be able to manage teams of people who are difficult to manage.

Your Key Employee Team

As you begin adding key technical employees to your payroll, you will be looking primarily for technical competence. However, do not overlook that team-player quality that you sought in your management team. You will want the entire enterprise to share the vision and live the mission of the business.

Two qualities you should require are energy and enthusiasm. Employees with these attributes know no limits, think that they can do anything, and often come pretty close to doing so in practice. Especially amazing is the extreme productivity of some of the younger and less experienced employees who often exhibit this pure energy and enthusiasm. These individuals, usually hired at relatively low entry-level salaries, often rapidly become key employees in a business, and they deserve to be treated and financially rewarded as such. Do not hire solely on the basis of age, however. Age discrimination is illegal, and clearly not all young people are energetic and enthusiastic. Many older individuals still have that energy and enthusiasm you are looking for, in addition to their valuable experience. Also, while many young free spirits may produce terrific results for you in the short term, their long-term interests may reside elsewhere. The turnover of new college graduates (those holding their first jobs) can be quite high.

Board of Directors

Power of the Board
The board of directors determines how much you will be paid and has the power to replace you as the CEO, so it is natural that you would want to control who gets on your board. When your company is first incorporated and before it is capitalized, you are the only significant shareholder and can appoint whoever you want. In California, you can be the entire board of directors by yourself if you so desire.

A board of directors is elected by the shareholders of the company and is empowered to carry out certain tasks as spelled out in the corporation's charter. Among such powers are: appointing senior management, naming members of executive and finance committees (if any), issuing additional shares, and declaring any dividends. Boards normally include the top corporate executives (the inside directors), as well as outside directors chosen from both the business community and the community at large to advise on matters of broad policy. You should discuss with your advisors whether only you as the CEO, or other members of your management team as well, should be on the board.

What a Board Should Do
The best-utilized boards will provide objectivity and sound judgment. Directors will question your assumptions, contribute to the resolution of specific problems, and bring new ideas to the table. Expect the board to review financial performance, marketing plans, key hiring decisions, and any other major development affecting the business.

How Often Does a Board Meet?
Venture-backed start-up boards usually try to meet every four, six, or eight weeks, or quarterly, but this varies significantly.

How Long Does a Board Meet?
Board meetings should last an hour and a half or, at most, two hours, but many run the better part of a day in start-up situations when many issues, including operational matters, are to be discussed.

Selection of Directors

Because they generally want to retain some control over their investments, you will probably end up having investors on your board. It is generally wise to get concerned board directors, and your investors will certainly fall into that category. Whether or not they will have too much vested interest in looking out for their finances is pertinent. A typical Silicon Valley start-up board comprises only the funding venture capitalists and the CEO.

Investors regularly demand seats on the board as a condition for investing, even if they do not have a majority of shares to elect themselves on board. For example, it is not at all unusual for investors' preferred series shares to have expanded voting rights over the common shareholders to facilitate their own board membership and increased control of the board.

If you have investors on your board, try to get individuals who are experienced in your industry and can genuinely help. These people will have run companies themselves. You will want someone on your board who understands financial affairs and the problems of running a business profitably. You should find individuals with sound judgment and who hold positions of leadership in your field. All directors should be relatively free from conflicts of interest and be able and willing to devote the time required.

It is also recommended that you strive for diversity on your board. Areas of expertise that are most valued are legal, finance, management, marketing, and human resources. An ideal board for a high-technology firm might consist of a venture capital firm partner, a university president, a *Fortune* 500 company financial strategist, an operations manager from your industry, and a retired CEO of a related company.

The board of directors is important in the long run, and having a supportive and knowledgeable board is crucial to the success of a company and the well-being of its founders.

Edward Roberts of MIT, in examining high-technology companies, found that boards typically comprise six to seven members (both outside and inside) with a variety of backgrounds. Representative professions prevalent on boards were, in order of frequency:

1. finance (venture capital, banking, private investing)
2. in-house
3. business (company-related, general)
4. consulting
5. academia
6. law

In addition, you should select directors who treat others the way you would like to be treated. For example, in one case where the CEO had to be replaced, the investor board member insisted that the company provide this individual with an office and secretarial support for the better part of a year, provide six months' severance pay, and allow the CEO to continue vesting in his stock during the severance period. One objective was to make the involuntary parting as amicable as it could be. They wanted the outgoing CEO to sincerely speak well of the company and its backers. That is the action of a first-class investor and director who is thinking of the longer term.

A board of directors can be a very powerful source of ideas, guidance, and leadership. The wrong board can be a nightmare. Most boards prefer to let the CEO run the business, and only step in on a more frequent basis when they see problems. As CEO, you should be on the board, and you might very well occupy the position as chairman of the board. Practically speaking, however, the chairman position carries little additional power, especially if you are already the CEO.

How Many Members Should Be on Your Board?

A start-up company can do well with a small board. A good recommendation would be to have between four and six directors. Janet G. Effland of the venture capital firm Patricof & Co. Ventures, Inc., prefers to see five or seven since with an odd number there is always resolution of a controversial subject. One workable combination for your initial board would be:

- you
- an outside financial advisor (perhaps your part-time CFO)
- your first-round investor
- a highly respected business advisor (a potential second-round investor would be ideal, but be aware that most active investors do not have time for noninvestee boards)

Compensating the Board

If a board member is a significant shareholder in the company, no compensation is required. He or she will have the motivation to be active, be attentive to the business, carefully review documentation, attend meetings, and perform committee work. If a director is not a stockholder, you will want to offer cash compensation or stock options (or possibly both, though you may only be able to afford the options in your start-up phase). Reimburse your directors in phases to make sure that those who stick with you get their rewards. While people will often serve on boards of large, prestigious companies for little or no compensation, more than likely you will need to compensate your nonstockholder directors. The American Electronics Association's 1991 *Executive Compensation in the Electronics Industry* survey publication reports that of its 423 reporting private companies, 379 (90%) provided no compensation for inside directors. Fifty-two percent provided no compensation for outside directors. Even when compensation was provided for outside directors, the average annual retainer was only $5,430. Twenty-seven percent provided stock benefits. AEA private companies include some pretty large businesses, along with some smaller start-ups, so compensation for the board of your start-up will probably fall below the AEA average. In contrast, AEA public companies provided stock benefits to 61.3% of their board members.

Management of the Board

Primarily, your management of the board will consist of making sure that it is composed of competent people who will put the time and energy into helping your enterprise. You do not let directors run the business on a day-to-day basis unless a problem arises.

You should also set the tone for board meetings and try to organize the agenda to focus on crucial issues. It helps to give assignments to directors for them to complete prior to the next board meeting. Do not turn the director's meeting strictly into a show-and-tell for your investors.

Prepare for Meetings

By properly preparing for board meetings, you will help to manage the board more efficiently. Providing updated financial statements and updates on major developments and carefully selecting the issues to bring to the board's attention will assist you in thinking through your business.

Before a board meeting, consider each issue and the options involved. Know what actions you want from your board, and let them know their part up front.

It helps to get premeeting information to your directors a minimum of two days before the meeting so they can be prepared. Keep in mind also that your company's attorney (often a difficult person to schedule) often acts as secretary to the board.

Legal Liability for Directors

Since boards are legally responsible for the actions of the corporation, many people will not formally serve due to legitimate concerns for liability. While a 1988 California law enables companies to reduce exposure to board members with an appropriate amendment to the articles of incorporation, members still do remain somewhat exposed. Purchasing director's liability insurance, while it sounds like a good idea, will most likely be beyond your initial financial capability. (You will need it, however, one year before your IPO.) The expense of liability insurance is reflected in AEA statistics that show that only 8.3% of private AEA members provide liability insurance. Consult your legal counsel to determine how you should best address this issue in your start-up.

Advisory Board

Many companies form executive advisory boards or scientific advisory boards to bring additional consulting expertise into the company at low cost. Because these boards have no legal purpose they invoke very limited legal liability exposure, and many individuals would be honored to be included in such a manner. These experts can be quite useful as technical consultants to your company, and if properly motivated (make them stockholders), they can do wonders for your image in the industry and trade press.

Mentors

If you have managed to form a mentor relationship during your career, be sure to include your mentor in your start-up business activities, perhaps as chairperson of an advisory board. This is the time to reward such a valuable individual with some stock options and to keep him or her interested and involved in what you are doing.

9

Evaluate Markets
and Target Customers

*"It is better to select an audience and fit products to it
than find a product and fit an audience to it."*
— Freeman F. Gosden, Jr.

Traditional Business Model

The traditional business model strategy for starting a firm suggests that you:

- Stake out a niche market in which you will have dominance from the start.
- Serve your market through increasingly better customer service and support.
- Develop a refined grasp of your market's distribution channels.
- Create product identity, company identity, and customer loyalty.
- Establish insurmountable barriers to entry by competitors.

Your first task, then, is to establish a market niche in which your technology and product can profitably play. To do that, you need to know your customers and markets.

Customers and Markets

Customers

When launching your start-up, you must have at least a vague idea of who your first customers could be. Your persistence and enthusiasm do not guarantee that these customers really exist. Some start-up entrepreneurs have no idea to whom they will sell their first product or service, what the customer will pay, what problems will be solved for the customer, or what the customer's alternatives are. Even worse, more than one entrepreneur has believed that everyone will want to buy his product. Not since *Life* magazine has anyone sold anything to everyone. Today, markets are more specialized; customers demand products and services that will deliver to them exactly the benefits that they require. If your technology is going to result in a product that is going to be successful, you must identify a realistic, specific target audience—a niche. You must have a crystal clear vision of your customer. Sandra L. Kurtzig of ASK Computer said it well: "One sobering aspect of choosing ASK's market was the realization that we couldn't be all things to all people."

Know Your Customers

Before launching your company you should get to know some of your customers personally. Talk to several potential customers about your planned product or service, and emphasize that you want to know how you can help solve his or her problems. One hint: do not sell too hard. Let the customer do most of the talking (if he or she will), and listen. Ask for elaboration on any point on which he or she seems hesitant or searches for words to describe. Repeat what you believe the potential customer said in your own words: "If I understand you correctly, you feel. . ." Then listen again for a confirmation or clarification.

Some general questions to ask are:

- What problems do you need solutions for?

- Why does our product appeal or not appeal to you?

- Is there anything you see that is unique about our product?

- What should this product cost, and how could you justify the investment to purchase it?

- When would you need delivery? Would you be interested in acting as a beta test site (for preproduction evaluation)?

- How will your needs change in the future?

- What are your concerns or worries about our product?

- Will you be a repeat buyer if you are satisfied, or would you only need one of these products?

- What are your alternatives if you do not buy our product?

Markets

Beyond examining individual customers, you will want to look at the overall market characteristics for the product or service being offered.

- Is it a high-growth market?

- What are the market opportunities and risks?

- Are there many competitors in this market?

- Does your company have a market niche to itself?

- Is your business in a crowded market with numerous well-established competitors (for example, hard disk drives for personal computers)?

- Will your market endure over time?

- What are the risk factors for failing?

These critical customer- and market-related issues are addressed in more detail in Chapter 11. Professional investors, such as venture capitalists, will especially scrutinize market issues as part of their due diligence process prior to committing any funds to your start-up. They are probably in a better position to perform such evaluations than you are since they have access to expensive market research studies and industry association reports (not to mention their extensive network and investment experience). If you can confer with your start-up's potential investors early on, you may uncover some very pertinent market information.

Competitive Market Analysis

In addition to identifying a healthy, growing market, you will want to carefully evaluate your competition within to make sure you have a perceived distinctive competence. Figure 9-1 illustrates most of the important questions you should be asking as you evaluate different markets or analyze how a particular product idea might work.

Your business plan, discussed at length in Chapter 11, will contain the results of your analysis. You will need to be able to give an account of other industry participants and prove that you either have a distinct competitive edge or a viable niche to yourself. You should compile separate profiles of each competitor (keep a separate notebook for each, noting niches served, market share, etc.) and a tabular comparison of the strengths and weaknesses of products and companies.

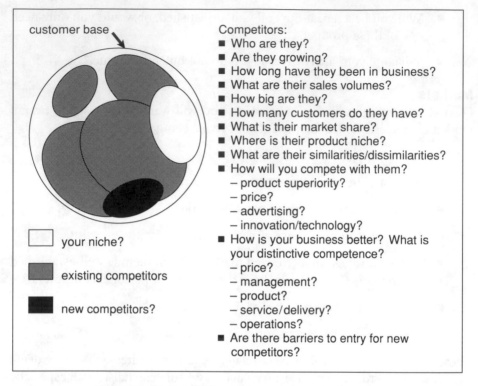

customer base

Competitors:
- Who are they?
- Are they growing?
- How long have they been in business?
- What are their sales volumes?
- How big are they?
- How many customers do they have?
- What is their market share?
- Where is their product niche?
- What are their similarities/dissimilarities?
- How will you compete with them?
  - product superiority?
  - price?
  - advertising?
  - innovation/technology?
- How is your business better? What is your distinctive competence?
  - price?
  - management?
  - product?
  - service/delivery?
  - operations?
- Are there barriers to entry for new competitors?

☐ your niche?

▨ existing competitors

■ new competitors?

Figure 9-1 Competitive Forces in Your Marketplace

In your analysis, do not:

- assume there is no competition

- miss any major players

- underestimate the strength of competitors

On the other hand, you should:

- be aware of competitors' product plans and market strategies

- develop your own marketing strategy for counteracting existing and new competitors

- make perfectly clear to yourself and to your investors (in your business plan) what exactly will make your product better (i.e., how you will compete)

Marketing versus Sales

Many people confuse marketing with sales. *Sales* is dealing directly with customers and is a developed art form. *Marketing* is enticing customers to consider buying a product and is an acquired discipline. More broadly, marketing is characterized by the "four P's":

- product (what to sell)

- place (where and how to sell—distribution channels)

- price (how much to sell for)

- promotion (how to raise awareness, gain acceptance, and make people want to buy)

Marketing decisions determine what products a company is going to develop and sell, how they will be positioned, to whom they will be sold, how they will be priced and distributed, and how their existence and features will be communicated to the market. Having the right products at the right price and the right programs to effectively and profitably sell those products is fundamental to any business.

Marketing Strategy

How are you going to enter the market, obtain a niche, maintain a market share, and achieve your stated financial projections? Figure 9-2 illustrates the infrastructure you will need to build to support your marketing goals. Taken as a whole, this will be your marketing strategy, and it will find its way into your business plan.

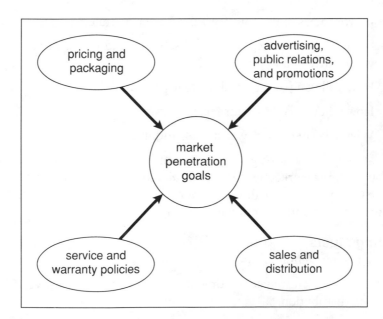

Figure 9-2   Marketing Strategy

Based on your analysis of Figure 9-2, some questions you need to ask are:

- What is the sales appeal (special qualities or uniqueness) of your product?

- How will you attract, maintain, and expand your market?

- What are your priorities? Again, do not think that everyone is your customer. You cannot be everything to everyone.

- How will you reach decision makers?

- Will you sell via salespeople, in-house staff or manufacturing representatives, direct mail, telemarketing, or trade shows?

- To whom will you sell—value-added resellers (VARs), systems integrators, or original equipment manufacturers (OEMs)?

- How, where, and when will you advertise—in trade journals, in magazines, or on television?

- How will you generate leads? How many leads are needed per sale? What is the cost per lead?

- How long is your selling cycle?

- How big will your orders be?

- How will you pay commissions?

- In what areas of the country will you concentrate?

- What are your prices, volume discounts, and dealer discounts? Will you be involved in price wars?

- How will you package and present your product?

- How will you collect your receivables?

- What level of service, warranties, and guarantees need to be offered?

As you can see, the marketing side of your business will consume a lot of your time. You can hire a marketing manager to take some responsibility in these areas, but as the CEO you have the ultimate obligation to make sure your business can sell, as well as make, an exceptional product.

Marketing Musts
Here are a few marketing musts.

- Do not underestimate the time required to establish a network for sales and distribution.

- Do not attempt to fill too many unrelated market gaps.

- Do not try to justify customer price by the cost to produce.

- Do justify price by the value to your customer.

- Do promote the marketable differences of your product.

- Do develop attractive packaging and establish brand recognition and loyalty among your customers.

10

Define Your
Product or Service

*"A rat trap? A rat trap? I thought
you said you wanted a cat trap!"*
— Terry Furtado,
Mechatronic Technologies, Inc.

Overview

Almost everyone, especially an engineer, figures they need to invent that perfect
new product idea to start a business. This is not so! The sections on market pull
and technology push in Chapter 4 emphasize that you should strive for superb
execution in developing and marketing a perhaps less-than-exceptional product
for which there exists a market, rather than a less-than-exceptional execution of
a superb product for which there may be no customers without missionary sales
efforts.

The purpose of this chapter is to understand a little bit more about:

- choosing the right product for your start-up

- marketing and competitive-analysis considerations in light of your chosen product

- exceptional product attributes
- producing your product

Choosing the Right Product

Products or Services?

You will note that this section discusses only products. This is because in a sense a service is also a product. Ideally, if your business provides a service, it can be replicated and marketed much like a product, and, also like a product, it can represent a high-growth, high-profit-margin opportunity.

The term *growth* is the key word here and was discussed in detail in Chapter 5. A service business is a perfectly acceptable way to create wealth so long as it is a growth business. Many franchises fall into the category of service businesses. It follows, then, that the way you make money is not to buy franchises, but to sell them.

Assuming you have selected a product upon which to start your business, do not forget the concept of service altogether. However, service for your product is not to be overlooked. Good service is an extremely powerful differentiator, as Davidow emphasizes in *Marketing High Technology*.

> The key is to convert great devices into great products. When a device is properly augmented [with service] so that it can be easily sold and used by a customer it becomes a product.

It is worth noting that very successful companies such as IBM have knowingly sacrificed technology leadership in order to attain service leadership. The combination of good service and a good basic product usually works better than a poorly serviced, exotic, high-technology product.

Finding Good Product Ideas

Studies by Edward Roberts of MIT indicate that most high-technology product ideas for new companies come from positions held with previous employers (source organizations) of the start-up's founders and key employees. Most entrepreneurs get an idea for a product or service based on their current employment.

Other sources of product ideas are customers, customer-sponsored research and development, and product line evolution. The market- and customer-oriented product ideas usually prove to be the best. In fact, at ASK Computer, Sandra Kurtzig was quoted as saying, "Virtually every ASK product evolved from discussions with and suggestions from our customers."

Attendance at technical conferences and trade shows is always a rewarding, if exhausting, exercise, where you will see the latest products being offered.

You should also subscribe to all the trade and business magazines related to your technology area in order to keep aware of new competitive products and trends. Most of these magazines are free controlled-circulation publications. To qualify for higher-level magazines such as *Electronic Business*, you may have to use your imagination in filling out the reader qualification card. In other words, claim that you do recommend, purchase, and authorize purchases for most products and services listed in all the little boxes you checked.

Subscribe to targeted periodicals related to your technology. For example, if your technology or skill is focused on developing programs for the Apple Macintosh computer, you will want to read every issue of *MacWeek, MacWorld*, and *MacUser*, as well as technical society journals such as the Institute of Electrical and Electronic Engineers' *Computer, Communications of the Association of Computing Machinery*, etc.

Finally, subscribe to general business periodicals such as *Business Week*, the *Wall Street Journal, Inc.,* and *Success. Forbes* may be too *Fortune* 500 oriented, and *Entrepreneur* may be too blue-collar, small-business oriented for your tastes.

Do You Offer the Drill Bits (Means) or the Holes (Ends)?

Apply your technology to develop a product that delivers a benefit to your customers. The most important lesson for an engineer to learn is that one does not sell technology, one sells benefits. There is a saying that "the hardware store owner does not sell drill bits, he sells holes!" You need to first find the holes in your market that need filling with your technology, then you can design and develop your product. Again, your company must be market- and customer-driven and technology-fueled. This is not to say that you need to be marketing-driven. A good product that fills a need and delivers a benefit can be sold with normal marketing effort. You will note that almost all discussion on selecting a product takes us back to marketing principles—not to the state-of-the-art of technology.

Do Not Confuse One Product with a Business

Many engineers have a good idea for a single product. Your market analysis will tell you whether or not you will be able to grow a business based on a single product. In almost every case, though, you will need to identify a family of related products to build a solid business. Always be thinking in terms of a product family and growth potential. This simple observation is often overlooked in the excitement of a start-up.

It is a good idea to have two folders on your desk labeled "next year" and "five years out." Put ideas and thoughts as they come to you in these folders for future analysis. Keep clippings, too, of articles that relate to your technology and marketplace. Brainstorm, and constantly consider new products your company could develop and produce. Today's innovative corporations, such as Minnesota Mining & Manufacturing (3M), derive more than 30% of revenues from products produced in the past five years. Hewlett-Packard gets more than 50% of its annual revenue from products introduced within the previous three years. Follow the successful models.

Marketing and Competitive Analysis Considerations

Product Positioning and Your Competition

Your temptation to develop a particular product based on your technology fuel must be viewed in the light of product positioning analysis. Figure 10-1, motivated by Francis and Heather Kelly's *What They Really Teach You at the Harvard Business School*, illustrates that a successful product must have a perceived benefit to the customer over other similar products in terms of price and/or performance (as evidenced by feature differentiation).

Competing on the basis of cost alone is clearly an option. Commodity products such as computer memory modules often gain market share primarily on the basis of price. If your technology enables you to produce a needed product at a cost advantage, then that is a reasonable candidate for your start-up's first product. Cost advantage alone will not guarantee you a market presence, however.

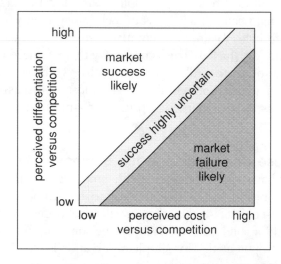

Figure 10-1   Cost versus Perceived Differentiation Model

Even if you could develop a software program equal in functionality to Microsoft Word or Excel and sell it at half the price, it may not take off. Customers know the Microsoft brand name, place emphasis on the de facto standard, and perceive a better deal due to better customer service, extended product life, and future product upgrades. Never forget: perception is reality.

Competing based on perceived differentiation of product features and performance is your alternative. Differentiating features can be solely product related and highly visible, for example, adding three-dimensional data representation and charting capabilities to a traditionally two-dimensional spreadsheet program. Or, differentiating features could be less tangible, such as your company's reputation, service, delivery, training, or product support. Figure 10-2 illustrates the positioning of Adam Osborne's low-cost computer programs offered by his Paperback Software International, Ltd. How do you think he did?

His product positioning was unique. Paperback's products were clearly differentiated by cost, and their functionality was perceived to be almost as good as that of his more expensive competitors. The company, although new, was well-known because of Osborne's acclaimed reputation (Osborne Computer

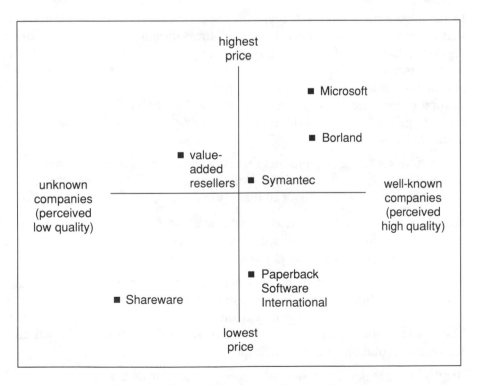

Figure 10-2   Positioning of a Software Product

Professional Publications, Inc. ▪ Belmont, CA

Corporation offered the world's first portable personal computer with full software for under $2,000) and extensive press publicity. It was destined to be a clear win, except that his competitors sued him for copyright infringement and won. The business did not succeed.

Before you launch a start-up with your product, plot its positioning with regards to your competition and know that there will be sufficient perceived benefits in cost and features.

Maintain a Proprietary Advantage, or Patent Protection

Investors like to hear that their potential entrepreneurs have technical reasons why their product can deliver better benefits to customers and that they can protect those advantages through either trade secrets or patents. Patents and trade secrets will provide entrepreneurs with an opportunity for a head start on their competitors, along with a period of time where they alone can handsomely profit. Many prescription drugs fall into this category. While they are under patent protection, the manufacturer can often charge aggressive prices for those products in heavy demand. Look at your product ideas in this light and try to identify similar opportunities.

Evaluate your proposed product against the competition. One rule of thumb is that a new product should have three to ten times the advantage in terms of price and/or performance of an existing product for a customer to switch. A popular story illustrates this point. Ely Callaway, a 72-year-old former textile tycoon and newcomer to the golf business, catapulted his eight-year-old Callaway Golf Company from a tiny specialty outfit selling mostly novelty clubs into the fastest-growing golf club maker in the country. Callaway explained in a *Business Week* interview:

> You've got to create a product that is demonstrably superior to what's available in significant ways. And—most important—it has to be pleasingly different. That's all there is to it. Simple.

His golf club is more than twice as expensive as a normal driver, but it has a much sought-after larger sweet spot due to its revolutionary design consisting of a larger head with better weight distribution.

However, be careful about claiming design superiority—it can come back to bite you if a competitor later claims you have infringed his patent. The competitor can use your statement to support a claim that he deserves high royalties—you have admitted the design's superiority; obviously, he deserves to be compensated for such a revolutionary and superior idea.

Are you going to develop new word processing software for a personal computer? Your potential customers likely may not consider buying a new, unknown word processor even if it is faster, more functional, and less expensive than what is now being used. The point here is to not become too attached to your technology, invention, or product. Take a good, solid, objective look at what you will produce and the value and benefits it will deliver to the marketplace.

Play in a Large Enough Market

One of the biggest mistakes engineers can make is to try to start a business in which they will develop a specialized product that has a worldwide market potential of only a couple of million dollars. Not only should your target market segment be large enough, it should also be healthy and growing.

Avoid Playing in a Marketing Market

Marketing-driven companies (such as ones selling cigarettes, food products, or perfume) thrive not only on the quality or uniqueness of their products and services but also on their unique methods of promoting and selling their products. This is not the market you should be in.

You may have a technical idea for a new razor blade that will work better than any on the market. To sell this razor blade, however, you would need to compete against giants who spend tens if not hundreds of millions of dollars to introduce such new consumer items. As a technically oriented entrepreneur, you should stick to items that do not compete in the everyday consumer market.

Identify Concrete, Real Customers

If you can list the names and phone numbers of two to five people who, when asked, "Would you buy this product for this price now if it were available from this person?" would respond "Absolutely, yes!" then you are on the right track. Having these customers lined up will do amazing things with regards to investors' reception of your business plan. In fact, some of these potential customers are good candidates themselves for seed-level funding sources.

It is also important that you understand the buying cycle of your customers. Many big ticket items are dearly wanted by customers, but they have to budget for them. This can easily add one year to their purchase action. Also, there is the uncertainty of capital expenditure cycles, which ultimately influence buying behavior in every industry.

Make Your Product Easily and Clearly Understandable

Many engineers concoct elaborate product ideas. That is, when asked "What do you intend to develop or sell?" they need five minutes to answer.

You must be able to describe your product and its benefits with utmost clarity. As one venture capitalist is fond of telling his courting entrepreneurs, "When you tell me what your product does and why someone needs it, I want to hear an answer that's as clear as if you were describing the function of a parking lot; everyone knows what parking lots are used for, and why they are needed." If you cannot describe your product in simple understandable terms, it is unlikely that your potential customers will even know that they need your product.

Exceptional Product Attributes

Developable and Producible in a Timely Manner

Heavy investment in plant and equipment, such as that required in semiconductor manufacturing, is risky and expensive. Software, on the other hand, has almost no production costs, yet development and maintenance of the product can sometimes be difficult to manage. Make sure that you do not select a product that will take too much time and money to develop and produce. Again, to yield high returns on investment, you need to attain rapid profitability.

Time to market is critical in this day of time-based competition. You need to be able to produce your first product in a short time to compete. Kurtzig of ASK Computer stated the case well:

> The faster my rudimentary product hit the market, the more money my potential users would save—and, of course, the faster I'd begin earning royalties. I didn't want to fall into the R&D trap of trying to create the perfect mousetrap. The trick is to be in the marketplace just as the demand for it is accelerating. By the time VisiCorp finally came out with their IBM product, VisiOn, Kapor's software, Lotus 1-2-3, owned the market. Adam Osborne, on the other hand, was right on time with the first portable computer. But Osborne then took too long to respond to the trend to IBM compatibility, and within another year his company had gone bankrupt.

High Gross Margins

Software is probably one of the highest gross margin businesses an engineer can start. Because you are small and have limited capital, you need to be able to rapidly produce your first products at low cost and sell them for an aggressive price.

Substantial Collateral Revenue

A good product generates revenue from collateral items such as service and maintenance contracts, accessories, updates, and operating supplies. You want your customers to keep coming back to you.

Clear Distribution Channels

Before making a final decision to sell a particular product, it helps to visualize how that product will ultimately be marketed and sold. For example, if your product will sell for $50,000, it will most likely have to be sold through direct sales representatives. That means hiring and training an expensive staff of sales people who will draw salaries for a long time before sales generate enough contribution margin (gross profit) to cover salaries and commissions for the sales force. A product selling for less than $5,000, on the other hand, will almost always have to be sold through distribution. That is, you would engage either independent distributors (who technically buy the product from you, and take title to the product), or independent sales representatives (who represent your company's products, as well as other competitive products, perhaps). Either way, you will give up typically 40% of the sales price for their efforts. While this seems expensive, being able to identify and use a known, proven distribution channel that will readily accept and promote your product will be very helpful. Proof of an existing distribution channel will also be a selling point with your investors. Many a start-up has produced a great product, only to begin a very long, missionary sales effort that took the company under. Time is money, and trying to establish an in-house sales force or to enlist a reluctant distribution channel can cost you plenty. Produce a product that you know can be readily sold.

Producing Your Product

Assume now that you have zeroed in on a good product idea. You have talked to possible customers and established to your satisfaction that there is a large and growing market where this product can solve real problems. This product could also be the basis for a lucrative product family. Compared to the competition, you seem to be well positioned and protected. The product is easy to describe, and its benefits are obvious. It can probably be developed and produced rapidly, and it has the potential for high gross margins and substantial collateral revenue. Now you have to lay the plans for actually producing your product.

Statement of Requirements

The initial step when devising a development plan for your product will be to give it a very specific description. This can be done by generating a *statement of requirements* document. This document describes the general requirements of your product and is to be used by engineering, marketing, and sales personnel during the product development, testing, and market introduction stages. While this document is primarily a marketing statement, it does cover engineering topics too. Much of this information can be extracted directly from a well-researched and well-written business plan. A good number of start-ups neglect to produce this document, which should not take more than one month to generate if the overall business is well planned. Start-ups lacking a carefully planned product description usually pay the price by heading off in a wrong direction. The statement of requirements gives your development team the direction it needs to make progress without your constant supervision. Figure 10-3 is a sample outline for the statement of requirements document adapted from a successful developer of industrial software.

What is the product?
    features
    applications and uses
    benefits delivered
    needs met
Market analysis and requirements:
    competition
    pricing
    Who is the user?
    Who makes/influences the purchase?
    What are likely sales channels?
    marketing communications and public relations literature
    distribution channels
Product requirements:
    competitive positioning
    target production costs
    Who installs the product?
    training and field support requirements
    customer support requirements
    warranty policy
    upgrade policy
    user, reference, installation manuals
    product packaging
    copy protection policy (for software)
    maintenance considerations
    expected product life
    release schedule (alpha, beta testing, first release, etc.)
    future product enhancements and extensions
Functional requirements:
    performance requirements (responsiveness, accuracy,
      reliability, mean time between failure, etc.)
    systems requirements
    human factors
External requirements:
    environmental requirements
    office, factory, etc.
Other requirements:
    regulatory requirements
    international and export considerations

Figure 10-3   Sample Statement of Requirements Outline

Functional Specification

Following the generation of the statement of requirements, a *functional specification* document should be produced. This is more of an engineering than a marketing document, stating in greater detail requirements relating to the product's function (but not the product's form) such as:

- how fast a machine must process parts, or how fast software must execute instructions or perform mathematical calculations

- how accurate (with what precision) a computation must be

- how repeatable a mechanical part positioning must be

- how a device or program must be controlled by an operator and what operating options must be presented

- how long an instrument must operate before calibration is required

- how heavy a device can be

- how much space a product may occupy

Figure 10-4 is an abbreviated sample outline for a typical functional specification document, again adapted from a successful developer of industrial software.

```
Terminology
Hardware platform
Operating system
User-interface standards
Help system
Input devices supported
Copy protection
Product features (an itemized feature list related to
    the application)
Documentation, comment, and annotation facilities
Cross-reference facilities
Debugging support
Fault detection and handling and error recovery
Cut and paste interfaces
Language specifications
Instructions supported
Limitations and restrictions
Program inputs and outputs
Operating environment
Reliability considerations
International language version considerations
Development notes
```

Figure 10-4   Sample Functional Specification Outline

Professional Publications, Inc. ▪ Belmont, CA

The functional specification can turn out to be a crucial document. If it is too vague, the customer will use it as a hammer against you—what started out as a bicycle could turn into a Mercedes (both are vehicles with wheels that transport a passenger from point A to point B), and you (the designer) could be required to pay for upgrading it.

A really good functional specification will be broken down into as many sub-specifications as one can reasonably think of. In addition, it will also have three performance target specifications (the data often being listed in three columns) as depicted in Figure 10-5. For this reason, a functional specification is often also referred to as a *performance specification.*

In regard to Level 1 in Figure 10-5, be cautious. This is a danger area for technology companies. The developing company's engineers have been known to get together with the customer's engineers and begin adding bells and whistles ("gee, if we just tweaked this a little bit here, it could do this, too...")—significantly increasing development time without having management pass along the price increase to the customer.

For Level 3 in Figure 10-5, make sure you look at how much time you add to the development project as well as how much you add to the cost—and price it accordingly. Cost overruns occur because no one did a realistic cost analysis or time analysis, or if they did, the analysis was not updated.

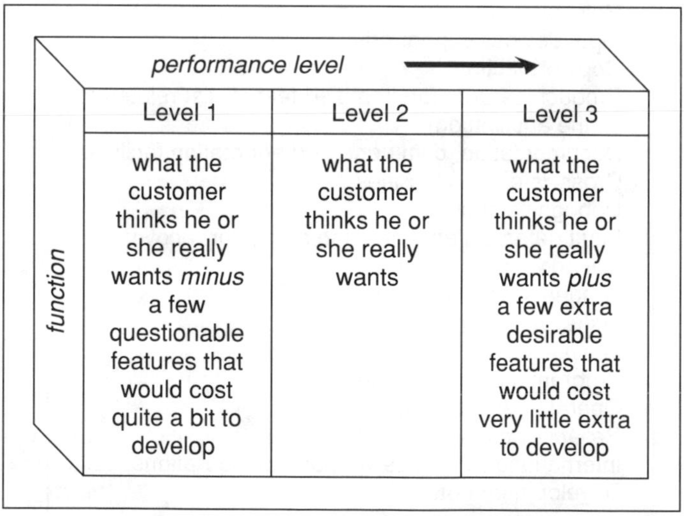

performance level →		
Level 1	Level 2	Level 3
what the customer thinks he or she really wants *minus* a few questionable features that would cost quite a bit to develop	what the customer thinks he or she really wants	what the customer thinks he or she really wants *plus* a few extra desirable features that would cost very little extra to develop

function

Figure 10-5   Performance Specifications

Professional Publications, Inc. ▪ Belmont, CA

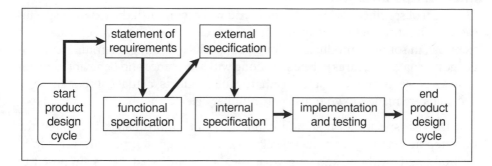

Figure 10-6   Product Design and Development Methodology

As illustrated in Figure 10-6, these documents represent only two of the important stages involved in a good product design and development methodology. Some of your documents will be living documents. That is, they will never be entirely completed and will always be changing. Yet it is important to be diligent in producing and maintaining these vital documents that state what the product is supposed to do, and why. Producing drawings, sketches, and more detailed designs will further propel you toward a closer understanding of the product development task that awaits. Without such documentation, you run the risk of producing what is instead easy, convenient, or interesting to produce as time passes, not what you know your customers want, need, and will buy!

External Specification
You probably do not need to get into this level of planning at business launch time, but you should know that an external specification document is often developed to translate the "whats" in the functional specification into more specific "hows." The external specification states everything about the product that can be seen, felt, measured, or touched by the customer—that is, seen externally.

For example, if a functional specification says to keep the weight under 100 pounds, a corresponding external specification might stipulate that a frame be made of lightweight aluminum. Statements of speed requirements might translate into the types of motors to be used, and statements of accuracy required might translate into the specification of the use of air-guided, frictionless bearings. For software, the external specification might consist of pictures of all menus, displays, dialog boxes, etc., with which a user would interact to perform the function specified.

Internal Specification

This level of specification explains how you will accomplish the external specification. The customer typically does not see or care about this level of detail. For example, in software products, an internal specification might stipulate the language and data structures to be used, along with the names and behavior of major routines, objects, modules, etc. For hardware products, actual component-level decisions are made, down to the part number level if possible.

The internal specification should come last, but unfortunately it is often the first step in a start-up's product design effort. It is very tempting to get started on building it without knowing what the "it" is and what "it" is supposed to do. Writing internal specifications (or worse, building your product prototype) before understanding what benefits the product must deliver by solving which customer problems is exercising poor judgment.

Implementation and Testing

This step should be unambiguous. There should be no more questions about how well the product is to operate, with what parts, and how everything interconnects. If the preceding specifications are implemented properly, the rest should be simple, and major milestones should be met on schedule. Of course, adjustments are constantly required because nothing can be precisely specified in advance and market needs are continually-moving targets. Be sure the best job possible is being done on each level and that the tasks are being undertaken in the proper order. It is amazing how many companies try to start by "hacking" a product without following any design methodology. Most of these enterprises are likely to fail.

If your start-up seems to be working from the bottom up, watch out! You cannot build a product from the pieces until you know what it is supposed to do in some detail. Most inventors are not good product development engineers. If your engineers do not understand the essential role of marketing's input to product specification and do not practice a top-down process of specifying, designing, and developing a product, the business may fail even if the product idea itself is fantastic.

One recent alternative to the traditional top-down method is a rapid prototyping methodology whereby, through iterative experimentation, one converges on a satisfactory design. This method has found some success in today's rapid-time-to-market environment, especially in software projects where one has to discover many of the hows through experimentation. This method is often justified on the basis that many software engineers and programmers are not very manageable anyway, and they tend to produce what is at the moment challenging and of interest to themselves. While there may be some basis for that reasoning, it is still essential that the programmers in this case have a keen sense of what the market needs. Those businesses that have successfully used rapid prototyping follow the rule that designs (the prototypes) are to be reviewed often, and any software written is to be reusable.

Sometimes a *skunk works* is allowed to exist. This is a slang term for an unofficial effort that is allowed to exist more or less out of sight. Unfortunately, out of sight means without much management direction and control. This model might work in some start-up situations where each employee is an exceptional team player, communications are superior, and there is a good sense of the market. If you choose to operate a skunk works, you had better be an active participant.

11

Write Your Business Plan

*"It's not the writing
that's difficult—it's the thinking."*
—James Leigh

Form versus Content

This is the longest chapter in the book. That is not because writing a business plan is complicated in itself, but because the business planning process (content generation) behind the writing (the form) is very difficult. Determining the appropriate form of your plan—which topics to put in, in what order, and with what emphasis—is important. Even more important, however, is that the content of your plan conveys an intimate understanding of what will make your business succeed. Much of what is covered in this chapter involves the content as well as the form of your business plan.

Types of Business Plans

First, know that there are two types of business plans: a general *planning and funding* document written to plan for the beginning of the business and to raise funds, and an *operational* business plan to monitor and control the growth of the company. In launching your start-up, you will be working with the former, and therefore that is the one addressed in this chapter.

Other than your last will and testament, the most important document you will ever write is your business plan. A business plan gives birth to your start-up. It enables you and your team to envision and plan how the business will be run and to raise funds. Because both you and your investors have similar questions, one business plan serves both parties. Later, your operational business plans (which can be less comprehensive) will enable you to monitor, plan, and adjust to changes in the growth of your business.

Getting Started

Chapter 6 describes the financial stages of a company's growth. It is important to understand that there are also five operational stages to your company's growth. C. Gordon Bell's *High-Tech Ventures: The Guide for Entrepreneurial Success* clearly describes these well-recognized operational stages, as illustrated in Figure 11-1.

You will be writing your business plan during a concept stage, before you have received outside funding. During a good part of this period you may still be employed.

The *concept* stage is the period during which you and your founding management team develop an idea and write the plan to implement that idea. The financial purpose of the plan is to seek funds for seed-stage testing and refinement of the idea. In some cases, the seed stage can be skipped.

In the *seed* stage your ideas are refined, and an even more detailed business plan may be written for the start-up funding round.

In the *product development* stage your product is developed, tested, and refined before any real sales are made.

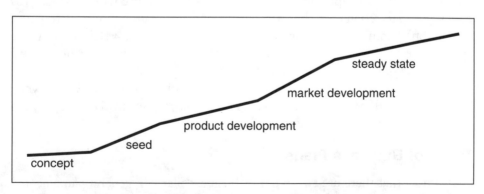

Figure 11-1   Operational Stages of Company Growth

Professional Publications, Inc. ▪ Belmont, CA

The *market development* stage arrives when the product is sold and you beome profitable.

Steady state is reached as the business matures and sustains itself. It should still be growing at this time, and the original investors may decide to exit or cash out.

Find a Team and Write a Plan, or Write a Plan and Find a Team?

You are encouraged to build your founding team as soon as possible. If you cast the vision and establish the mission together, you probably will be more successful. A 25-year study of high-technology companies by MIT professor Edward Roberts shows that multiple founders increase a start-up's chances for success. Larger founding groups start with more capital, generate more sales earlier, and can work longer hours. In one subgroup of 20 young companies, 63% of those with more than two founders performed better than average, while only 20% of those with one or two founders exceeded average performance.

Not only will you need help to write a good plan, you will need help in raising funds. Therefore it is a good idea to team with partners who can assist you in attracting funds. Investors do not throw money at glossy business plans; they invest in teams with plans to exploit market opportunities. This subject is also discussed in Chapter 8, which deals more extensively with creating winning management teams.

When to Write the Plan

When do you write the business plan, and with whom? If you are currently employed, can you take the time and energy to write your business plan and not have a conflict of interest or commitment with your employer? During the plan-writing phase you will need conduct extensive research, talk to potential customers and investors, and understand your market better. Rarely can all this be done successfully on a part-time basis.

Silicon Valley trade secrets and unfair competition lawyer James Pooley addresses the legal implications of when you must leave an employer:

> You may find that planning your move while you're still working for the company is somehow unethical. Deliberate, careful planning of your new enterprise is neither illegal nor immoral. Unless you are independently wealthy, you must do it while you still have an income and before you burn any bridges. As long as you don't actually begin your competing business or start recruiting your team from your employer's staff while still on the payroll, you should be clear.

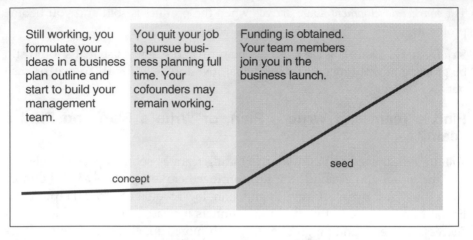

Figure 11-2   Start-Up Scenario

The start-up scenario illustrated in Figure 11-2 shows that at some point in time you must quit your job and dedicate yourself full time to engineering your start-up. It is for this reason that there are thousands of voyeurs and would-be entrepreneurs who will never start that business they constantly dream of. It indeed takes quite a sacrifice and risk to start your own business, especially for the first time. For this reason, many start-up founders are people who have been fired or come from other failed start-ups. In fact, many people claim that the purpose of starting your first business should be to really achieve success in your second. Viewed from this perspective, if you are not yet sufficiently committed to quit your job and launch your dream, maybe you should consider joining someone else's start-up as a key employee or cofounder. That way you would only need to quit your job after seed funding has been obtained, and you would know where your next paycheck is coming from.

How Long Should It Take to Write Your Plan?

You should plan to spend three to twelve full-time months in the unfunded concept stage of your business while you write your business plan and launch your start-up. Michael O'Donnell says, "A typical time frame for writing a plan would exceed 300 hours over one to six months, depending on how much time can be devoted to the research and writing." Ronstadt and Shuman state that "[in] our experience [the time required to write a business plan] ranges from 100 hours to nearly 2000 hours." Your founding team members, as you convince them to join your venture, will of course help you to write the plan. As the CEO, however, the burden is squarely on your shoulders to take the risk and ensure that the plan gets written.

Essential Tools

Almost everyone, especially an engineer or a scientist, has access to a personal computer today. If you do not own a computer and good word processing and spreadsheet software, you must go shopping. These are essential tools of the trade these days. Invest in (or at least obtain easy access to) a good printer also, preferably a laser or ink-jet printer rendering 300 dots-per-inch resolution. Your plan should reflect both good form and good content. Ignore the form and you will lose many potential investors. You know it makes good business sense to dress for success, so dress your business plan as well; it is an extension and reflection of yourself. Like a resume, it introduces you and says, "This is the very best I can do; now do you want to talk to me further?"

A sidebar to this chapter reviews some excellent commercially available word processing and spreadsheet templates to aid in organizing your business plan that you will definitely want to look at.

Good Business Planning

There are dozens of good business plan models and actual business plan samples to be found in literature. If you have access, try to rummage through other private business plans to find examples that are especially relevant to your start-up situation. By now you should be networking with potential team members who have access to a variety of business plans.

Rummaging through other private business plans to which you have access can be dangerous if it results in illegal misappropriation of another's trade secrets. Watch out for violating confidentiality agreements when you do this.

The following are business plan basics and some good sample outlines.

Business Plan Basics

This book is built around six elements of success of a start-up business:

1. management teams
2. markets and customers
3. products
4. plans
5. funding
6. luck and persistence

These success elements map into the four substantive sections of any business plan:

1. management team
2. marketing

3.   products

4.   financial projections

Your business plan must clearly cover these critical sections, and there are several variations in format. As you choose a plan format, never lose track of the following basic messages you need to give:

- an executive summary compelling the reader to study the plan

- a management team that will guarantee success in the venture

- a market opportunity that gives this business a distinct competitive advantage. You should state who will buy your product and whether it is in a new or existing market. (Chapter 9 contains more extensive material that should be included in your plan.)

- a product that is producible and merchantable (state whether this is a new or existing product)

- financial projections that satisfy return-on-investment objectives, are achievable and believable, and obviously do not violate rule-of-thumb sanity-check ratios

Plan Emphasis

Emphasis in a business plan is usually put on either the management team or the growing market opportunity. Decide what you are offering to your investors, and structure your plan accordingly. If your management team is inexperienced and this is your first business launch attempt, you must focus on your unique market opportunity and how your high-technology product will make the business successful. Sometimes, personnel resumes are buried in a plan. Since many investors want to read about the management team first, if this material is hard to find, your plan may not go very far. If you have a successful management track record, on the other hand, or your combined management team looks very appealing, definitely highlight this asset as the first and most visible section of the plan by placing it immediately after the executive summary.

Different investors have differing postures on the relative importance of a management team versus a growing market opportunity. You will often hear statements such as, "we invest in people, not ideas; we assume the product idea can be built," "the market is number one," or "lack of a management team is the number one company killer."

If your start-up has a strong management team and if you are playing in an attractive, growing market, then the Genµs example illustrated in one of this chapter's sidebars should suit you well. You can make your plan short and compelling, especially if you have a strong story to tell. Like a powerful person speaking in a soft voice, it forces everyone to listen attentively. A plan that is too comprehensive, discussing every operations detail, can come off like a not-so-powerful person who is trying too hard. You are selling yourself, your team, and your unique market opportunity, not a used car. Prepare and present your plan accordingly.

There exist dozens of comprehensive plan outlines for the general planning and funding type of business plan. Three of these outlines are presented in this chapter. The detailed, lengthy, comprehensive plans are not recommended. If nothing else, the items your investors will be looking for (people, financial projections, and unique market opportunity) will be too difficult to find amid a long plan. However, you can use these more detailed plan outlines as checklists to see that nothing important has been missed.

New Venture Business Plan Outlines

JIAN's BizPlan*Builder*™ suggests the following business plan outline:

    A. Executive summary
    B. Present situation
    C. Objectives
    D. Management
    E. Product/service description
    F. Market analysis
        1. Customers
        2. Competition
        3. Focus group research
        4. Risk
    G. Marketing strategy
        1. Pricing and profitability
        2. Selling tactics
        3. Distribution
        4. Advertising and promotion
        5. Public relations
        6. Business relationships
    H. Manufacturing
    I. Financial projections
        1. 12-month budget
        2. 5-year income (profit and loss) statement
        3. Cash-flow projection
        4. Pro forma balance sheet
        5. Break-even analysis
        6. Sources and uses of funds summary
        7. Start-up requirements
        8. Use of funding proceeds

    J. Conclusions and summary

    K. Appendix

Adapted from JIAN BizPlanBuilder^{TM}, with permission.

Institutional Venture Partners' Suggested Business Plan Contents

The following business plan outline was recommended by Norman A. Fogelsong and Kenneth J. Kelley from Institutional Venture Partners. IVP is a leading venture capital firm in Silicon Valley specializing in investments in start-up and early stage high-technology companies.

    A. Executive summary with 5-year milestones

    B. Product or service description

    C. Business strategy overview

    D. Marketing and sales plan

       1. Market size, projected growth, and segmentation

       2. Competitors and their market shares

       3. Strategic positioning and marketing plans

       4. Channels of distribution

       5. Sales strategy and 5-year sales forecast

       6. Customer references or references on market potential

    E. Operations plan

       1. Development and engineering programs

       2. Manufacturing and materials programs

       3. Facilities plan

       4. Product service or maintenance programs

    F. Management and key personnel

       1. Organization

       2. Detailed resumes with personal references

       3. Staffing plan

       4. Stock option plan or incentive program

    G. Financial statements and projections

       1. Historical and current financial statements

       2. Annual projections of income statement, balance sheet, and cash flow for next 5 years

       3. Monthly projections of income statement, balance sheet, and cash flow for next 1 or 2 years

       4. Existing shareholders and ownership percentages

H. Proposed financing
    1. Amount and terms
    2. Post-financing capital structure
    3. Use of proceeds
  I. Appendices

In a recent address to a Silicon Valley engineering management society meeting, Fogelsong and Kelley of IVP gave the following hints for engineers wanting to start their own companies. First they said that an attractive business plan will exhibit:

- a talented management team with entrepreneurial skills

- a large market need with high growth potential (we are looking for a $50 million to $100 million company valuation in five years)

- a unique and/or proprietary technology

- sound and executable plans

- attractive financial returns (we are looking for 10 times returns over five years)

They also claim that the keys to your success will be:

- Vision: You need a clear vision of what the company should be.

- Commitment: You need the commitment to work hard to succeed.

- Focus: You need to focus on the task at hand.

- Execution: You need superb execution of your plan.

A Personal Favorite

The following combined business plan outline and checklist has been used in a number of successful high-technology engineering start-up opportunities. Again, do not attempt to cover every item listed; use this outline to verify that you have not missed any important topics for your business situation.

A. Executive summary
    1. Objective of the business
    2. Background and unique opportunity and market
    3. Management team
    4. Products
      a. Initial
      b. Future
    5. Marketing strategy
    6. Producing the product

    7. Investment sought and return
    8. Use of proceeds
  B. The company's objectives
    1. Origin of business idea and mission
    2. Current status; immediate and long-term objectives
    3. Meeting a new/existing market's needs
    4. Raising seed money
       a. Mission statement (must be clear, precise, and compelling)
       b. Approach for initiating new organization
       c. Time schedule for starting the business
       d. The unique opportunity
       e. Description of business objectives in clear, simple, nontechnical
          terms
       f. Long-range objectives
       g. Short-range goals
       h. Character and image of business
  C. Background and the market opportunity
    1. The competition
    2. A growing market
       a. Meeting competition
       b. Market growth data
       c. Competition (include printed material in appendix)
       d. Who buys product now, for what, where, and when?
       e. Needs and wants of intended market segment
       f. Market survey data used to develop plan and select market niche
  D. Personnel
    1. Qualifications to run the business individually and as a team
    2. Organization of the business at present
    3. Organization of the business after funding
    4. President and CEO
    5. Marketing manager
    6. Treasurer
    7. Secretary
    8. Engineering management
    9. Board of directors
       a. Resumes of management team and qualifications track record
          (select a consistent, powerful format)
       b. Organization chart (pre-funding, post-funding) of officers, board
          of directors, key employees
  E. Product description
    1. First product
    2. Design drawing (attached; investors love to see pictures, sketches,
       and drawings in business plans)
    3. Functional specifications

    4. Sample (mock-up is okay) advertising brochure including sketch or photo
       a. Description of product with drawings, sketches, pictures, or illustrations
       b. Desirability, advantages of product
       c. Present state of the art, trends, predictions for your place or niche
       d. Patentability or uniqueness of product (Do not include too much technical information in your business plan. Specifically, technology-related details that you consider trade secrets probably should not be written down in your business plan. Business plans frequently circulate far beyond your wildest dreams.)
       e. Describe a family of (future) products (one product usually does not make a business)

F. Marketing strategy
    1. Distribution arrangements
    2. Direct sales, rentals
    3. Sales channels, costs, and calls per salesperson per year
    4. Unique promotional concepts
    5. Delivery, field support, and maintenance emphasized
       a. Marketing approach (market segment and distribution channels)
       b. Basic selling approach (lead generation, cost per lead and cost per sale, lead generation time, and sales cycle time)
       c. Market share expected over time (By the way, overestimating this number has discredited many financial projections.)
       d. List of three to five people who will buy your new product (Get their names and permission to call them; some investors rely heavily on potential customer testimony for their due diligence.)
       e. Pricing

G. Development and operations plan
    1. Personnel staffing requirements
    2. Facilities and equipment required to develop and produce product
    3. Make versus buy strategy
    4. In-house production and subcontracting
    5. Research and development required (Keep this to a minimum: investors want a product fast! However, if time plans are not realistic, problems will quickly develop as milestones are missed.)
    6. Operations and manufacturing considerations unique to the product

H. Financial pro formas
    1. Assumptions (State these clearly and explicitly. Format your financial templates so you can easily change any assumption and have the effects immediately filter throughout all spreadsheets. Spend time to set up your spreadsheets right; otherwise minor changes will be hard to accommodate later.)

   2. Profit and loss for 5 years
      a. By quarter, years 1–2
      b. By year, years 1–5
   3. Cash flow and sources and uses of cash for 5 years
      a. By quarter, years 1–2
      b. By year, years 1–5
   4. Balance sheet for 5 years
      a. By quarter, years 1–2
      b. By year, years 1–5
      c. Financials (State assumptions; compute return on investment for
         your sanity check but do not include in plan. This is explained
         later in this chapter.)
      d. Profit and loss statements (sales and profits)
      e. Balance sheets
      f. Cash-flow analysis
      g. Break-even chart for minimum sales goal
      h. Fixed asset acquisition schedule by month (item and amount)
      i. Ownership interest reserved for founders
      j. Capital needed
      k. Founders' share of initial capital investment
 I. Capitalization plan
   1. History, funding plan, capitalization, and current ownership
   2. Authorized, outstanding and reserved stock, warrants, and options;
      certain loans and other financial transactions
   3. Use of proceeds
 J. Summary and Conclusions
   1. Unique opportunity
   2. High-risk, high-reward investment
   3. Investor qualifications
   4. Time schedule for funding
 K. Appendix
   1. Articles from trade journals
   2. Competitors' literature
   3. Resumes (if not included in body)
   4. Product design drawings, photos
   5. Sample brochure (dummy okay)
   6. Customer references

Adding or Highlighting Sections

It is important for you to take the time to work up an outline before you write
your plan and to customize that outline to fit to your situation.

If you attempt to include all of the topics suggested thus far in this chapter, you
will have a plan that is much too long and too difficult to assimilate. Know what

aspects are important to your business' success and document those. For example, if your start-up will be capital-intensive, a capital equipment acquisition schedule and cost sheet would be exceedingly useful in addition to the standard financial pro formas.

One start-up business had a customer list of five *Fortune* 100 companies from earlier contract work and added a section to its business plan entitled "Existing Customer Base." It made quite an impression on investors. Here were good references that could be checked during due diligence, along with important evidence that this start-up had a head start. Everyone looks for such an advantage. If you make use of customer lists, make sure you do not violate noncompete agreements or misappropriate trade secrets.

Another company was modeled after others in a very successful industry (although they were not to be direct competitors). It added a section entitled "Why We are a Good Investment," which tabulated sales levels and company valuations over a period of time for these model companies. Investors clearly associated with these success models, and it made the start-up's pitch more credible.

A third company had not only a strong management team, but an active and capable board of directors who truly helped to manage the business. It had a section in its plan entitled "Management and Board of Directors."

Are your product development plans especially complex, or are you proposing to develop a complex process? If so, you will want to convince your investors that you can get there in a reasonable time frame since rapid profitability is the key to high return on investment. You could consider adding a section on schedules and milestones.

Identify the strengths and selling points of your business proposal and promote them in your business plan. Identify any perceived weaknesses in your venture and adequately defend them. Make sure this important material is highlighted in your executive summary and is easy to find in the body of the plan. Use existing guides to assist you and to help you check for completeness, but do not let them bind you.

Classic Problems

Your new venture could fail for several reasons. In preparing your business plan be on the lookout for the following classic problems:

- inadequate market knowledge
- ineffective marketing or sales approach
- inadequate awareness of competitive pressures

- potentially faulty product performance

- rapid product obsolescence

- poor timing for the start of a new business

- undercapitalization due to unforeseen operating expenses, excessive investment in fixed assets like buildings or land, or other financial difficulties

Use Standard Ratios

Use standard and expected ratios in your financial cost estimates. For example, if the expenses for marketing and sales in your industry typically run 16–17%, you will have much explaining to do if you show less than 10% or more than 20%. Sophisticated investors examining your financial projections will take you for an amateur if you are too far off on common expense ratios. The same goes for revenues and gross and net profit margins. Study the trade and financial literature in your industry to find numerous ratio examples such as the following.

Marketing, sales, and general and administrative costs as a percent of total revenue:

- HP, a large, stable company, spends about 25% of total revenues for marketing, sales, and general administrative costs.

- DEC's selling and administrative costs in 1989 were 31% of revenues; for Sun Microsystems, the figure was only about 24%.

- SG&A (selling, general, and administrative) is normally high in a technology-based company: about 35–40% of product revenue.

- In the computer business it is common to spend more than 20% of revenues on direct sales, service, and post-sale support.

- High-technology companies often spend 10–20% of revenues on direct sales.

Gross and net margins as a percent of total revenue:

- HP showed a gross margin (total revenues minus cost of goods sold) of approximately 50%.

- A net margin (after-tax profit) of 10% is often considered substantial.

- Net margins (after tax) should usually exceed 10% for a software company.

Research and development (R&D) expenses as a percent of total revenue:

- HP spends about 8% on R&D.

- R&D is normally 15–20% of product revenue in a technology company.

Revenue ratios:

- Revenue from maintenance for a software company might equal 10–18% of the product cost and be subscribed to by 50% of all customers.

Advertising and promotion:

- In technology-oriented companies, a large sum will be spent on documentation, while only a small amount will be spent on advertising and promotion. Most marketing expenses are earmarked for direct sales, training and supporting distribution channels, customer education and application support, service, and post-sale support.

- In consumer businesses, promotional costs can exceed 10% of revenues.

Sales per employee:

- Typically, a company in the expansion stage and beyond will have $150,000 to $200,000 in revenue per employee. Revenue of $300,000 per employee is not unheard of in software companies.

This last ratio of revenue (sales) per employee is very important. You need to obtain industry figures for your business to make sure your plan makes sense. For example, Figure 11-3 (reported in *Electronic Business*, July 22, 1991) clearly shows not only that revenue per employee is high in the electronics industry, but that it is climbing even higher. If your business falls in the area of electronics and your plan shows revenues of only $100,000 per employee, you may not be taken very seriously.

Are you projecting revenues or profit margins above or below investor expectations? Miss these marks and your plan could be quickly dismissed.

It is not difficult to obtain information on these ratios. Visit the library and obtain copies of other business plans from your associates and team members. You should also evaluate several annual reports of young, growing public companies in your industry. You can obtain these reports from any public companies just by calling them up and asking for the investor relations department. Tell them you are a private investor and wish to receive copies of the latest annual report and any subsequent quarterly reports. Ask for their 10K and 10Q, which are more complete versions of these reports that they are required to submit to the SEC and make available to anyone who asks for copies.

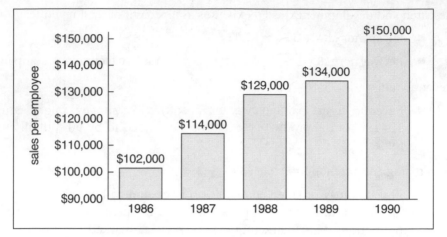

Figure 11-3   Productivity for the Top 200 Electronics Companies

See Table 11-1 for some excellent benchmarks if you plan to launch a software-based business. These typical operating expenses as a percent of revenue for software companies come from the September 1991 issue of David Bowen's *Software Success* survey, where he compiled responses from 50 of his subscribers. There are very few financial benchmarks of this quality available for small software companies, and this information can be critical to the successful management of your business.

Looking Like an Amateur

It is difficult not to look like an amateur if you admittedly are one. Most engineers attempting their first start-up will not have had the operations and business experience needed to prepare a first-class business plan, attract capital, and pull off the execution. This is why it is important to build a strong management team to help you launch your start-up. As discussed in Chapter 2, you might even want one of your team members to be the CEO while you take on the position of engineering vice president.

Financial Pro Forma Documents to Generate and Master

Balance sheet, profit and loss (P&L) statement, and sources and uses of cash (and cash flow) are the three basic financial statements that must be clearly understood by the start-up entrepreneur. If you rely on someone else to generate these statements for you, you will not understand them and you will not be able to defend them. Worse, you will not be able to use them to control your business. If you wonder why a fresh MBA gets paid a lot of money to run a company while

Table 11-1 Operating Expenses for Software Companies
as a Percent of Revenue

Category	1991 (%)	1990 (%)
revenue		
product revenue	76.8	84.0
support revenue	15.4	8.0
professional services	7.8	8.0
	100.0	100.0
cost of sales		
hardware	5.9	3.0
royalties	4.4	4.0
other cost of goods sold	5.5	7.0
total cost of goods sold	15.8	14.0
gross margin	84.2	86.0
marketing expenses		
salaries	3.0	6.0
promotion/lead generation	11.1	11.0
	14.1	17.0
sales expenses		
salaries	5.6	8.0
commissions	4.5	2.0
other	0.6	0.0
	10.7	10.0
support expenses		
salaries	8.6	8.0
other	1.0	1.0
	9.6	9.0
development expenses		
salaries	15.0	13.0
computers	3.0	3.0
other	1.7	1.0
	19.7	17.0
administrative expenses		
salaries	6.8	9.0
facilities	5.3	4.0
other	7.0	8.0
	19.1	21.0
total expenses	89.0	88.0
profit before tax	11.0	12.0

Professional Publications, Inc. ▪ Belmont, CA

engineers seem to be relatively underpaid and have to struggle to get promoted, the MBA's understanding of financial controls is part of the answer. While it takes no genius to get an MBA degree (most engineering degrees are harder to earn than most MBAs), the MBA often has the financial edge. It is suggested that you attend several night school college classes in finance and accounting before you try to start your own company. Your investors will be looking for someone with financial control skills to run your business. Even if one of your team is financially experienced, all founders will benefit from familiarity with financial jargon and procedures.

Working Backward

As you start to prepare the financial projections for your business, it is tempting to work backward from the answers. For example, you may have figured out that in five years you need to have revenues of $50 million and 10% post-tax profits in order to allow your investors to obtain a compounded 25% return on investment. If you iterate through a spreadsheet to calculate the required sales price of your product to meet these goals, all you have is a number that works in the model, not in the market. It is okay to calculate this number as a sanity check, just do not use it in your model.

Get Good Data

The hardest part of preparing financial projections is not in the mechanics, but in getting good data. "Garbage-in, garbage-out" is an old computer programming expression that doubly applies here. In the preceding example, you must determine your sales price from the market. What people will pay for your product is based on what benefits it delivers to them and what alternative products cost. You must clearly understand your market and competition before you can create your financial plans. Engineers in particular tend to ignore the marketing side of a business, figuring that sales problems can be dealt with later.

Do Not Ignore Your Own Data

After you know what the market will pay for your product, you can look at your cost-of-goods and backward-computed required price to see if you have a viable business plan. If you do not, you must seriously rethink whether your business is viable or not. Keep in mind that the most important purpose of the business plan is to convince yourself that this is a reasonable thing to do; selling your ideas to investors is secondary. Start a business for which your numbers initially tell you that you will fail and you will probably fail. Many failed start-ups likely had initial business plans that indicated a flaw which was ignored.

Writing a business plan forces you to consider every aspect of your proposed business. Any information you put into the business plan should confirm and reinforce information you earlier relied upon. Resolve any discrepancies to your satisfaction before proceeding.

Balance Sheet

The balance sheet financial report is sometimes called a *statement of condition* or *statement of financial position* because it represents the state of the business at a point in time. This snapshot of your business differs from a profit and loss statement, for example, which summarizes activity over a period of time. A balance sheet shows the status of your company's assets, liabilities, and owners' equity on a given date, usually the close of a month or year. One way of looking at your business is as a mass of capital (assets) arrayed against the sources of capital (liabilities and equity). Assets must always equal liabilities plus equity.

Your balance sheet lists the items that make up the two sides of this equation. To efficiently analyze a balance sheet, you need to compare it to prior balance sheets (e.g., to see an improvement or degradation in various positions and ratios) and other operating statements (e.g., profit and loss, sources and uses of cash, etc.).

The sample balance sheet shown in Figure 11-4 indicates the level of detail you should strive for. The actual numbers are relatively meaningless, and are included only as examples. Your business needs will dictate what values should be inserted. Lines with zero amounts should be included so your reader will not think you missed something. In addition to projected balance sheets for the end of each of your first five years, you will also want to prepare quarterly sheets for the first two years. Some investors will insist that you prepare these quarterly balance sheets. Again, your worksheets should be assumption-based, allowing you to quickly enter different estimates to immediately see the results as they filter throughout all your linked financial pro formas.

Profit and Loss (P&L) Statement

The P&L statement is a summary of the revenues (sales), costs, and expenses of your company during an accounting period. The P&L is sometimes called an *income statement, operating statement, statement of profit and loss,* or *income and expense statement.* Look at the annual reports from a variety of public companies until you become comfortable with the various names and formats for the P&L. It is the easiest of the three statements to comprehend.

The sample P&L (income) statement in Figure 11-5 shows what you should strive for. While this figure illustrates a less detailed profit and loss statement by year for five years, you will also want to prepare a more detailed statement by month and quarter for the first year and by quarter for the second year.

	Year 1	Year 2	Year 3	Year 4	Year 5
Assets					
Current Assets					
cash	$10,000	$10,000	$10,000	$10,000	$10,000
investments	$1,800	$2,700	$4,050	$6,075	$9,112
accounts receivable	$29,500	$47,200	$75,520	$120,832	$193,331
notes receivable	$5,000	$5,000	$5,000	$5,000	$5,000
inventory	$45,000	$60,750	$82,013	$110,717	$149,468
total current assets	$91,300	$125,650	$176,583	$252,624	$366,911
Plant and Equipment					
building	$175,000	$175,000	$175,000	$175,000	$175,000
office equipment	$62,000	$62,000	$62,000	$62,000	$62,000
leasehold improvements	$18,500	$18,500	$18,500	$18,500	$18,500
less accumulated depreciation	$0	$0	$0	$0	$0
net property and equipment	$255,500	$255,500	$255,500	$255,500	$255,500
Other Assets	$0	$0	$0	$0	$0
Total Assets	$346,800	$381,150	$432,083	$508,124	$622,411
Liabilities and Owner Equity					
Current Liabilities					
short-term debt	$13,500	$13,500	$13,500	$13,500	$13,500
accounts payable	$22,500	$29,250	$38,025	$49,433	$64,262
income taxes payable	$1,500	$1,500	$1,500	$1,500	$1,500
accrued liabilities	$0	$0	$0	$0	$0
total current liabilities	$37,500	$44,250	$53,025	$64,433	$79,262
Long-Term Debt	$22,000	$19,800	$17,820	$16,038	$14,434
Owner/Stockholder Equity					
common stock	$250,000	$272,340	$307,526	$363,199	$451,370
retained earnings	$37,300	$44,760	$53,712	$64,454	$77,345
Total Liabilities and Owner Equity	$346,800	$381,150	$432,083	$508,124	$622,411
Ratios					
current ratio = (total current assets/total current liabilities)	2.43	2.84	3.33	3.92	4.63
quick ratio = (cash + accounts receivable + notes receivable/total current liabilities)	1.19	1.41	1.71	2.11	2.63
return on assets = total assets/net income					

Figure 11-4 Balance Sheet

Notice how much easier your tabular data is to comprehend when you make it into a graph as shown in Figure 11-6. Good business plans should be highly pictorial and easy to read.

	Year 1	Year 2	Year 3	Year 4	Year 5
Sales					
product or service A	$58,000	$95,700	$157,905	$260,543	$429,896
percent of total sales	58%	61%	66%	69%	72%
product or service B	$22,000	$28,600	$37,180	$48,334	$62,834
percent of total sales	22%	18%	15%	13%	11%
product or service C	$20,000	$32,000	$45,000	$67,500	$101,250
percent of total sales	20%	20%	19%	18%	17%
total sales	$100,000	$156,300	$240,085	$376,377	$593,980
Cost of Sales					
materials	$21,500	$33,325	$51,654	$80,063	$124,098
percent of total sales	22%	21%	22%	21%	21%
labor	$31,000	$44,950	$65,178	$94,507	$137,036
percent of total sales	31%	29%	27%	25%	23%
overhead	$18,500	$24,050	$31,265	$40,645	$52,838
percent of total sales	19%	15%	13%	11%	9%
total cost of sales	$71,000	$102,325	$148,097	$215,215	$313,972
Gross Profit	$29,000	$53,975	$91,988	$161,162	$280,008
gross margin	29%	35%	38%	43%	47%
Operating Expenses					
selling costs	$2,000	$2,500	$3,125	$3,906	$4,883
percent of total sales	2%	2%	1%	1%	1%
research and development	$2,800	$3,780	$5,103	$6,889	$9,300
percent of total sales	3%	2%	2%	2%	2%
general and administrative	$4,100	$4,102	$4,103	$4,105	$4106
percent of total sales	4%	3%	2%	1%	1%
total operating expenses	$8,900	$10,382	$12,331	$14,900	$18,289
percent of total sales	9%	7%	5%	4%	3%
income from operations	$20,100	$43,593	$79,657	$146,262	$261,719
percent of total sales	20%	28%	33%	39%	44%
interest income (expense)	($5,000)	($4,999)	($4,998)	($4,997)	($4,997)
income before taxes	$15,100	$38,594	$74,659	$141,265	$256,722
taxes on income	$5,889	$15,052	$29,117	$55,093	$100,122
Net Income	$9,211	$23,542	$45,542	$86,172	$156,600
percent of total sales	9%	15%	19%	23%	26%

Figure 11-5   Profit and Loss (Income) Statement
Adapted from JIAN BizPlan*Builder*™ with permission.

Revenue versus Income

Many people are confused by the terms *revenue* and *income*. In the business situation, revenue denotes the gross figure, namely the sales from the business. Income denotes the net figure: the sum remaining after expenses or cost-of-goods-sold have been deducted (namely the profit). However, there are many different accounting, financial, and common definitions of these terms, and gross income can certainly mean the same thing as revenue in some contexts. Do not be

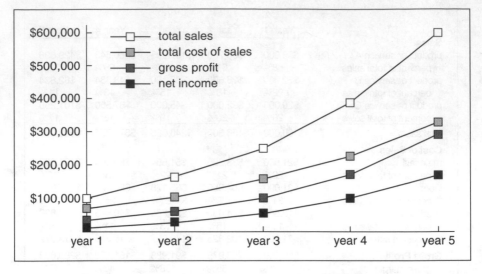

Figure 11-6   Plot of Profit and Loss (Income) Statement

embarrassed if you find yourself confusing the two. Perhaps because salary is often informally equated with personal income, many first-time entrepreneurs correspondingly confuse what one might call a business' sales income (i.e., its revenue), with the business' income. If you study the following equations, the confusion quickly dissipates. In a simple salaried situation, you have no deductible costs associated with producing the services for which you are paid. Thus, your revenue for working is equivalent to your income.

General Terminology	Salaried Terminology	Business Terminology
gross revenue	salary or personal income	sales income or revenue
less cost of providing goods or services	less cost-of-services-provided ($0)	less cost-of-goods-sold (COGS) ($ > 0)
equals income	still equals income	equals profit or income

Sources and Uses of Cash (and Cash Flow)

This is the most difficult of the three financial statements to understand. While it is relatively simple to generate and understand a cash flow statement, the more modern sources and uses of cash statement, which includes cash flow, requires a deeper understanding of finance. You can master the sources and uses of cash statement with practice and disciplined study of each line item.

Sometimes called the *sources and uses of funds statement* or *source and applications of funds statement*, this statement allows you to analyze the changes in the financial position (represented by the balance sheet and the P&L statement) of your business from one accounting period to another. You will find that these statements are now required in the annual reports of all public companies, and it is suggested that you study several of them.

To understand the sources and uses of cash statement, you first need to know what working capital is. Working capital is equal to current assets minus current liabilities, and it finances the cash conversion cycle of your business. The cash conversion cycle includes the time required to convert raw materials into finished goods, finished goods into sales, and accounts receivable into cash.

If you are unfamiliar with any of the preceding terms or with concepts such as depreciation, net income, etc., you should pick up a pocket dictionary of finance and investment terms. The sources and uses of cash statement has two parts: the sources of funds summarizes the transactions that increase working capital such as net income, depreciation, the issue of bonds, sale of stock, or an increase in deferred taxes; the uses of funds or applications of funds summarizes the way funds are used, such as for the purchase or improvement of plant and equipment, the payment of dividends, the repayment of long-term debt, or the redemption or repurchase of shares.

The sample sources and uses of cash statement shown in Figure 11-7 again indicates what you should strive for. While illustrated here is a less detailed yearly statement for just the first three years, you would prepare a sources and uses statement by month or quarter for your first two years, as well as yearly statements for five years.

Many people break out a simple cash flow statement by month or quarter for the first year or two (illustrated in Figure 11-8) which gives a clearer picture of your net cash balance over time (which is of significant interest if you want to quickly see that you can make every payroll). Data from June through November are suppressed to improve readability. Earlier business plans often include only a cash flow projection.

While the cash flow statement shows actual cash requirements, the sources and uses of funds includes noncash expenses like depreciation and therefore shows more clearly cash availability and expenditure.

	Year 1	Year 2	Year 3
Source of Funds			
income after taxes	$54,500	$163,500	$490,500
depreciation and amortization	$22,000	$22,000	$22,000
operating cash flow	$76,500	$185,500	$512,500
increased long-term debt	$40,000	$40,000	$40,000
issuance of stock	$100,000	$50,000	$100,000
total source of funds	$216,500	$275,500	$652,500
Use of Funds			
marketing and advertising	$25,000	$37,500	$88,000
salaries	$15,000	$15,000	$60,000
facilities	$65,000	$70,000	$90,000
capital equipment	$18,000	$22,500	$101,000
research and development	$20,000	$40,000	$85,000
operations expenses	$22,500	$23,500	$66,000
cash dividends	$0	$0	$0
increased working capital	$51,000	$67,000	$162,500
total use of funds	$216,500	$275,500	$652,500
Summary of Changes in Working Capital			
decreased cash	($20,000)	($20,000)	($47,000)
increased accounts receivable	$32,000	$30,000	$181,000
increased inventory	$40,000	$58,000	$52,500
increased accounts payable	($16,000)	($16,000)	($39,000)
decreased notes payable	$15,000	$15,000	$15,000
increased working capital	$51,000	$67,000	$162,500

Figure 11-7   Sources and Uses of Cash Statement
Adapted from JIAN BizPlan*Builder*™, with permission.

Again, it is helpful to show your reader this data in graphic form, as shown in Figure 11-9. JIAN states that:

> The cash flow projection incorporated in BizPlan *Builder*™ by most standards is a hybrid. Several categories are broken out to make it easier to project cash requirements based on decisions regarding advertising, sales commissions, salaries, equipment leases/purchases, and office lease. These expenses are the ones most often under direct management control. They are the ones (in addition to cost of sales) where funding will directly apply, and among other things, [which] you must convince your investors to fund.

> Outside of operating cash flow, your money and that of your investors is entered in beginning cash balance, sale of stock, and proceeds of bank loan. Work with these numbers to maintain a positive net cash

	Jan.	Feb.	Mar.	Apr.	May	Dec.
Beginning Cash Balance	$10,000	$44,174	$32,317	$19,459	$10,950	$46,061
Cash Receipts						
sales	$31,500	$34,650	$38,115	$41,927	$46,119	$89,873
interest income	$44	$193	$141	$85	$48	$202
total cash receipts	$31,544	$34,843	$38,256	$42,012	$46,167	$90,075
Cash Disbursements						
accounts payable	$15,800	$16,748	$17,753	$18,818	$19,947	$29,993
advertising	$1,200	$1,200	$1,200	$1,200	$1,200	$1,200
commissions (10% of sales)	$3,150	$3,465	$3,812	$4,193	$4,612	$8,987
salaries	$2,500	$2,500	$2,500	$2,500	$2,500	$2,500
other expenses	$3,100	$3,162	$3,225	$3,290	$3,356	$3,854
tax payments	$1,500	$1,500	$1,500	$1,500	$1,500	$1,500
total cash disbursements	$27,250	$28,575	$29,990	$31,501	$33,115	$48,034
Net Cash from Operations	$4,294	$6,268	$8,267	$10,511	$13,052	$42,040
equipment lease	$125	$125	$125	$125	$125	$125
equipment purchase	$1,995	$0	$3,000	$895	$18,500	$4,400
office lease	$3,000	$3,000	$3,000	$3,000	$3,000	$3,000
short-term loan repayment	$15,000	$15,000	$15,000	$15,000	$15,000	$15,000
sale of stock partnership units	$50,000	$0	$0	$0	$0	$0
proceeds of bank loan	$0	$0	$0	$0	$25,000	$0
Net Cash Balance	$44,174	$32,317	$19,459	$10,950	$12,377	$65,576

Figure 11-8   Simple Cash Flow Statement
Adapted from JIAN BizPlan*Builder*^{TM}, with permission.

balance; a rule of thumb to use is to raise between 50–100% more cash than the cash flow statement indicates you will need.

Break-Even Analysis

Since becoming profitable as soon as possible is the most important goal you can make if you want to optimize the valuation of your business, you and your investors will want to know when your business will break even. Break-even occurs when sales equal costs. A break-even analysis determines this point by computing the volume of sales at which fixed and variable costs will be covered. All sales above the break-even point produce profits; any drop in sales below that point will produce losses. A break-even analysis is a rough but important gauge of the volume of sales you need to attain profitability. Break-even for an imaginary company is shown in Table 11-2.

Fixed costs include such items as rent, management salaries, utilities, insurance, taxes, and depreciation. Variable costs include items such as supplies, outside labor, raw materials, production wages, advertising, and maintenance.

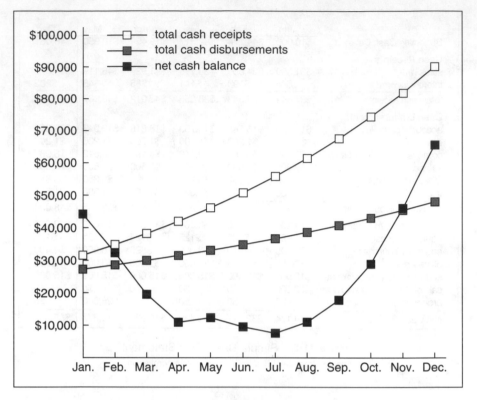

Figure 11-9   Cash Flow Projection Chart

Again, it is important that you prepare a break-even chart similar to the one shown in Figure 11-10. Nothing is more frustrating than trying to see what numbers mean in tabular form. All modern spreadsheet programs support charting from your raw data. By example, each of the charts you see in this chapter was created in just a few minutes using the data in the example financial pro forma spreadsheets.

Investor's Hurdle Rate of Return on Investment

It is to your advantage to know what measures investors use in determining which companies they will invest in, how you can compute these measures, and how you can use them to evaluate and help sell your business plan. If your venture's rate of return on investment does not exceed your investor's hurdle rate (i.e., the minimum needed to be considered), your plan will not be given further consideration.

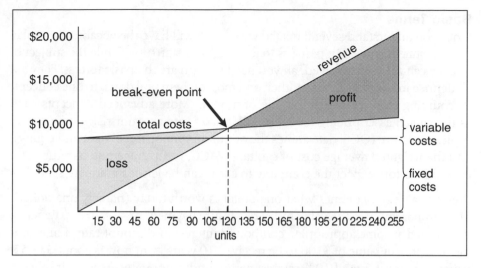

Figure 11-10   Break-Even Analysis Chart: Realistic Case

Table 11-2   Break-Even Analysis

	Per Month Optimistic	Per Month Realistic	Per Month Pessimistic
Fixed Costs			
administrative costs	$225	$563	$1,406
R&D investment	$2,800	$4,200	$6,300
selling costs	$2,100	$3,150	$4,725
total fixed costs (TFC)	$5,125	$7,913	$12,431
Variable Costs			
cost of goods sold	$4,490	$6,735	$10,103
total variable costs (TVC)	$4,490	$6,735	$10,103
Pricing & Unit Sales Variables			
selling price (SP)	$79.00	$79.00	$79.00
number of units (U)	600	500	400
variable costs per unit	$7.48	$13.47	$25.26
break-even unit volume	72	121	231
gross profit	$37,785.00	$24,852.00	$9,066.00

Adapted from JIAN BizPlan*Builder*™, with permission.

Basic Terms

Once you understand several related terms, you will have the vocabulary to play the investment game as it pertains to funding your start-up. While the subject of finance can get very involved, all you need to learn are the basic terms. They are all defined in relation to one another, and most of them boil down to one concept: discounting cash for the time-value of money. More advanced concepts such as the capital asset pricing model (CAPM; takes into account risk), the optimal capital structure (OCS; determines the optimum proportion of debt and equity), and the weighted average cost of capital (WACC; the average rate of return that capital investors expect the company to earn) can be left for graduate school.

Present value (PV) defines what one dollar is worth today (namely one dollar). More important, it is the value today of a future payment or stream of payments, discounted at some appropriate compound interest or discount rate. For example, the present value of $100 to be received 10 years from now is about $38.55, using a discount rate of 10% interest compounded annually. This is simply the time-value of money. If you were to put your savings in a riskless (before-tax) 10% annually compounded savings account, it should make no difference to you if you received $38.55 today or $100 in 10 years.

I = cash invested at the beginning of a holding period

PV = discounted value of a future payment or series of payments

Future value (FV) is simply the amount to which an investment will grow at a future time if it earns a specified interest that is compounded annually. It can easily be shown that the FV of an initial investment I compounded annually at rate i for n years is:

$$FV = I\,(1 + i)^n \tag{1}$$

= cash yielded at the end of an investment holding period

Cash-on-cash returns (COC) is the simplest measure of an investment return. It is widely used to describe venture capital investments.

$$COC = \frac{FV}{I} \tag{2}$$

As you can see, COC does not take into account the time-value of money. Therefore, investors often describe their performance goals in terms of COC and a period of time. For example, if you hear that an investor expects a 10 times return in five years, that means COC should equal 10 after a five-year holding period.

One can easily compute the actual annual compounded rate of return, i, achieved by a particular COC return over a period of n years from the preceding equations. Financial calculators or tables are usually consulted.

From Equation [1],

$$(1 + i)^n = \frac{FV}{I}$$

Substituting Equation [2],

$$(1 + i)^n = COC$$
$$(1 + i) = COC^{\frac{1}{n}}$$
$$i = COC^{\frac{1}{n}} - 1 \qquad\qquad [3]$$

Thus, in the example of COC = 10 in n = 5 years,

$$i = (10)^{\frac{1}{5}} - 1$$
$$= (10)^{0.2} - 1$$
$$= 1.584893 - 1 = 0.584893$$
$$= 58.4893\%$$

Under the net present value method (NPV), the present value (PV) of all cash inflows from an investment is compared against the initial investment (I). The net present value (NPV) is simply the difference between PV and I.

NPV determines whether an investment is acceptable. To compute the PV of cash inflows, a discount rate called the *cost of capital* is used for discounting. Under this method, if NPV > 0 (or equivalently, PV > I), the investment should be made.

Rate of return or rate (of return) on investment (ROI) is equivalent to the internal rate of return (IRR) needed for the net present value of one's investment to be zero. Any financial calculator will spit out that number. This is sometimes a difficult concept to understand. Working through a few examples in a finance textbook will make this relationship clear.

Thus, IRR is the discount rate at which the present value of the future cash flows of an investment equal the cost of the investment. When the net present values of cash outflows (the cost of the investment) and cash inflows (returns on the investment) equal zero, the rate of discount being used is the IRR.

When IRR is greater than the investor's required return on investment (called the *hurdle rate* in capital budgeting) the investment is acceptable.

An investment can profitably be made when IRR exceeds the cost of capital.

Investors May Examine Your Financials First

Some venture capital investors will assign a part-time junior assistant (usually an MBA student) to first examine your financial pro forma documents (informally referred to as your *financials*) before attempting to understand your business (i.e., your market, your product, or the strength of your team). This is done with the thought that if your numbers do not reflect the return needed to meet their ROI hurdle criterion, they would not invest in your start-up. For this reason alone, you must do your best in preparing your financial projections.

Because the investor's ROI depends on his or her percentage equity ownership and price per share paid (items yet to be negotiated), ROI does not fall out of any of the business plan financial pro forma projections.

You could compute ROI for a given investment scenario and include this in your plan, but most people do not. Including investor's ROI in your financial section forces you to make a presumption on the valuation of your company, and many investors prefer that you do not do that for them. While it might seem to make sense to include this information to prove that you know that this is a good investment, do not do so. If you want VCs' money, play by their rules. In oral presentations to VCs, be prepared to respond to questions concerning ROI.

Valuation

Investors want to calculate their ROI themselves based on their valuation calculations and using their methods, and they probably figure that in doing so they have a little edge on you. Calculating an investor's ROI is akin to computing someone else's income taxes without knowing their income (because investors will discount your projected revenues to a level they feel is attainable, and you will not know what discount they used). Because no two people would likely give your company the same valuation independently, calculating an ROI for your investors is indeed presumptive. Chapter 17 contains essential information for you to understand exactly how investors put a valuation on a company (the methods differ widely). Only when you understand how much your company is worth to your investors can you begin to estimate how much equity you should give up for your seed or start-up capital. Without this knowledge, you may just have to settle for a rule-of-thumb explanation for any proposed pricing, and your stock will likely be underpriced. Unfortunately, supposed rule-of-thumb valuations have funded more companies than you might imagine.

While you will not include ROI in your plan, you must calculate it to make sure your plan will not be rejected. It is surprising how many entrepreneurs neglect to compute ROI.

A company's ROI can be expressed as a percentage earned on the company's total capital (its common and preferred stock equity plus its long-term funded debt), calculated by dividing total capital into earnings before interest, taxes, and dividends. It should be easy enough to calculate ROI for a company. However, while this number might be an overall useful measure, for the individual investor it does not answer the question, "Should I invest in this company?"

When an individual investor computes his or her ROI, the thinking is, "How much will my return be in compounded annual terms, in so many years, when I cash out?" To figure this out, one needs to know:

- How much is paid per share at year 0?

- What can a share be sold for at year N?

From these two valuation-related numbers, you can see that ROI is the internal rate of return (IRR) needed for the net present value of one's investment to be zero. Any financial calculator will furnish that number.

- Given a target IRR, one can compute the purchase price per share needed for an assumed cash-out price and holding period.

- Given a target IRR, one can compute the cash-out price per share needed for a given purchase price and holding period.

- Given a target IRR, one can compute the maximum holding period one can tolerate in order to cash out at an assumed cash-out price for a given purchase price.

- IRR can be computed by setting any other target variable and making estimates of the others.

Your potential investors will attempt to compute your company's future valuation, figure in their required percentage ownership, and determine what would be a fair purchase price reflecting a judgment of current valuation. Again, Chapter 17 contains detailed information to enable you to attempt this same feat.

Table 11-3 shows an investor's IRR for several investment scenarios. Your task is to show that your company will generate such good profits so rapidly that the investor's hurdle rate of return on investment criterion can be met without needing to acquire an unreasonable percentage of your company in the seed or start-up round.

Table 11-3 shows cash flows from the investor's pocketbook. Assume that $10 is paid per share in year zero. For simplicity, no additional cash exchanges hands during years one through four. In year five, anywhere from $10 to $150 is returned to the investor at cash-out time. The investor's corresponding IRR is shown in the right-hand column.

Table 11-3   IRR for Given Cash Flow

year 0	year 1	year 2	year 3	year 4	year 5	IRR
($10)	$0	$0	$0	$0	$10	0.00%
($10)	$0	$0	$0	$0	$11	1.92%
($10)	$0	$0	$0	$0	$12	3.71%
($10)	$0	$0	$0	$0	$13	5.39%
($10)	$0	$0	$0	$0	**$14**	**6.96%**
($10)	$0	$0	$0	$0	$15	8.45%
($10)	$0	$0	$0	$0	$16	9.86%
($10)	$0	$0	$0	$0	$17	11.20%
($10)	$0	$0	$0	$0	**$18**	**12.47%**
($10)	$0	$0	$0	$0	$19	13.70%
($10)	$0	$0	$0	$0	**$20**	**14.87%**
($10)	$0	$0	$0	$0	$21	16.00%
($10)	$0	$0	$0	$0	$22	17.08%
($10)	$0	$0	$0	$0	$23	18.13%
($10)	$0	$0	$0	$0	$24	19.14%
($10)	$0	$0	$0	$0	$25	20.11%
($10)	$0	$0	$0	$0	$26	21.06%
($10)	$0	$0	$0	$0	$27	21.98%
($10)	$0	$0	$0	$0	$28	22.87%
($10)	$0	$0	$0	$0	$29	23.73%
($10)	$0	$0	$0	$0	$30	24.57%
($10)	$0	$0	$0	$0	**$31**	**25.39%**
($10)	$0	$0	$0	$0	$32	26.19%
($10)	$0	$0	$0	$0	$33	26.97%
($10)	$0	$0	$0	$0	$34	27.73%
($10)	$0	$0	$0	$0	$35	28.47%
($10)	$0	$0	$0	$0	$36	29.20%
($10)	$0	$0	$0	$0	$50	37.97%
($10)	$0	$0	$0	$0	**$70**	**47.58%**
($10)	$0	$0	$0	$0	**$100**	**58.49%**
($10)	$0	$0	$0	$0	**$150**	**71.88%**

How Big Does ROI/IRR Need to Be?

Obviously, investors would like to hit all home runs. Ideally, an investor would get 10 times his or her money back in five years, as shown in Table 11-3; a yield of 58.49% compounded return. In reality, though, the numbers are lower. While VC fund returns may be single digit, VCs still will not invest in any single venture unless they see five to ten times returns (40–60% annually) due to the fact that some investments will fail and others will not perform as well.

A number of years ago, venture capital funds were expected to get 25% returns, meaning that they would triple their investment in five years. Returns of 40–50% were not uncommon, as reported by the *Wall Street Journal*, June 20, 1991. More recently, single digit returns are more usual, returning anywhere from 1.4 to 1.8 times an initial investment over a five-year period. Investors are often finding that they need to stick with a start-up longer than expected. You can imagine that an additional couple of years' holding period drastically lowers returns.

Acquisitions are increasingly the exit vehicle most often available for venture capitalists, as opposed to initial public stock offerings. Unfortunately, cash-on-cash return (i.e., return not discounted for time value) for an IPO is typically seven times the original investment ($70 in the year 5 column in Table 11-3, yielding a 47.58% IRR), whereas an acquisition typically delivers two times the original investment ($20 in the year 5 column in Table 11-3, yielding a 14.87% IRR).

Actual returns earned by venture capital firms are less than might be imagined. Many of the funds formed in the early '80s returned 25% annually or more. The generation of funds formed from 1983 through 1987, known as the *lost generation* of funds, is averaging less than 10%. Many other venture funds formed after 1983 are permanently under water (i.e., are worth less than what they started with) and many will be lucky to earn a 5% return.

Exit Strategy

More and more entrepreneurs are including a section in their business plan that recommends a preferred exit strategy: for example, acquisition by a large company that is also a strategic partner. This is a change from a few years earlier when few gave thought to whether (and if so, how) the business would be sold. The reason for this new awareness is probably that more start-up entrepreneurs see starting a business as a means to an end, not an end in its own right.

Private Placement Memorandum

You may see a variation of the general business plan designed for subsequent rounds of funding for ongoing start-ups from the venture capital community and from sophisticated individual investors. In these cases, the plan is targeted toward these sophisticated investors and serves multiple functions:

- It embodies major sections of the company's general business plan.

- It is a selling document, and thus supposedly represents reality.

■ It is a legal document, meaning that it is the basis for an investor's decision. Because charges of fraud and securities violations can arise from misleading statements or omissions in such a document, it will be a more honest accounting of the business.

Such a business plan will often be entitled a *private placement memorandum*. Here will be described the number and kinds of shares (equity) and notes (debt) authorized, issued, and offered, and at what prices. The legal structure of the business is also described in more detail. Copies of key manager employment contracts (if they exist) will be included, too, along with remuneration schedules of key managers. Terms of stock option arrangements for key managers will be precisely described. Actual past financial statements are presented. Finally, names of accountants, attorneys, and bank officers will be set forth.

In conclusion, as you can see, a well-planned business requires a lot of home-work. If you understand all the issues explained in this chapter, you are indeed very well prepared to proceed. If your start-up does not have a well thought-out business plan, you may be taking a big risk. You will have presumably generated more information by this time than you thought possible and will know whether to proceed.

Business Plan Writing Aids and Financial Planning Aids

There now exist good computer planning aids that will minimize your writing and financial planning efforts. BizPlan*Builder*™ by JIAN, Tools for Sales, along with Tim Berry's *Business Plan Toolkit*™ by Palo Alto Software, are worthy of your consideration, and both are available for either the PC or the Macintosh. Each of these provides a complete business plan text template you can use with almost any word processor to guide you through the construction of your plan. While specific wording with blanks is often provided, you do not have to use the templates' words; you can instead just substitute your own. In other places you will find well-marked reminders to make sure you have considered important points. When you are satisfied that you have included the information needed, or determine that a particular section does not apply to your business situation, merely delete the reminder text.

For more information, contact the following:

- JIAN, Tools for Sales, 127 Second Street, Top Floor, Los Altos, CA 94022, (800) 442-7373, (415) 941-9191, $129.00.

- Palo Alto Software, 260 Sheridan Avenue, Suite 219, Palo Alto, CA 94036, (800) 229-7526, (415) 325-3190, $149.95.

BizPlan*Builder*™

This comes with a complete manual on how to write a business plan along with extensive suggestions for wording to be used in your plan. The following is a sample of this tool's excellent text-writing aid for the executive summary.

Executive Summary

- This section is an abstract of your company's present status and future direction.

- It is usually written after the plan is completed because it gives readers an overview of your business and it indicates how your business plan is organized.

- Edit to about two pages.

In 19___, _____ (your group, company, product developers) were formed to _____ (purpose of activities).

Now, (Company) is at a point where _____.

- Corporate mission statement covering the line of products and services—what kind of company do you want to be?

Background

For many years people have _____.

- How people are managing to do without.
- How and where a similar product or service is now being used.

We have just started/completed the development/introductory phase of (product/service)—a novel and proprietary _____ (e.g., soap for cleaning vinyl). Our operation was producing _____ (sales, units, products) by 19__, and has operated at _____ (financial condition—profitable, break-even, etc.) ever since. Revenue projected for fiscal year 19__ without external funding is expected to be $_____. Annual growth is projected to be _____% per year through 19__.

Concept

The state of the art/condition of the industry today is such that _____.

- Explain your place in the state of the art.
- Description of product or service.
- Desirability of your product or service.

Compared to competitive products (or the closest product available today) our (product/service) _____.

The ability to _____ is a capability unique to (Company)'s products/services.

- How would your customers compare your product with those of competitors?
- Advantages product or service has—its improvements over existing products or services.

Our strategy for meeting the competition is _____ (lower price, bigger/better—your unique selling proposition).

(Company)'s target market includes _____ (types of customers). (Company) is rapidly moving into its _____ (marketing phase).

This approach is generating a tremendous amount of interest throughout our industry.

_____ follow-on products/services, _____ (product) is a _____ and is especially useful to _____ (prospective customers) who can now easily _____.

Other products/services include _____.

All products from (Company) are protected by the trademark and copyright laws, and _____ (patents, etc.).

Responses from customers indicate that _____ (product/service) is enjoying an excellent reputation. Inquiries from prospective customers suggest that there is considerable demand for _____. Relationships with leading OEMs (original equipment manufacturers), retailers, major accounts, manufacturers, and distributors substantiate the fitness of (Company) for considerable growth and accomplishment.

Objectives

- Near term and long term

Our objective, at this time, is to propel the company into a prominent market position. We feel that within _____ years (Company) will be in a suitable condition for an initial public offering or profitable acquisition. To accomplish this goal we have developed a comprehensive plan to intensify and accelerate our marketing activities, product development, services expansion, engineering, distribution and customer service. To implement our plans we require an investment of $_____ for the following purposes (choose the activities pertinent to your goals):

- Build manufacturing facilities and ramp up production to meet customer demands.

- Maximize sales with an extensive campaign to promote our products/services.

- Reinforce customer support services to handle the increased demands created by the influx of new orders and deepened penetration into existing accounts.

- Augment company staff to support and sustain prolonged growth under the new marketing plan.
- Increase research and development to create additional follow-on products/services as well as to further fine-tune our competitive advantages.

Management

Our management team consists of _____ (how many) men and women whose backgrounds consist of _____ years of marketing with _____ (*Fortune* 500 company names always look great here), _____ years of corporate development with _____ (more *Fortune* 500 company names look great here too), _____ people with _____ years of engineering and design with _____, a chief financial officer with _____ years of _____ with _____.

- Actually, any good company backgrounds pertinent to your management team's functions are good references to demonstrate a solid background and assure a higher probability of future success.

Marketing

_____ (research firm, industry report, trade journal study) research projects a worldwide/nationwide market for _____ (product/service) to be approximately $_____ by the end of 19___. Conservative estimates suggest (Company)'s market share, with our intensified and accelerated marketing plan, product/service development, manufacturing, and customer service would be about _____%—generating $_____ by the end of 19___.

- Describe the projections and trends for the industry or business field.

The fundamental thrust of our marketing strategy consists of _____ (unique selling basis).

We intend to reach _____ (market segment) by _____ (marketing/sales/promo tactics).

- Who are your customers? Where are they and how do you reach them?
- Are they buying your product/service from someone else?
- How will you educate customers to buy from you?

Our company can be characterized as a _____ (the business and image for customers to see).

(Company) enjoys an established track record of excellent support for our customers. Their expressions of satisfaction and encouragement are numerous, and we intend to continue our advances in the _____ (marketplace) with more unique and instrumental _____ (product/services).

A partial list of customers includes:

_____

_____

Also, _____ prospective clients presently evaluating _____ (product/services) for use are _____ (actual customers).

■ List customers in customers section.

Finance

■ Briefly forecast financial expectations.

In _____ years we will have _____ (achieved goal) and our investors will be able to _____ (collect their return on investment).

Adapted from JIAN BizPlan*Builder*™, with permission.

Business Plan Toolkit

Business Plan Toolkit for the Macintosh contains a much less lengthy suggestion of text segments for you to go through, but does provide a useful HyperCard utility for collecting and sorting your thoughts on electronic notecards. When you are finished making your electronic cards, they can be automatically collated into one text file for polishing and merging with other financial and graphic data. The HyperCard utility might be attractive to regular HyperCard users, but the small editing window and scantiness of text suggestions may be somewhat of an annoyance, especially on a large screen Macintosh. A screen shot of this tool's HyperCard aid for writing the executive summary is shown.

You can simply click with your mouse on the folder tab buttons to open any of the business plan sections (Summary, Company, Product, Market,

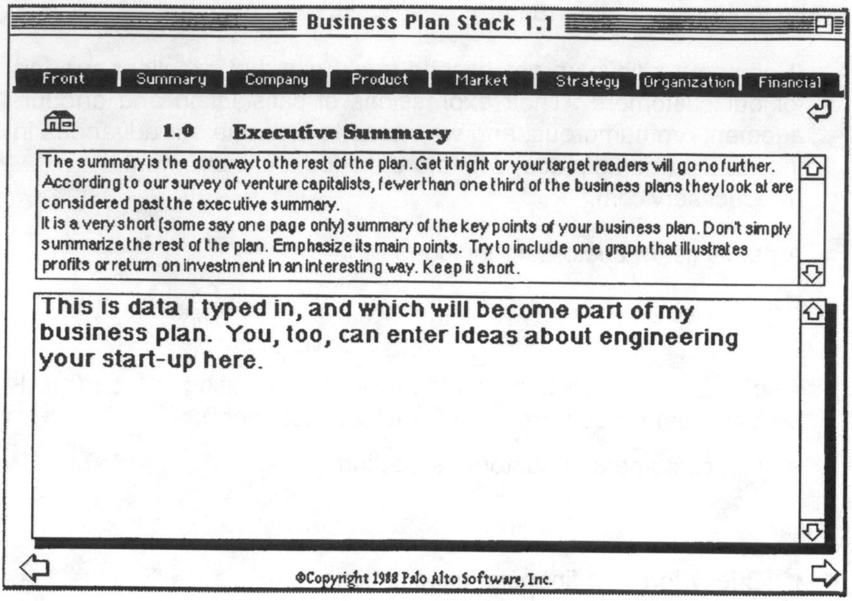

Figure 11-11   Business Plan Toolkit Screen
Adapted from *Business Plan Toolkit*[TM], by permission
from Tim Berry, Palo Alto Software.

Strategy, Organization, or Financial) and enter a new HyperCard prompting script such as that shown for the executive summary.

Business Plan Toolkit's sample text files can also be used to guide your writing process without the HyperCard aid, as shown (again, this is an example for the executive summary).

Executive Summary

- Acme Widget Company (AWC) produces industry-specific widgets from standard widgets. It has its main offices in Upscale, CA, and maintains a small manufacturing and assembly plant in Standard, CA. Its products are sold through distributors and direct-response marketing.

- This business plan is part of our regular business planning process. We revise this plan every quarter.

- In the next full year we intend to develop two new widget products and to improve revenues to more than $250,000 monthly.

- Our keys to success and critical factors for the next year are, in order of importance:
  Product development
  Sales to dealers in volume
  Financial control and cash flow planning

- AWC is a growing concern that has been profitable for the last five years. Figure 1 illustrates highlights of our financial performance over the last three years. Sales have grown to more than $440,000, while net profits are up to more than $50,000.

Also included in *Business Plan Toolkit* and BizPlan*Builder*™ are spreadsheet templates for your financial pro formas. While you can certainly make your own, why not take advantage of good tools created by others? "The right tool for the job" is an expression that applies here. Do not get stingy with a hundred dollars now when time and completeness are so critical for your success. You are likely to find these packages for sale at discount software stores for as low as $79.

Ronstadt's Financials also markets financial planning tools that are designed more for managers and business professionals who cannot afford to spend time learning to use or write formulas and format their own spreadsheets. Ronstadt's Financials is available from Lord Publishing, 49 Eliot Street, Natick, MA 01760 or P.O. Box 806, Dover, MA 02030, (508) 651-9955. It costs about $119 and includes Ronstadt's book, *Entrepreneurial Finance*. When ordering, specify 3.5″ or 5.25″ diskette. This package is designed for the PC only. You use it by entering your business' operating assumptions on a single form. The program automatically generates cash flow statements, balance sheets, and income statements.

In order for you to get a better feeling for the value of the financial planning parts of the two packages reviewed, a few examples have been included. Both are very well done.

BizPlan*Builder*™'s templates consist of both a large integrated template that includes all the schedules in one and individual nonlinked schedules. These represent two fairly different ways to construct your financial pro formas. In the integrated template method, one changed entry automatically updates all the other fields (wherever it is used), but only within this one very large integrated template. That is, rather than using external links between different smaller spreadsheets, there is just one large integrated spreadsheet. To use this spreadsheet you need a fully functional product like Lotus 1-2-3 or a compatible spreadsheet such as Excel. The integrated spreadsheet is recommended unless your spreadsheet program will not support it, in which case you can use the individual nonlinked spreadsheets. However, since you will be using this tool almost daily in your business and there is absolutely no time for errors or delays when you are writing your business plan, it is strongly recommended that you obtain a modern spreadsheet product.

Finally, BizPlan*Builder*™'s templates are built on an assumption-driven model with slots to fill in for your expected starting values and growth rates for all key variables, which can be an exceptionally useful feature.

Business Plan Toolkit's templates consist of an integrated template externally linked to many smaller input schedules; thus, all estimates and changes made in any individual worksheet schedule (sales, for example) show up in the integrated document. In addition, macros are provided to automatically open spreadsheets and charts. For some, the *Business Plan Toolkit*'s multiple-linked-document product represents a somewhat better, more modular approach than BizPlan*Builder*™'s single large integrated template. *Business Plan Toolkit* does require Lotus 1-2-3, Microsoft Excel, or a compatible spreadsheet on the PC, or Microsoft Excel or Works, Lotus 1-2-3, or a SYLK compatible spreadsheet on the Macintosh. At the time of writing, *Business Plan Toolkit*'s templates were based on an older version of Excel (revision 1.5, which still works with newer versions), and a new product release was in the works.

In conclusion, if you are writing your first business plan, then owning one of these two tools is essential.

More experienced entrepreneurs might already have their text and financial templates from previous start-ups, but they would still benefit from the ability to do an on-line check for completeness with either one of these excellent tools.

A third useful package is one that has been adapted from Michael O'Donnell's *Writing Business Plans That Get Results*, a highly recommended workbook. His book has also been marketed as a business plan writing aid by Ronstadt's Financials under the title *Business Plan for Start-ups*. Their version provides word processing software for O'Donnell's book and includes many commonly asked questions.

To obtain this business plan writing diskette, send $14.95 to Lord Publishing, 49 Eliot Street, Natick, MA 01760 or P.O. Box 806, Dover, MA 02030, (508) 651-9955. Specify 3.5″ or 5.25″ floppy.

One Venture Capitalist's Perspective on Plan Emphasis

Addressing the Silicon Valley Engineering Management Society in 1990, Michael Moritz, partner of Sequoia Capital, a Menlo Park, CA firm, stated some interesting opinions:

> In selecting an investment it's all in the timing. Investments in word processing software, for example, a few years before its time, resulted in big losses, whereas at a later point in time they were attractive.

> We ask where is the market, where are the customers [with discretionary funds], where are the [customers'] wallets, what is the product [and how long will it take to ship, especially for software?], and who is the management?

It is interesting that this statement puts less emphasis on management than most. Management and markets, not necessarily in that order, are usually listed as the two most important factors in evaluating a business opportunity.

> First, the market must be right! We want to achieve scale in a few years. Management must be of high quality, and we must see an exit strategy.

> We look for unexploited niches [networking utility software for business was mentioned as one good example].

> We want to see a substantial market potential, a proprietary product or service, existing channels of distribution, and high gross margins.

Moritz cited software as having good gross margin potential; hardware has less, since disk drives look unattractive at 28% gross margin (unless one captures over 50% of the market share). Radius at the time was an exception, having 37% gross margins.

> After the last financing round, 25–30% of the stock should stay with management.

> Our objective is to turn $1 million into $10 million.

> We will typically spend one to two months on due diligence before we invest in a start-up.

Different areas are hot at different times; we like communications, semiconductors, software [prefer existing software], computers and associated peripherals, medical- and health-related technology [instrument] companies, and biotechnology.

A Strong-Management Strong-Market Business Plan

Genµs, Inc., a successful public Silicon Valley company, was incorporated in 1981. It raised $9.5 million of venture capital in just four months based on the strengths represented in a short business plan. To give you a feeling of the importance of strong management and unique market opportunity, look at the following summation of their plan.

Section Title	Number of Pages	Comments
executive summary	2	It is compelling and powerful.
marketing analysis	15	This section is comprehensive (the only section with subsections); it appears first, and it comprises a full one-third of the plan. It is illustrated with many charts and touches on sales and characteristics of the industry. It also lays out the unique market opportunity: • history • direction • market data • similar equipment • target markets • competitive analysis • target market forecast • sales level and strategy
product analysis	4	This section contains enough information to describe what the product will do, but says nothing about how it will be developed or invented. Technology alone is not being sold here.
operations plan	1	It is obviously assumed that the strong management team members, with their proven track records, can administer operations.

Section Title	Number of Pages	Comments
management and key personnel	8	Three two-page resumes for the president/general manager, the V.P. finance, and the V.P. engineering, plus an organization chart succinctly says it all. These managers have performed before and investors know they will perform again. No mention is made of any key engineers who might actually design the product.
financial data	12	Essential and basic information—standard financial pro formas along with: • bookings/backlog forecast • capital/leasehold plan • staffing plan This section tells investors how much money the business is going to make and when, and also what will be spent to make it happen.

Summary of Genµs, Inc., business plan reprinted by permission
of William W. R. Elder, Chairman and CEO of Genµs, Inc.

12

Funding Issues

*"Business? It's quite simple.
It's other people's money."*
— Alexandre Dumas

Investment Criteria

Investors determine how much money they will invest based on your minimum needs, considerations of return on investment, and considerations of risk. Obviously the best opportunity with the lowest risk will attract the most funds. This is why your business plan must reflect your very best effort, and why you should have already made progress in building your management team. You are selling an opportunity, and the evidence of this opportunity and your potential for success is reflected in the essential elements of your business plan as detailed in Chapter 11. A marketable business plan will clearly reflect:

- a unique market/business opportunity
- a complete and experienced management team with a solid track record
- attractive markets and a high likelihood of selling and distributing successfully to identified customers

- sound plans and the technological basis for developing and manufacturing the proposed products

- a clear vision and an operations plan for carrying out the business

- clear financial business objectives and an understanding of the funding requirements to make the venture successful (largely the subject of this chapter)

Cheap Start-Ups are Finished

Unfortunately, the days are past when you could start a high-technology company in your garage or spare bedroom and grow to be a leader in your industry. Stories beginning, "Founded in 1939 in a Palo Alto garage by Stanford electrical engineers William Hewlett and David Packard. . ." are history. Increased competition demands a more professional approach if you are to successfully compete for declining venture capital and other sophisticated investment resources.

A well-known general partner of a prominent Silicon Valley venture capital firm recently stated, "There will be no more successful stand-alone start-ups." By this, he meant that because competition is now so strong and so global, a successful start-up must from its beginning have plans for strategic partner relationships with customers (for product specification and distribution), manufacturers (for low-cost manufacturing), and the government (for plant construction and so forth).

He concludes,

> The rules have changed. While the pace of start-ups has actually turned up, we see more experienced teams starting ventures. Start-ups need at least two initial venture capital investors plus plans for follow-on financing. The big opportunities—and there are big opportunities, such as in pen computing, the life sciences—are still there.

Looking for Seed Cash

Your business plan pro forma financial documents should tell you how much cash you will need to get your venture to the break-even point, i.e., where your revenues will balance your expenses. However, this amount of cash may not represent what you should have to start. Realistically, you may have trouble raising that much seed cash. And, if you did raise that much cash, you might have to give up too much equity to do so. Even if you raised enough cash to take you to break-even, you would need even more cash to finance growth. So how much money should you seek to seed your venture, and from whom?

How Much Money?

It really is impossible to specify an exact number here without knowing more about your business plans. Many small software companies are entirely funded by custom development contract work from one or more of their customers. This strategy gets a prototype built without giving up any equity. Usually, though, additional funding will be required. It is extremely important that you never run out of cash; that would be your worst nightmare.

Ideally, you would like to have enough cash to operate for at least six months (see your cash flow statement). You do not want to interrupt your development schedule any earlier than necessary to go fund raising. Realize, however, that you will always be raising funds until your company is self-sustaining. You can make a good rough estimate of how much you will spend monthly based on head count alone. Unless you have better regional and industry statistics available, use the rule of thumb that a business will need to spend about $10,000 per month per employee including all overhead costs. For high-tech companies in high-cost geographic locations with large capital equipment needs, $20,000 would be a more typical target. Since you will likely have no significant income during your seed and start-up phases, your cash outlays dictate your cash needs. Therefore, a six-person start-up operating for six months, at 60% salaries, would consume about

$$6 \times 6 \times \$10,000 \times 0.6 = \$216,000$$

This estimate is consistent with the fact that a large fraction of private investor initial deals are for $50,000 to $300,000, and that most seed venture capital funds typically invest from $200,000 to $500,000 at the initial stage of a new company. Several additional rules of thumb can be found in literature, which may be useful:

- Have enough cash to attract key employees to the business and to look good enough to prospective creditors and landlords that you can rent space and equipment. Be able to make promises you can keep concerning payroll, taxes, and rent for the near future.

- If funded entirely through personal funds and funds from relatives, be able to show a bank balance of at least $100,000 at the formal launch of the venture.

- If funded by an angel or other sophisticated investor, try to raise a minimum of $300,000 before the launch.

- If funded by venture capitalists, try to show a bank balance of $500,000 to $1 million at the formal launch of the venture.

Seed, Start-Up, and Subsequent Funding Rounds

Your seed round financing should take you through the point where you can prove your product concept. These funds may involve product development, but they rarely involve initial marketing.

Although your start-up round financing will probably be a separate round following seed, ideally the two are combined so that you can concentrate on executing your plan instead of constantly looking for funding. Because the recent trend is to parcel out even smaller chunks of cash, you would be very lucky to secure a combined seed and start-up round these days. Start-up round funds are used for product development and initial marketing, assembling the key management team, perhaps preparing more detailed business plans, completing market studies, and generally preparing to do business.

First-stage early-development funds are then solicited to initiate commercial manufacturing and sales. You probably will not be profitable in this stage.

Expansion financing for your second-stage, third-stage, and fourth-stage financing steps follow the start-up phase.

The Nightmare: Running Out of Money

While you hope to get each round funded in a timely fashion and for an adequate amount, there will be times when you are close to running out of cash and unable to make a payroll. One reason you want to structure your business for rapid profitability is to avoid this nightmare. If you run out of cash, you will be faced with the dilemma of trying to raise funds under duress while trying to keep the doors open. To avoid this, you need to raise enough funds, get profitable fast, and keep looking for money.

Where to Get Money

Savings, Mortgages, Friends, and Relatives

A study of 600 high-tech firms by Edward Roberts of MIT shows clearly that personal savings provide the primary source of seed capital (see Figure 12-1). John Ward at Loyola University's Graduate School of Business states that parents constitute the largest single source of start-up capital in the country. Most likely, you will be risking your savings, and those of your loved ones, to launch your new business. Sandra Kurtzig, the founder of ASK Computer Systems, financed her $400-million business with a $2,000 commission check from a previous employer and a loan from her father for $25,000.

The most successful entrepreneurs (those whose companies grow most quickly), however, initially had money from venture capitalists and angels. Once again it is

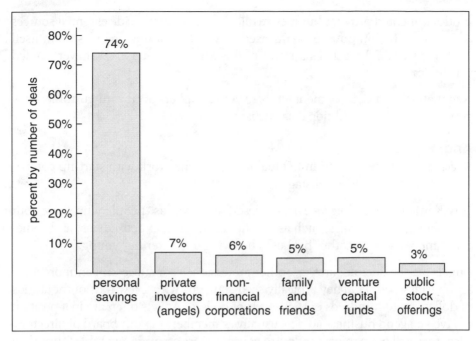

Figure 12-1   Primary Sources for Seed Capital for High-Tech Companies

emphasized that you try to start your business with a team. Find members who can help you attract investment funds.

Accountants and family business consultants will tell you that if you decide to borrow money from relatives, the only hope of making the loan work lies in being very explicit about the conditions of the deal in writing. Popular literature (*Inc.* magazine, *Success*, etc.) is littered with tragic stories of families torn apart from misunderstandings about money loaned to business start-ups.

Customers and Suppliers

A powerful source of capital in your seed and start-up stages can be your first customers. Getting customers to pay fat deposits up front with their orders (in return for discounted prices, for example) can relieve you of the need to raise substantial funds. Alternatively, instead of a cash deposit, you might request that your customer give you a letter of credit for a down payment which you could take to a bank and borrow against, thereby enhancing your funds and credit history simultaneously. Early customers also can provide an important revenue stream to your business if you provide them with services associated with the use of your product. Income from such services can be used to finance the continuing development of your products. At some point you might want to sell off such income substitution branches of your business to facilitate more product-oriented growth, but meanwhile, services can provide essential sources of funds. ASK Computer Systems used service bureau income to sustain itself in its early days. Largely as a result of this service income, ASK never needed venture capital.

Negotiating extended payment terms to your suppliers until your customers pay you can provide an additional cash cushion.

Angels

Angels are wealthy, private-individual investors who work with start-up companies, often at the seed-level stage.

Guy Kawasaki, in *Selling the Dream*, describes angels as "people who share your vision and provide *wings*, such as emotional support, expert advice, and sometimes money—as a mother bird uses her wing to shelter her young."

Angels may be doctors, lawyers, other professionals, or successful entrepreneurs and businesspeople. They typically seed start-ups with a few tens of thousands of dollars up to hundreds of thousands of dollars. Angels often are in a position to give you good business advice, usually as members of your board of directors. Also, they will often inject funds into your business on more favorable terms than some venture capital firms. You will find angels in all walks of life, and it is often up to you to structure and propose a deal to them. Most angels, unfortunately, will not be in the best position to introduce you to the next round of investors.

By accepting angel money you will have started your business with a knowledgeable resource and minimal dilution. However, this often leads to the venture capital catch-22 problem (discussed after the venture capital section of this chapter). Some angels repel venture capitalists; the venture capitalists often prefer not to invest along with certain people, so be careful that your early angel is not an albatross.

Despite all the attention paid to venture capital firms, angels back more than 30,000 new and emerging businesses a year with about $10 billion, while venture funds back only about 2,000 with $2 billion, says William E. Wetzel, professor of management and director of the Center for Venture Research at the University of New Hampshire. Figure 12-2 illustrates how important angel capital is.

However, angels, while they may be easier to catch, can also be harder to please. Investors must typically be prepared to inject additional funds equal to double or triple their initial investments, and they will have to ride the company through rough times. Many angels do not have the investment experience to realize that these things will happen, while venture capitalists are almost always more experienced, their funds more heavily financed, and more able to adapt. Unlike

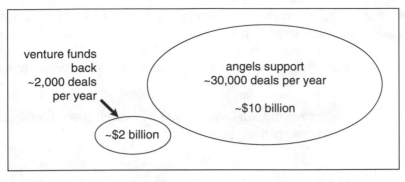

Figure 12-2   Angels versus Venture Capital Support

venture capitalists, who may have worked with start-ups for years, inexperienced angels often cannot provide essential business advice. Venture capitalists are in tune with the specific markets they invest in. However, seasoned angels know what to expect also.

Angels who overprice seed deals may seem a delight to you, but to a venture capitalist looking at your start-up round, that may be reason enough to pass you up. If a venture capitalist does come in for your second round of financing and then reprices the deal, your angel will get diluted more than expected. If you anticipate this, but a nonsophisticated angel does not see it, fix that angel up with more shares if necessary (see ratchets in Chapter 14 or warrants in Chapter 16 for two mechanisms that can be employed).

Private Stock Offerings

As you investigate approaching a few angels for seed or start-up capital, you may be tempted to try to sell stock in your company to an even larger number of individuals. A private stock offering is sometimes made through the drafting of a Rule 504 private-placement memorandum that allows you to raise up to $1 million without too much trouble from the Securities and Exchange Commission. If you attempt this, you most definitely need to work with an experienced lawyer. Table 12-1 summarizes the major exemptions to registration with the SEC, along with comments on how they work.

Fortunately, in early 1992, SEC chairman Richard Breeden proposed relaxing the rules to help small companies raise capital. Under these new proposals:

- Small companies seeking seed capital could issue up to $1 million in unrestricted securities per year.

- Companies could canvass the public for interest in the securities before making the offer.

- Regulation A, which allows companies to use a simplified disclosure document for limited public offerings that are directed mainly toward big investors, would be raised from $1.5 to $5 million. Also, information could be published to gauge investor interest before filing the offering.

- New, simpler registration forms would be created based on the size of the company rather than the size of the offering.

Table 12-1 Summary of Exemptions to Registration with the SEC

	Exemption Limit	Limit Number of Investors	Documentation Required
SEC Rule 504	$1 million	none	Disclosure document must be cleared by one or more U-7 states; SEC Form D must be filed after sale.
SEC Rule 505	$5 million	none if all investors are accredited[a]; 35 if nonaccredited	SEC Form D if investors are accredited; if not, form S-18
SEC Rule 506	none	35 experienced[b] investors; no limit on accredited investors	Form S-1 for experienced investors; Form D for accredited investors
1933 Act 4(2)	none	fewer than 25	whatever attorney deems necessary to protect exemption
1933 Act 3(a)(11)	none	none if all reside in the same state	Varies from state to state. Company must keep good records on investors and use of proceeds to protect exemption.

[a] *Accredited* investors are institutions or individuals with at least $200,000 in annual adjusted gross income or with a net worth of at least $1 million. The $1 million net worth does not include the worth of a personal residence.

[b] *Experienced* investors are people capable of evaluating the merits and risks of a prospective investment.

Source: Drew Field/Direct Share Marketing, San Francisco.
Reported in *Inc.*, December 1991.

About 21 states have adopted a little-known funding process for small businesses known as the SCOR (Small Company Offering Registration) process. Also known as ULOR (Uniform Limited Offering Registration), SCOR enables small companies to go public and raise up to $1 million with less difficulty and expense than a traditional securities offering usually involves. The *Wall Street Journal*, January 21, 1992, reported that only a few dozen companies have tried to use SCOR. Washington state was most active. While SCOR offerings suffer from the absence of an active aftermarket for the underlying securities, the process is reported to work well where there is already a large group of customers or employees who are potential investors. According to the North American Securities Administrators Association, the following states have adopted the SCOR process.

Alaska	Massachusetts	South Dakota
Arizona	Mississippi	Tennessee
Idaho	Missouri	Texas
Indiana	Montana	Vermont
Iowa	Nevada	Washington
Kansas	North Carolina	Wisconsin
Maine	North Dakota	Wyoming

Selling stock in your start-up company is a very difficult thing to do; also, your stock will have no market, and you and your new company will have little reputation to attract such investors. Although many firms exist for the sole purpose of helping you make these private placements, even they tend to have limited success for the average engineer starting his or her first company. Save such excursions for your second start-up when you become famous from your first success, or at least wait a year or two until your company has a track record. At that point, a private placement service certainly can work. Private placements are a little like going public on a small scale. While this is an exciting idea, it is not practical for you now. Save your time and more than a little money.

Finally, do not make the mistake of thinking you can bypass or disregard the securities laws; the penalties are severe. Also, watch out for things like rules against advertising investment opportunities.

Venture Capitalists (VCs)

Venture capital firms are a kind of funnel that gathers money from limited partners and then distributes funds to a large number of carefully selected growing businesses. The venture firm managers, known as general partners, raise this money from pension funds, insurance companies, university endowments, corporations, wealthy individual investors, etc.

A typical VC fund raises $50 million from limited partners and invests in up to 35 companies for 10 to 12 years. (These days, 35 companies would be a lot to invest in, since VCs are having to stick with their portfolio companies much longer before they can cash out their investments.) By the end of that time, the companies will have either succeeded (returning a profit to the fund through a public stock offering or sale to a larger company) or they will have failed and been written off.

VC firms can make money in three ways: management fees, carried interest, and stock price appreciation after a company goes public. A standard 3% management fee once provided venture capitalists with a monthly draw. A 20% profit participation in each deal (called *carried interest*) was the real payoff. Appreciation from the public stock from companies going public before funds were distributed to the limited partners provided additional profits. More recently, however, the pension fund limited partners have negotiated management fees to just 1% or 2%, and while keeping carried interest at 20%, many now insist on a profit distribution immediately after each initial public offering.

Kurtzig, who grew her business completely without venture capital funds, has an opinion on venture capitalists:

> Nowadays it is venture capital that keeps you in business in the early going. But venture capital is impatient money, and I doubt many venture capitalists would have stuck with ASK as it continued to redefine itself in its first four years. Not having venture capital means never having to say you're sorry.

Few software companies really achieve the $50 to $100 million sales levels that VCs want to see in companies they will fund.

While returns of venture capital firms were once as high as 40–50% annually, single digits are more common now (reported by the *Wall Street Journal*, June 20, 1991). In the five years that ended in 1990, venture capital funds collectively posted losses of an average of 3.8% a year (estimate by Morgan Stanley & Co., the *Wall Street Journal*, February 11, 1992).

A number of publications list current venture capital investments. The *San Jose Mercury News*, for example, runs excellent quarterly reports on the venture capital money tree. These reports show what is hot and what is not in the investment community, which can be valuable to you in your search for funds. For example, from the decrease in the number of new listings and the reporting of additional rounds on older deals, it was obvious in 1991 that investments in new computer-related seed deals were declining. To those keeping tabs, the trend was clear, as illustrated in Figure 12-3.

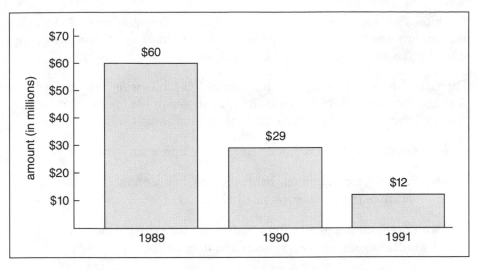

Figure 12-3   Computer-Related Seed Deals Closed

In 1991, only two dozen deals were consummated, each drawing an average of $500,000.

Nationwide, investments by venture capital firms peaked at $3.9 billion in 1987. That figure tumbled to about $2 billion in 1990, according to the market research firm Venture Economics, Inc., of Needham, MA. Reports in early 1992 showed a continued severe deterioration of venture capital disbursements to a level of just $801.4 million for 1991 (reported in *Venture Capital Journal*).

In 1991, the venture firms themselves attracted only about $1.34 billion from new investors (source: Venture Economics, February 1992). This figure is down from $1.8 billion in 1990 (source: the *San Jose Mercury News*, December 2, 1991 and February 24, 1992).

Only 35 partnerships raised money in 1991, a sharp decrease from 105 in record 1987 (source: Venture Economics, February 1992). Six big funds, including Oak Investment Management Co., Institutional Venture Partners, and Summit Ventures, accounted for more than half the total funds raised. In a dramatic unexpected turnaround, at the end of 1991, venture funds were expected to bring in as much as $2 billion in the first six months of 1992 (source: *Venture Capital Journal*). For perspective, a record $4.2 billion was raised in 1987.

Another positive trend for start-up engineers: early stage funds are back in vogue. Venture Economics says that of the total raised in 1991, 35% (nearly $470 million) was committed to partnerships investing in start-ups. That is a big increase from the $180 million or so committed to partnerships in 1990!

The most significant trend in Silicon Valley in the fourth quarter of 1991 was the amount invested in software companies—$62.4 million, more than any quarter since 1986 (source: the *San Jose Mercury News*, February 24, 1992).

The rate of money flowing into and out of VC funds will vary from year to year and the overall flow will be cyclical, as shown in the Figure 12-4 (source: Venture Economics, Inc., Venture Economics Publishing Co.).

Other statistics from Ernst & Young show more important trends:

- Funding for computer hardware and semiconductors continues to shrink as these industries mature.

- Communications is an important sector with sharply increased demand for computer network systems and fiber optics.

- Venture funding for biotechnology and medical products declined as these companies obtained more money from initial public stock offerings.

- Software continues to attract the biggest share of venture funding, reflecting a strong demand for new programs and the small amount of investment needed to start a software business. (Obviously, software companies continue to provide the best paths for engineers wanting to start their own companies.)

As reported in *Venture Capital Journal*, July 1991, the sharp, pervasive reductions in venture capital disbursements are illustrated in Table 12-2.

Table 12-2   Recent Reductions in Venture Capital Disbursements

Industry	Disbursements in Millions of Dollars		
	Dollars Invested (1990 Q1)	Dollars Invested (1991 Q1)	Percent Change
commercial communications	23	0.9	−96
biotechnology	48	6	−88
medical/health care	94	19	−80
consumer-related	84	17	−80
software and services	108	62	−43

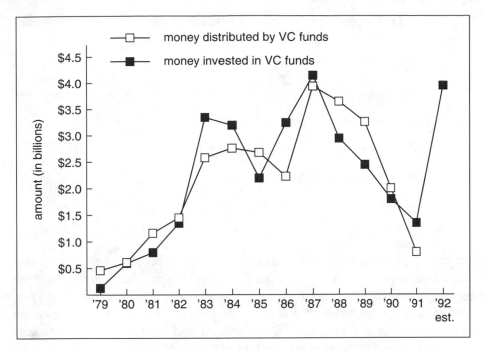

Figure 12-4 Venture Capital Funding Cycle

Seed disbursements fell more rapidly than the market as a whole. Only seven companies were the beneficiaries of seed investments in the first quarter of 1991 ($4.2 million), versus 21 in the first quarter of 1990 ($16.9 million). Likewise, start-up investments totaled just $9 million in the first quarter of 1991 versus $41 million in the first quarter of 1990. The huge declines ran through all industry categories. Software and services received the lion's share of the dollars disbursed.

Receiving any venture capital investment in early 1991 was quite an accomplishment. Ten companies pulled in a total of only $87 million; this represented almost one-half the entire amount disbursed. Three of the ten largest deals involved software companies.

Remember, the venture capital business is very cyclical, and by the time you read this book, venture funds could again be more widely available. It is essential that you keep abreast of these trends so that you do not waste time chasing improbable funding sources. This information will also be extremely valuable to you in setting realistic expectations for your start-up. There are many industry-specific publications that you might want to consult. *Computer Letter*, based in New York, covers the computer-related industries, for example.

You will find that venture capital investments are usually listed by the following categories:

- computers

- peripherals

- semiconductors

- communications

- biotechnology and medical products

- software

- miscellaneous

Very often a company founder finds it exceedingly difficult to raise funds, especially from sophisticated venture capital sources. Despite the connotation of the name, venture capital is not the reckless business of throwing money at speculative deals. A great deal of due diligence goes into evaluating an investment option, and risk is always carefully calculated and factored into the structure of investments. Investors want assurances that they will get a return on their investment. As stated previously, they want to see a management team that has performed well in the past and that will do so again in the future. They want to see you working in markets that are growing and in which you have distinct competitive advantages. They are interested in proprietary technology that offers that competitive advantage, but not technology for technology's sake.

Sophisticated investors also want to see product prototypes—evidence that you can produce what you say you can. In short, they want to bet on a horse that looks like it will cross the winning line. But how can you demonstrate this confidence without expending initial funds? Since you cannot, you get some angel's or relative's money and do your best, thinking that soon you will really impress the pros. Ideally, your initial seed funds will produce a believable product prototype and you will be ready to shop your business plan.

The catch-22 comes in when a sophisticated investor, now considering your plan, exclaims that "this looks pretty neat, it is too bad that you went ahead and got these unsophisticated (angel, relative) investors involved; that muddies the waters for us—they are hard to work with." It is a catch-22 since you often cannot get the attention of venture capital (new money) until you have produced something, and you cannot produce something without getting seed funds (old money), but venture capitalists often do not like to mingle with amateur investors.

There are ways out of this catch-22, however:

- The new money can cash out the early stage seed investors, but you should prepare your seed investors for that possible preference before they invest in your business. This is the cleanest move and makes sense. Your seed investors make a quick return and everyone should be happy.

- The new money can help convert the seed investors' equity position into a debt position, but this should be done only if that would match the seed investor's investment objective.

- The new money can convert the old money's preferred equity position into a common equity position. If this happens, make sure that your loyal seed investor is compensated for the new, riskier common position through the conversion of the preferred equity into a significantly larger (typically three to ten times) number of common shares.

- The new money can live with the old money—the venture capitalists and seed investors can share board seats and vote together. This last option is usually satisfactory when the seed investor is a veteran angel, but it is rarely satisfactory when inexperienced relatives and friends are involved.

It is best to get a seed-level venture capital firm involved in your business at the earliest date possible. It will have the networking connections to assist you in getting your second round of financing, and will see that all subsequent financing rounds are equitable. Getting a quality investment firm involved from day one, however, probably will require that you have formed a complete and experienced management team containing at least one individual who was successful in an earlier start-up. Again, if you try to do everything yourself, the growth of your business will likely be limited.

Shopping versus Selling Your Business Plan

Shopping a plan in the venture capital trade means sending it out to too many investors at the same time. Because of the close-knit nature of the venture capital community, it is not at all unusual for these people to share information about potential deals. If you give your plan out to multiple venture sources at the same time and they know about each other, no one may give you the attention you are looking for since each wants to invest time on deals that they likely can close on if they become interested. Similarly, if your plan has been in circulation for a long time, it will be labeled shopworn. No one wants to spend time evaluating a plan that 100 other investors have passed on. This section is about how to sell your business plan without overshopping it.

Norman A. Fogelsong and Kenneth J. Kelley of Institutional Venture Partners offer the following formulas for how to get started in business and how to approach a venture capitalist.

Getting Started

- Plan on establishing a serious partnership with your investors and your management team that will last at least five to seven years.

- Make the firm decision to start a business; your start cannot be contingent on "ifs" and "maybes."

- Get the support of your family (this is absolutely essential).

- Establish very clearly your *raison d'être* (your unique contribution and business mission).

- Identify the market opportunity, develop the product definition, and build the founding team. (It cannot be emphasized enough how important building a team is.)

- Write the initial business plan.

How to Approach a Venture Capitalist

- You should first select no more than three to six venture capital firms whose investment profiles fit your start-up's needs, and be sure that each has a good philosophical fit and compatible style with your team and business.

- It is essential that you obtain a personal introduction from another investor, entrepreneur, accountant, or lawyer.

- Phone to briefly discuss the business and determine if there are any conflicts. (Venture capitalists will not invest in competing companies as they want to focus all their assistance on just one.)

- Bring a business plan and personal references to the first meeting.

- At the first meeting, give a brief product overview of the plan and identify the key reasons for your success (this is not the time to go into detail). Tell them what is unique. What do you have to offer that others do not? Why will you succeed?

- Arrange for follow-up meetings; expect them to take place over a few weeks.

Venture Capital Directories

The preceding information suggests that you prudently and carefully present your plan to investors. First, make sure that the investment group you are approaching invests in your type of company. You do this by consulting some of the many venture capital directories and lists available. Your library should have pointers to more venture capital directories. The following are the three most useful and popular directories:

- One excellent venture capital directory, especially for those in Silicon Valley, is available for $50 and is updated yearly (usually in early May). You can get it by contacting Western Association of Venture Capitalists— Directory of Members, 3000 Sand Hill Road, Building One, Suite 190, Menlo Park, CA 94025, (415) 854-1322. Make sure you invest in the most current directory as these become obsolete very quickly.

- A national directory is also available, entitled *National Venture Capital Association Directory*. To obtain this directory, write to: NVCA, 1655 North Fort Myer Drive, Suite 700, Arlington, VA 22209.

- *Pratt's Guide to Venture Capital Sources*, updated annually, is available in some bookstores (see References and Suggested Readings) for $145, or by writing to Venture Economics, Inc., 451 Buckminister Drive, Norwood, MA 02062.

You can obtain directories in computer-readable form from a variety of sources. They claim to have database sorting capabilities that are available on both IBM- and Mac-compatible disks. Scan the latest issue of *Inc.* magazine for advertisements or new programs. The following are two useful references. (Note, however, that you will be wasting your time if you buy an electronic directory to use as a broadband mailing list to send out 100 business plans.)

- *VenCap Data Quest*, from Artificial Intelligence Research, in Mountain View, CA. A larger database ($89.95) has information on 399 venture capital firms. A smaller database ($49.95) has information on about 250 firms. Quarterly updates sell for $69 and $39, respectively.

- *The Financing Sources Databook*, from Data-Merge, in Denver, CO, contains information on about 750 venture capitalists, banks, and finance companies, and gives less complete detail on more than 2000 additional sources. The cost is $399 for the basic product. A version with fewer listings is $139. Updates are $75 and $49, respectively.

These directories will tell you:

- who the officers or partners are
- what kind of company it is and how long it has been in business
- its investment posture in terms of minimum and maximum initial investment and desired total commitment (average and maximum) over time to any one investee company
- the maturity of company desired (seed to buyouts)
- special help that can be provided in addition to venture capital

- areas of preferred investment
- areas avoided for investment

Do not begin searching for a venture capitalist without first consulting a directory.

Over the Transom

Over the transom refers to the submission of unsolicited business plans (also known as *cold deals*)—those that appear on an investor's desk without any introduction or explanation. An unsolicited business plan submitted to a venture capital firm has almost no chance of being funded.

Many entrepreneurs have wasted months sending unsolicited business plans to venture capital firms, only to get polite declines in the mail (if they hear anything at all). To make progress in getting a business plan read and taken seriously, you need either yourself or a team member to have a reputation or name recognition quality, or an introduction.

Investors, for the most part, simply will not take the time to study a plan from an unknown entity.

Introductions and How to Get Them

Getting introductions is difficult. This is not something you wait to worry about after you have finished writing your plan. You need to work on introductions long before you attempt to launch your own venture capital-backed company. Besides asking every friend you know who might know investors (your banker, doctor, associates, etc.) you need to make more friends. This is done through the process called *networking*.

Networking and Name Recognition

Attending professional association and business club meetings might seem unpleasant, especially for a technically inclined engineer or scientist. But if you want to start a venture capital-backed start-up, you must play the role of a businessperson. That means going out and meeting other businesspeople, and getting your name recognized.

Delivering a speech or a technical presentation (perhaps on the challenges of applying your technology) will go a long way in opening doors. This enables you to introduce yourself to investors. If you have given a paper at a conference, make reprints and send them to 20 or 30 potential investors with a note saying that you thought they might be interested in the topic. If you do this several times over a couple of years, your name will eventually have recognition value in their minds. An investor might not remember how he or she knows you, but your name will become familiar enough to at least glance at your business plan when it finally appears.

Looking the Part

Dress for Success is an old book, but it contains good advice. When an investor talks to you about your business idea, does he or she see an engineer or an entrepreneur? An entrepreneur knows how to sell, and you are selling yourself now. You have to offer the customer what he or she wants, not what you want him or her to want! A few years back it was somewhat classy in Silicon Valley to wear tennis shoes and try to start a computer company. It is still entertaining to incorporate fun with business, but this is only appropriate with friends.

If you obtain an interview with a potential investor, you had better look the part. For men, a modern, clean, pressed suit is mandatory, and a woman should wear a business suit. Men should wear long socks. Investors actually say such things as "Joe (the engineer) had a really good idea and a well thought-out plan, but he was wearing short socks." Little things, like a gold Cross pen in your pocket, say that you are a businessperson who should be taken seriously. Your commitment to projecting a professional appearance can yield a high return on your investment. This is not subterfuge; it is expected business behavior.

There is controversy over the "look successful—be successful" point of view. Some claim it should make no difference, but it clearly does to many investors. If you want their money, play their game. It is even suggested that you dump your 10-year-old Toyota and lease a new BMW (or at least a new Toyota). People observe how you appear personally, what you drive, and where you live. If you plan to start a business in your community in a few years, it would not hurt to be living where successful business people live when you go looking for money. Remember the saying that bankers only lend money to people who apparently do not need it? Investors often work the same way, so it helps to not look like you need their funding.

Unsolicited Business Plan

For unsolicited business plans that you submit to venture capitalists, you will seldom receive any comments to help you out, usually for one of two reasons:

- The investors did not have time to read or evaluate your plan, let alone write you a letter or talk to you on the phone.
- They do not want to risk litigation by commenting on your plan only to have you sue them when they back someone else's plan with your ideas in it.

This leads to the topic of confidentiality and nondisclosure agreements.

Confidentiality and Nondisclosure Agreements (NDAs)

Since your business plan is valuable to you and you do not want any competitors to get hold of it, you must print "confidential" on each page and treat your plan as a trade secret. You should never give your plan to anyone who does not promise (preferably in writing) that they will respect the document accordingly. This is good theory, but bad reality. Some investors will sign nondisclosure agreements (NDAs), but they are few and far between; further, they would be more comfortable with an NDA if they already knew you or the person making the introduction. If you submit an unsolicited plan to a venture capitalist with a cover letter asking him or her first to sign an NDA, the plan will likely be returned unopened. The reason, again, is the risk of lawsuits. Investors receive hundreds, even thousands, of plans each year and they cannot be expected to remember what information they saw where, or to whom they should not tell what.

It is exceedingly difficult (if not impossible) for an investor to evaluate your plan without disclosing its contents to others, and an investor is not likely to worry about putting everyone in the due diligence chain under NDA for you. The sad fact is that your business plan, especially if it is good, will probably be read and copied by many others. Most of these people will have good intentions and will not intentionally deliver your plan into the hands of a direct competitor, but it does happen.

Your best defense is not to include in your business plan your most sensitive market information or the technical aspects of building your product. Save this information for one-on-one discussions with interested investors. The purpose of a business plan is much like that of a resume: it gets you the interview. You sell and close after you get the appointment. There is no need to overdisclose confidential information in your business plan.

Negotiation Skills

Take the time to learn negotiation skills (such as Nierenberg's win-win approach to negotiating and deal-making). Both sides should act and feel like winners in a funding agreement. Kurtzig of ASK was a big believer of leaving something on the table in negotiations. She also wrote:

> To get in or out of a deal, there are four things necessary for a successful negotiation: good sense, guts, diplomacy, and leverage. You need good sense to know what to ask for, guts to ask for what you want, diplomacy to know how to ask for it, and leverage to get it.

Paying for Criticism?

A number of firms will offer to read your business plan, make suggestions for improvements, and presumably represent you to the investment community. The back pages of business magazines and newspapers are full of these ads. Some of these firms are legitimate, but many are just out to get your money.

It is true that you may have to pay for help to write a good plan. There are many financial advisors who can do a reputable job assisting you with your financial pro formas, for example, if that is a weak area for you. Seek out specific advice as you need it, and pay for that, but do not pay big bucks for general advice. (It would be wise, too, to request that these advisors sign an NDA).

It is better, however, to get good, experienced businesspeople to work with you who will give you their money and their advice (rather than you paying them). These individuals are the angels discussed previously. Someone who is truly in a position to help to make you successful will share in the future riches he or she helps you achieve, not in your precious pre-seed funds.

Prenuptial Provisions

Venture capital ratchets (powerful instruments employed by most venture capital investors to ensure their stake in your business) are discussed in Chapter 14. A related concept (more in your favor) involves a provision in your contract with your seed and start-up investors that will ensure that they will stick with you when you need them in the future. While it is true that the investor will most likely propose the terms of any deal, everything is there for you to negotiate.

The typical scenario is that you raise some seed or start-up cash from an investor, a sort of marriage is established, and off you go on your honeymoon. But what happens later in the marriage?

As was mentioned earlier, your worst nightmare in a start-up is running out of money. What would you do if you were on plan, the time came to raise more cash, and your original investors no longer possessed the enthusiasm for your business they initially had? The marriage loses some of its passion. This situation can destroy a company, and it happens frequently enough that you need to plan in advance for it.

Individuals with significant financial assets frequently employ a prenuptial agreement before getting married. You should consider a similar agreement with your investors.

If you can negotiate it, insert a "pay to play" provision in your investment agreement that states the investor's responsibility to put in a pro rata share in future rounds of financing. If your initial investor can, and intends to, support you in subsequent rounds, put that intention in writing, and insert a penalty for a failure to perform. Penalties can be in the form of a loss of liquidation preferences or a ratchet to severely dilute and wash out shares. This provision is intended not to punish your seed and start-up supporters, but to apply financial pressure on them to set aside appropriate funds so that they can and will support you when you need them again in the future.

Software Success—Who Gets Funding How and Where?

Software Success is published monthly by marketing consultant David H. Bowen for a select readership—individuals and businesses marketing computer software. Together, through surveys and seminars, they investigate significant issues for success in the software business.

We earlier established that software is one of the easiest businesses for an engineer to start, due to low capitalization requirements, minimum manufacturing problems, and growing market interests and needs. In a recent issue of *Software Success*, Bowen reports some interesting statistics (derived from a survey of his readership) regarding funding issues for software entrepreneurs. These statistics represent an interesting slice of the real world.

Many of his readers are in the bootstrap (i.e., self-funding) stage (as you might be) or are determined not to use outside money if possible. Here is a breakdown of their company revenues by percent of Bowen's total responses:

Company Revenue	Percent Responding
< $250,000	21.7%
$250,000–$500,000	15.1%
$500,000–$1 million	21.7%
$1 million–$2 million	17.8%
$2 million–$5 million	12.5%
> $5 million	12.5%

Companies with greater revenue and greater revenue potential are more interesting to investors. Private investors typically want to see a potential for $5 million in sales so that the company can be sold to a larger company later. Venture capitalists want to see an absolute minimum annual revenue potential of $25 million and many have minimum limits of $100 million.

Paid-in capital is money invested in a company for equity and the most common amount for this survey is $10,000 to $100,000. This is a common range that founders can fund from their own personal savings. Many companies understate their capital because they do not pay themselves full salaries during start-up.

The most common form of ownership was several partners (42.1%), followed by one owner (29.6%). Less than 20% of the companies who responded have outside investors.

Software companies, while easy to start, are also difficult to find funding for. Most of the companies that have less than $100,000 in paid-in capital did not raise money from outsiders. The funding came from the principals and their family and friends. The more you are willing to invest in your business, the higher venture capitalists will value your business. Investors figure that their money is safer with you if you also have your own funds tied up (or those of your friends and relatives).

For the larger companies in the survey, 15.1% of the responding companies tried to raise over $1 million, but only 11.8% have over $1 million in paid-in capital. This is pretty close to the 11.2% who had either venture or public ownership. Venture capitalists are generally interested in deals greater than $1 million.

Mid-sized companies seeking $100,000 to $1 million need too much money for family and friends to help, and too little for venture capitalists. In this range, Bowen suggests that private investors can make sense. Of the companies surveyed, 10.5% had private investors as owners. Since 18.4% of the companies had $100,000 to $1 million in paid-in capital, Bowen guesses that 57% of these situations involved private investors (10.5% divided by 18.4%).

Of the companies, 43.4% have tried to raise money from private investors, and 52% of those who tried were successful; 15% raised less money than desired, 3% gave up more stock than planned, and 12% were unsuccessful. Another 17–21% appear to have given up. While Bowen concludes that his survey suggests that it is reasonable to raise private money for software companies, you certainly do not want to bet your next payroll on obtaining private financing.

There are numerous unfortunate situations where family members invested who could not afford to lose their investment, and where private investors were later severely diluted by venture capitalists in later rounds through ratchet clauses.

In the venture capital arena, 29.6% of the companies have tried to raise venture capital. Of them, 37.8% were successful, 13% obtained less money than desired, 22.3% had to give up more stock than desired, and 26.7% were not successful. The lack of revenue does not discourage people from approaching venture capitalists, but the success rate below $5 million in company revenues is under 20% of the companies that tried. For companies over $5 million in revenue, 45% of them succeeded in raising venture capital.

Professional Publications, Inc. ▪ Belmont, CA

On public offerings, only 4.6% of respondents even tried, but that represented 36.8% of respondents with over $5 million in revenue. Of those trying, 28.2% were successful.

Successful fund-raising takes time. The estimated average amount of time it took for successful firms to raise money was:

- one to three months for private investments
- six months to one year full time for venture capital
- more than one year to go public

Why were some companies unsuccessful in fund-raising? Too much work, did not want to give up control (the top stated reason), revenue potential not enough (probably the top real reason), did not need enough money, and weak management team were among the reasons cited.

Growth rates relate to fund-raising success. Having a high growth rate (> 30% annually) helps somewhat to raise private money. Of companies with over 30% growth rate expectations, 56% were successful in raising private money. Only 33% of the companies with 1–10% growth rate expectations were successful. In venture capital, a high growth rate is required. No one with expectations under 10% was successful in raising venture capital.

Bowen concludes with the statement,

> Fund-raising is the one task I believe the CEO must do himself. Investors want to talk to the person at the helm. In my experience, finders are rarely successful in getting companies funded.

Edward Roberts of MIT seems to agree. In his study, he found that of all referral mechanisms leading to 54 investments in 20 high-technology firms, finders played a role in only 6 of the 54 instances. Presumably, finders are best at earning one an introduction—the entrepreneur has to do the actual selling. Finders are believed to play a more effective role in securing overseas investments. It would be difficult to secure funding from a Japanese firm, for example, without the assistance of a respected Japanese consultant on your side.

Source: Statistics in this section are excerpted from the June 1991 issue of *Software Success,* with permission of David H. Bowen.

4

MAKING IT PAY

Part Four of this book (Chapters 13–18) covers the most important remuneration issues for you to consider in launching your start-up. You will learn to balance salary and equity rewards, learn what works and what does not, and understand what practices are followed in other start-ups. Chapter 13 deals directly with the important issue of salary and introduces the remaining (primarily equity-related) topics of Part Four.

13

Remuneration Practices
for Your Start-Up

*"When you can measure what you are speaking about,
and express it in numbers, you know something about it."*
— Lord Kelvin, 1824–1907

Salaries

Compensation and Benefits for Start-Up Companies

How much you will remunerate to yourself, your associates, and other employees in salary, fringe benefits, and other perquisites depends on your needs, your cash situation, the culture you have established in your company, and the preferences of your investors. There is always a balance between wanting to preserve precious cash and getting your due. If you do not pay fair salaries early on, sweat equity may never be fully compensated. If cash is initially tight, you might want to consider giving deferred compensation to balance cash-flow needs with the need for equitable compensation. The January–February 1989 *Harvard Business Review* article by Joseph Tibbetts, Jr., and Edmund Donovan entitled "Compensation and Benefits for Startup Companies: How to conserve cash and still attract the best executives" discusses the following key points:

- Be realistic about your limitations, but do not ignore the advantages of being small.

- No start-up is an island. Factor regional and industry trends into your salary calculations.

- Shares in a company that will never go public can actually demotivate your people.

- You cannot match IBM's benefits, so you have to be creative.

The wisest approach is to go slowly (make incremental enhancements) and factor in cash flow, taxation, and accounting implications while making your decisions.

Fringe Benefits and Salary vis-à-vis Stock and Stock Options

Salaries at start-ups should be reasonable and competitive. More established companies will offer superior fringe benefits that you cannot yet afford, such as retirement plans. You might think that you have to offer higher salaries to offset this difference, but this is not true. Your offsetting financial attraction is instead the potential for equity ownership that you can offer (the subject of Chapters 14 and 15). However, while your salary costs can be attenuated by the offsetting value of any stock or stock options offered, this is only true to the extent that the manager or employee understands and appreciates the potential value of his or her stock position.

Many younger and less experienced employees will have formed no notion or appreciation of the potential for wealth creation through equity ownership. Some start-up entrepreneurs choose to keep such employees in the dark, drawing them simply with good salaries and thus avoiding dilution of the equity pool. Other more knowledgeable entrepreneurs take advantage of the tremendous power of equity participation and educate their employees on this front. It is strongly urged that every start-up employee should have a potential ownership interest in the business, should know what that interest can be worth, and should be apprised monthly of the financial performance of the business. This strategy can work well to attract and retain strong team members who are dedicated to hard work to achieve their and your success.

If you have a candidate who hesitates to join your start-up (wanting extra salary for the extra risk and lack of benefits), you probably should not hire him or her. You want key managers and employees who thrive on the risk and excitement of a start-up environment and are motivated in part by visions of their stock appreciation.

Section 125 cafeteria plans, dependent care reimbursement plans, and 401(k) plans can be relatively inexpensive ways to offer competitive fringe benefits using your employees' own money.

Six-Figure Salaries

Since 1985, when many high-technology companies (and their stock prices) hit on hard times, high salaries for executives and key employees have become exceedingly commonplace. No longer are slave wages with sweat equity the only ways to moderate wealth. In the early 1990s, salaries for CEOs could easily run into six figures. Six-figure salaries for vice presidents also were not unheard of.

With the exception of the seed-level start-up funded exclusively by the founders' and their relatives' hard-earned cash, successful start-ups generally do not neglect wages for the founding and key management team. Since you and your key employees might never recognize a penny gain on your stock or stock options, go ahead and put a liberal salary high on your list.

There are a number of sources available to assist in setting up an equitable compensation plan. One excellent source of salary information can be found in the annual American Electronics Association (AEA) salary surveys. AEA also conducts seminars on this topic and many others. You soon will want to consider purchasing a corporate membership in AEA to access its extensive networking and publication opportunities. The surveys are a bit costly, however, so you may prefer to search your library or borrow the set of volumes from one of your human resource (HR) associates in a member company instead. Your HR contacts can be very useful in obtaining data on both salary and stock compensation practices in other companies. For yourself and your coexecutives, look at the AEA *Executive Compensation in the Electronics Industry* volume. Other useful volumes include: *Employee Benefits and Personnel Practices, Professional Engineers: Supervisory and Nonsupervisory Salary Survey, Benchmark Salary Survey of Supervisory and Nonsupervisory Personnel, Sales Salary Survey of Supervisory and Nonsupervisory Personnel,* and *Operating Ratios Survey.*

In presenting job offers, make sure that the potential employee appreciates that his or her new salary includes monetary and nonmonetary compensation elements (i.e., stock options and benefits are forms of compensation).

Salary Extremes

You want to get and keep good people at a low cost. At the same time, though, you will be tempted to hire superstars and pay whatever is necessary to attract and keep them. However, you will need to maintain perceived equity across the company. If employees think their salaries are inequitable, you can expect less work output from them, and your more valuable employees may show their feelings by leaving the company.

The fact that you need to maintain equity does not mean that you have to pay all employees on the same scale. Rather, it is important that employees perceive that the criteria used to determine how they are paid is fair and that those criteria are applied equitably throughout the business.

It has been said that you cannot win the remuneration game. You can go to great lengths to reward one outstanding employee who might still feel underpaid even after an exceptional salary action. Further, when or if the other employees find out, the added result can be that now everyone feels underpaid.

Keeping salaries secret in a small company is almost impossible, although most CEOs try their best. Legend has it that Steve Jobs, founder of NeXT Computer, Inc., posts all salaries on a bulletin board, but with mixed results.

Pay for Performance

Keep salaries competitive and in line with industry standards. Reward exceptional performance continuously—primarily with additional stock options (see Chapter 15). At times, hand an exceptional employee a check for, say, $1,000, perhaps grossed up to cover taxes. Some CEOs try to hand out these mini-rewards as nontaxable employee expense reimbursements (sort of like dipping into a big petty cash drawer), but that practice is not recommended. If the IRS does not catch you, your auditors might when they need to get clean financial statements for investors or a distant initial public offering. Look at each individual to see what motivates him or her, and use the appropriate vehicle for handing out effective rewards.

As an example, one key employee had a reputation for driving a junk heap, and he was continually fixing flat tires in the company parking lot. One day after that employee met an important deadline, the CEO had a local garage install four new tires on the employee's car. That gesture only cost a few hundred dollars, and it clearly said to the employee that his performance was valued.

Equity Ownership: Stock and Stock Options

Stock grants (see Chapter 14) and stock options (see Chapter 15) are major sources of future potential wealth for you and your employees. Many start-up entrepreneurs vastly underestimate the power of these instruments. Study the next two chapters closely if you are unfamiliar with the mechanisms and practices of stock grants and stock option grants (as most engineer-entrepreneurs are). In terms of direct financial payback, understanding and applying these equity-related concepts are every bit as important to your success as being customer- and market-driven.

Other Compensation

Other equity- and wealth-building vehicles (see Chapter 16) and fringe benefits (see Chapter 18) complete the remuneration spectrum. One needs to consider this entire spectrum when formulating a workable compensation policy.

Employment Contracts

While Chapter 18 covers the basics for employment contracts for yourself, try to avoid giving them to any others. Investors do not like them and they can be the cause of severe cash drains if you need to shake out nonperforming team members.

14

Stock Ownership, Grant, and Award Practices for Your Start-Up

"Change the rules—Win the game!"
—Jim Harper
CEO, Flexis Control Incorporated

Stock ownership is the clear differentiator of the start-up company. It is the quintessence of entrepreneurial activity. With stock you have a kind of ownership and pride in an enterprise that cannot be replicated in any *Fortune* 500 company environment. You have a deeper stake in the business, more potential wealth, and correspondingly more risk. Most start-up entrepreneurs have little experience or training to guide them in the areas of stock ownership, grant, and award practices. Through a careful reading of this chapter and the next, you will become much better armed in the knowledge necessary to leverage the power of equity to make your business a success in the way it is best measured, in the wealth generated for the start-up's founders and other stakeholders.

There are really two different perspectives in time from which you will want to address the distribution of stock and stock options. As a founder/owner, you view the new company as being yours because you (and your family and friends) provided the initial capital to get the company going. The business eventually gets to the point where it needs additional investment capital. Since you, as the founder/owner, own the lion's share of the company (at least initially), your objective is to bring in additional funds with as little dilution as possible. Founder/owners look at stock in their company as their investment capital.

Later, as a founder/employee, you can no longer think of the company as yours. It really belongs to your investors, since they will probably own about 75% of the stock. From this point of view, your new objective is to negotiate for as good a deal as possible for yourself and your associates. Founder/employees look at their stock and stock options as bonuses.

Table 14-1 provides an overview of the basics of stock and stock option practices. Stock and stock options are perplexing subjects. Key features of each type of stock and option are characterized in terms of the advantages and disadvantages of each type to the employer and to the employee. The remainder of this chapter and Chapter 15 provide more detail.

Risk-Reward Scale

First you need to understand more about the various stock weights that you will arrange to put on the reward side of your start-up risk-reward scale as shown in Figure 14-1.

You are starting your own business, so you will be the owner, right? Perhaps—if you intend to remain a small business. However, Chapter 5 establishes that you will want to grow for a variety of reasons. Growth requires capital, and that implies the presence of investors who will give you needed funds only in return for an immediate or optional equity interest in your company. Banks will not loan a start-up business money unless the entrepreneur personally secures the loan with personal assets (such as your house), so it looks like you will be stuck with co-owners in your business. You will have a founding team and other key employees who will be critical to your success. It is essential that they all be motivated by a share of the ownership of your business. Ownership in a business is reflected in shares of the company's stock. A founder of the business will usually be granted cheap founder's stock. Employees who join the business later will usually be granted options to acquire shares in the future (more on options in Chapter 15).

First, it is necessary to briefly review the different legal forms your business can take before illustrating how stock ownership can be equitably divided between you and your associates.

Table 14-1 Stock and Stock Options

Event Type	Employee Advantages	Employer Advantages	Employee Disadvantages	Employer Disadvantages
stock grants gift of stock	Immediate voting rights. Stock is free.[a] Stock in hand is easier to keep. No conditions for ownership.	Gets a more loyal employee. Book expense—reduces profits which can save taxes.	Tax liability. Repurchase agreement.	Dilution of ownership. Book expense—hurts paper profits.
or gift of right to buy stock immediately	Immediate voting rights. Stock is cheap. Stock in hand is easier to keep. No conditions for purchase.	Gets a more loyal employee. Gets small additional capital.	Tax liability. Repurchase agreement. Need to buy immediately.	Dilution of ownership. Book expense—hurts paper profits.
above stock granted can be: restricted	Section 83(b) election can eliminate future tax burden.	Can buy back stock if employee does not meet performance or vesting conditions.	Repurchase agreement. Pay a small tax up front.	
or transferable (generally cannot be done in start-ups)	Can dispose of shares anytime.		Immediate tax liability.	Loss of control of stock.
other stock acquisitions purchase (investments)	Immediate voting rights. Very high ROI possible. Can sell shares anytime.	Gets additional capital.	Need higher salary, and/or invest hard-earned cash.	Increased number of shareholders.
or via provision of property	Can dispose of shares anytime. Immediate voting rights. Sophisticated investment. Tax-free exchange possible.	Gets needed property.	Some investment risk.	Dilution of ownership.
stock option grants gift of incentive stock options (ISOs)	No income reportable (no tax) on grant or exercise. Options exercisable in any order. Taxed only when stock is disposed of. Vesting schedule negotiable.	Does not show as an expense, thus does not hurt paper profits. High likelihood option will not be exercised by employee. Exercise schedule not negotiable.	No voting rights until exercised. Taxed when disposed of. Many IRS requirements to qualify: option price > = fair market value, must exercise < = 10 years from date of grant, must be employee to exercise or exercise < 3 months after termination, need cash to exercise options before they expire, high risk of losing options. Exercise schedule is not negotiable.	Possible future dilution of ownership.
or gift of nonqualified stock options (NQSOs)	Options exercisable in any order. Vesting schedule negotiable. Exercise schedule negotiable.	Gets a more loyal employee. Book expense—reduces profits which can save taxes.	No voting rights (until exercised). Taxed at date of grant. Taxed when exercised. Taxed when disposed of.	Possible future dilution of ownership. Book expense—hurts paper profits. Exercise schedule negotiable.

[a] The IRS will not recognize stock grants as gifts in the classic sense—stock will most likely be treated as compensation to the employee (so he will owe income tax on its value); therefore, it is technically inaccurate to say the stock is free.

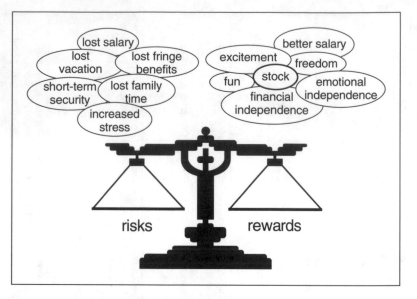

Figure 14-1   Start-Up Risk-Reward Scale

Corporations

Most product-related engineering businesses will need to be incorporated, if for no other reason, to establish an efficient mechanism for the ownership and distribution of assets and profits over time as the business grows. A corporation is perhaps best thought of as a fictitious being or artificial entity independent of the owners or investors. This artificial entity may conduct a business or businesses in its own name much in the way that a real person could. Business is done, assets are acquired, contracts are entered into, and liabilities are incurred, all in the name of the corporation rather than in the name of any individual. Other attempts to describe the theoretical nature of a corporation involve a description of the power of states to regulate corporations or the rights or duties of participants in a corporation among themselves. Ownership in a corporation is represented by shares of stock that are held by shareholders or stockholders, which is the main subject of this chapter.

Partnerships

Some service-related engineering consultancies could be operated as partnerships (where there is less need for capital), and a simple formula could determine how revenues would be divided. A partnership is the simplest form of organization involving more than one person. It is formed by agreement of the partners, who share the right to manage and the right to participate in the profits. Each also shares the unlimited obligation to answer personally for all the liabilities of the business.

It is true that many professional service businesses (including many law firms and some engineering consulting firms) share only profits rather than equity with business partners. The typical start-up entrepreneur, however, will be trying to build value in the equity of an incorporated (and usually product-related) business. That equity must be shared in order to motivate the key players and attract needed investment.

Limited Liability Companies (LLCs)

You might ask your lawyer about limited liability companies. At the time of writing, only eight states (Colorado, Florida, Kansas, Nevada, Texas, Utah, Virginia, and Wyoming) had authorized LLCs, but interest was growing. LLCs enjoy the best of both worlds: the tax advantages of a partnership and the legal safeguards of a corporation. Yet they face none of the drawbacks associated with forming a so-called subchapter-S corporation, which is also taxed much like a partnership. For example, S corporations cannot have corporate shareholders, but LLCs can. Because not all states recognize the limited liability of the partners, LLCs may not be suitable for companies doing business in a wide range of states.

Incorporate with a First-Class Lawyer

It is very tempting to incorporate your business yourself. While it is quite easy and fun to do, and there are dozens of books that will lead you through every step of the procedure in your state, you should incorporate with the aid of a good lawyer. Lots of businesses offer incorporation services for a hundred dollars or so, but do not be tempted to use them. You will need a good lawyer working with you over the next few years, and you need expert advice from day one. If you go to a good lawyer with your incorporation papers in hand and ask him or her to represent you, he or she will likely mark you as an amateur and at best assign one of the firm's youngest and least experienced associates to your case.

While using a first-class lawyer can consume a lot of money very quickly, it will be worth it in the long run if you plan to grow a successful company and take it to an IPO.

Many venture capital groups have preferred relationships with first-class attorneys that can help in setting reasonable limits on initial costs. The flip side is that this relationship could leave the entrepreneur on the outside if he or she is not prudent. For example, famous law firms such as Wilson, Sonsini, Goodrich & Rosati really work for investors, such as Adler & Company, who bring many deals to them. Choose your first-class lawyer with care.

Ownership Interest Over Time

Other stockholders will eventually own a good portion of your company, and through increased value of their shares will participate in the profits. While you may eventually also distribute dividends as a form of profit sharing, in your first years you will not even think of wasting precious cash doing so. So what do you need to know about stock ownership in order to launch your business successfully? Figure 14-2 shows qualitatively how stock ownership interests might change over time as your business grows.

In the beginning, the company you launch is clearly yours, and you call the shots. You may very well be the only stockholder, hold every office your secretary of state requires, and be the only board member. You own a very big piece of a very small pie. As you bring other founders, key employees, and investors on board, however, the picture changes greatly. The value of the company (the increasing area of the pie) and your percentage ownership (the ever smaller slice) will depend greatly on a number of factors.

How Many Shares Should You Grant?

The total percentage of stock owned or claimed by management and employees should equal 25–30% after the last round of financing, and about 4% after an IPO. With declining returns on venture capital funds, there is a trend toward reserving an even smaller portion for management and employees. At least one well-known venture capital fund tells entrepreneurs in advance that its general model is 80/20. Management and employees will likely get 20% maximum.

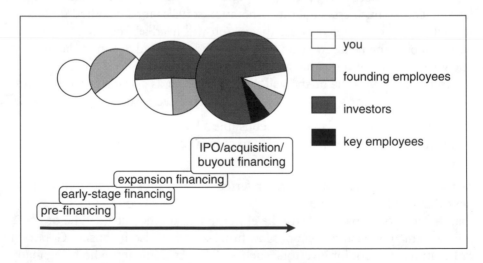

Figure 14-2   Business Ownership Interest Over Time

As the founder, you could initially own about one-half of all the stock granted to the cofounding team, and you could own as much as one-third of the total stock allocated to the management-employee pool (i.e., the noninvestors' shares) after the final round of financing (see Figure 14-2). These numbers will vary widely, and will depend greatly on who else cofounds or joins your business.

The absolute number of shares you can grant an employee or cofounder will be determined by the established price per share. The pricing of shares is completely arbitrary; only percentages really matter. One approach is to price your stock so that each founder has something approaching 1 million shares. This is a very powerful psychological threshold, as people can see their million dollars more clearly if they have a claim on 1 million shares of your stock. Even junior employees will be able to visualize their tens of thousands of shares being worth significant amounts. Anyone who thinks about it for more than a moment will realize that the number of shares really does not matter, but even you will be heartened by the thought of owning millions of shares of stock. Venture capital investors understand this psychology as well, and will often encourage you to play this penny stock game. When you take your company public in the future, however, reason calls for pricing stock in an accepted price range (typically $10–$20) which means you must do a reverse-split, significantly reducing the number of shares each employee claims. If not handled properly, this can cause employee animosity.

Some people advise avoiding the reverse-split ordeal by starting out with a price per share of exactly $1.00. That way, the company might be able to go public at a few dollars per share without going through any reverse stock split. The call is really yours, but the penny stock approach can be more exciting since it emphasizes the possibility of a real home run. A prominent Silicon Valley venture capital firm, for example, invested roughly $1 million in Aldus (the PageMaker software company) and the company was worth over $400 million when it went public four years later. Since returns of 300 or 400 to one are not unheard of, why not hand out a million shares worth a penny each that might be worth a dollar each some day?

Some entrepreneurs maintain a major ownership for years, even after the company goes public. In 1986, for example, Microsoft Corporation went public. Founder Bill Gates retained 43% of the company with 11 million shares worth $390 million on the day of the offering. In 1992, Gates was worth about $7.35 billion, and still owned about one-third of the software giant. The legendary David Packard was worth about $1.9 billion with his 13% ownership of Hewlett-Packard. Others will own less than 1% after years of work, which may or may not be enough.

Kurtzig from ASK Computer said of its day of public offering,

> For the 546,550 personal shares I sold, I was to receive a check for
> $5,580,276. And I still owned more than 3 million shares of ASK
> stock, 61% of the company.

Like a baby, you give this entity birth, and as it grows and matures it will grow
into its own. Enjoy and prosper from the journey and the destination of this
child!

Common and Preferred Stock

Preferred stock owners have certain advantages over common stock owners.
The owners of preferred stock have a first claim on the assets of the company
(after debts have been taken care of) should it ever be necessary to liquidate
the company. Some preferred stock issues also carry a dividend payable every
year on every share before any dividends can be paid to common stock holders.
Further, if the preferred stock is cumulative preferred, then any dividends not
paid in previous years would accrue and must be paid in full before the common
stock holders could get a penny in dividends. For these reasons, preferred stock
usually has a higher valuation or market value than common stock.

In some cases where investors or insiders have imposed unreasonable dividend
service to their preferred stock holdings, the common stock can be predicted to
have virtually no present or future value, barring some miracle in the fortunes
of the company. It is for these reasons that your investors, if they are at all
sophisticated and if they contribute any substantial amount of money, will no
doubt demand preferred stock, and will require you to hold common stock.

A rule of thumb is to assume that one common share is only worth between 10%
and 50% of one preferred share, depending upon the preferred dividend policy
and the maturity of the start-up. Generally, each share of preferred stock will be
converted into one share of common stock just before the company goes public
or is sold, at which time their values become equal.

Authorized and Outstanding Shares

When you and your lawyer incorporate your business, your articles of incorporation will specify how many common and preferred shares of each series
of stock you want, and which will be available for sale or distribution. This is
the number of authorized shares, and the number can be very large. It is also,
however, almost meaningless. It only temporarily specifies how many shares
can be sold in the future. At any future time when the company wants to sell
more shares, all it needs to do is modify its articles, specifying that more shares

are to be authorized. Do not use the number of authorized shares to compute anything.

The number of shares sold or given to people is the number of outstanding, or issued, shares. In calculating your present percentage ownership of the company, divide your share holdings by the number of outstanding shares. To estimate your percentage of ownership at some future point in time, divide your current share holdings by the sum of the number of shares currently outstanding plus any authorized shares that you estimate will be issued between now and that point in time (for example, to accommodate the exercising of stock options).

Acquiring Stock

One can generally buy stock at a fair market value at any time once a business is underway. Founders generally will divide up the business according to the perceived value each member is expected to bring to the party, independent of how much cash is provided. Founders providing excess cash can simply be treated in part like investors. One also can acquire an option (which is a right, but not an obligation) to buy stock in the future, usually at a discounted price.

Founder's Stock

When launching your start-up, you will grant to yourself and your founding team shares of stock called founder's stock. However, this does not mean that the shares are free from either a dollar point of view or from conditions.

For Founders

Founder's stock is loosely defined as cheap stock (received when fair market value is near zero). Founder's stock is usually available only to those who create or found a business and is granted in proportion to one's potential contribution. It is often purchased for a nominal sum or a token amount with no income tax liability. Purchase is made just after incorporation and before infusion of substantial outside capital.

For Key Employees

A key employee whom you hire later but choose to treat as a founder may still be granted cheap founder's stock even after infusion of outside capital. However, there will be income realized from the IRS' point of view, and taxes must be paid by the employee because the stock will be purchased at a price less than fair market value. Although as the employer you could gross up a paycheck to help the employee pay his or her taxes, this is not done frequently in practice because of the impact on cash. Therefore, from a practical income tax point of view, founder's stock is only readily available before the business is substantially capitalized.

Dollars

Founder shares are sold primarily to distribute ownership in the business equitably. Price is an issue only to the extent that, after founder shares are issued and before financing can be obtained, the company must end up with sufficient capital to be viable. Though many state laws specify no minimum level of capitalization, your lawyer will likely recommend that you and your cofounders scrape together at least a few thousand dollars at this step. He or she wants to be paid, as will many new service providers you will be engaging very soon. If you do not start with sufficient capital, you will find yourself lending money to the business very soon.

Anyone who loans money to a start-up (including yourself) should be compensated with a very high interest rate (like junk bonds) or an option to convert the loan into equity in the future. Take some caution, however, in compensating yourself with a high-interest-rate loan. Several items to be aware of are: the high interest rate may violate the usury laws; if the lender is also a corporate officer or director, charging a high interest rate may be a breach of fiduciary duty and open the door to a shareholder suit; high interest may run afoul of IRS rules on reasonableness; and the interest income could be treated as disguised wages (so the company would be liable for penalties for failure to withhold FICA, FUTA, FWT, etc.).

Conditions

Imagine that you and your founding team have come to an agreement. It is decided, for example, that as the president and chief executive officer, you should have twice as much stock as your vice presidents of engineering and marketing and sales. Your programming manager will have half again as much, and so on. Now, what happens if some of these key people leave the business: they quit, are fired, or become ill? Will they simply retain all their founder's stock and eventually benefit from the future years of labor of those remaining behind? This could happen if you do not impose some restrictions. It is wise to use a lawyer experienced in this area. Also, try to get on your board of directors someone who has experience in start-up businesses.

Restricted Stock Grants

To a founder or early employee, you may grant the right to purchase, sometimes at a very small nominal cost, restricted shares of stock.

If you are using the sale of founder's stock to substantially capitalize your business, you may find a few cases of financial hardship among your founders and key employees. For such individuals, the money they need to purchase their stock grants might be loaned by the company, and this loan might be forgiven over time in whole or in part as they acquire seniority with the company. Some key employees negotiate not only forgivable loans (which they never have to repay) but also zero interest (or forgivable interest) loans.

The IRS will impute interest (typically 9%) on zero interest loans. If you do not actually pay the interest to the company, you may be taxed on the equivalent income you realized.

Be careful not to run afoul of Rule 144 when using loans to fund purchases of restricted stock. Rule 144 restricts the selling of securities until certain conditions and time tests have been met. (Rule 144 has been modified somewhat by Rule 706.) Under Rule 144, if the loan is secured by the stock, the clock does not start running until the loan is repaid, so use something other than the stock as collateral.

In one case, a successful entrepreneur found that he had to exercise some stock options that had significantly appreciated before his exercise period expired. The bad news was that the exercise of these (nonqualified) options was a taxable event. Therefore he owed big taxes on big gains, but he could not sell the stock for another two years to get the cash to pay his taxes. Be careful not to paint yourself into such a corner. To avoid realizing taxable income through the acquisition of cheap stock, one rule of thumb is that the price of any share of common stock you purchase should be at least equal to 10% of the amount paid by investors for a share of preferred stock.

In any case, the shares you will be granting can be restricted in two senses of the word and you need to be aware of both.

Transfer Restricted Stock—Restricted Securities

State and federal securities laws dictate to whom outstanding shares in a corporation can be resold, under what conditions, and at what times. If you or your employees have received a stock certificate for the shares granted to you, these shares probably have not even been registered with the state of incorporation (depending upon the number and kinds of shareholders and the amount of capital accumulated). Since all shares have legal restrictions on their transfer, you can expect unregistered shares to be even more restricted. Thus, you should not be surprised to see printed on the top of your certificate in big bold letters and red ink something like the following:

> IT IS UNLAWFUL TO CONSUMMATE A SALE OR TRANSFER OF THIS SECURITY, OR ANY INTEREST THEREIN, OR TO RECEIVE ANY CONSIDERATION THEREFOR, WITHOUT THE PRIOR WRITTEN CONSENT OF THE COMMISSIONER OF CORPORATIONS OF THE STATE OF CALIFORNIA EXCEPT AS PERMITTED IN THE COMMISSIONER'S RULES.

There will also be over a dozen rules printed on the back of your certificate in very small letters, making reference to obscure sections of legal code understandable only by lawyers schooled in your state's securities laws. The bottom line is that, short of dying, you probably cannot sell or otherwise transfer your stock to anyone except the company, or possibly other qualified and sophisticated investors or shareholders. However, your major concern will be with the more common meaning of the word restricted, as described below.

Ownership Restricted Stock (Vesting)—Control Securities

You will generally be obligated to sell founder's shares back to the company, in whole or in part, until certain events have occurred or certain time has passed (i.e., until you have become vested). When you become vested in stock, you have the right to retain your ownership of the stock granted to you (i.e., which you have purchased) with no threat of repurchase by the company.

A repurchase agreement will be executed, spelling out the details of how and when the company can buy back these restricted shares (usually when one's employment terminates before a certain date). The terms of repurchase agreements are negotiable.

Rule 144 and the Sale of Restricted or Control Securities

Excerpts in this section are from Arthur Andersen's *An Entrepreneur's Guide to Going Public*, 1988, Subject File AA5490, Item 33 88-1003. This guide, and many more such useful guides, is available free by calling the Arthur Andersen & Company office in your area.

Securities purchased in reliance on the private placement exemption of the 1933 Act or Regulation D (restricted securities), and other securities held by persons controlling, controlled by, and under common control with the company (control securities) may not be resold in the public market unless they are registered under the 1933 Act or sold in compliance with Rule 144 or some other exemption from the Act.

In general terms, Rule 144 permits a person who has owned and fully paid for restricted stock for at least two years to sell during any three-month period up to the number of shares that equals the greater of 1% of the outstanding class or the average weekly trading volume of the security during the four weeks preceding the filing of the notice of sale required under the rule. Owners of control stock may sell up to the same number of shares and are not required to have held their control stock for any specified period of time. Officers, directors, and 5% owners may, however, encounter additional restrictions. If you obtained a loan from the company to purchase your shares, the Rule 144 clock will not start ticking until that loan is paid off. Rule 144 contains many technical provisions and is subject to constant interpretation. Accordingly, legal counsel should be sought before sales are made in reliance on Rule 144.

Future Tax Liability on Restricted Shares

If one receives restricted founder's shares, no tax is due immediately, since the shares may have to be returned to the company. However, the IRS will tax you when any of your restricted shares become tradable or are not subject to a substantial risk of forfeiture. Therefore, a few years after you receive your shares, you may be in for quite a surprise as you become vested. The difference between what you paid for your shares and their new current fair market value is taxed to you as ordinary income, even if you do not sell a single share. In fact, it may not be practical or legal for you to sell shares even if you wanted to, but you will still owe taxes. Unfortunately, that holds even if the stock later becomes worthless.

Section 83(b) Election

Luckily, you can partially avoid the preceding tax liability problem (and almost everyone who is aware of this alternative does so) by ignoring the transferability limitations and risk of forfeiture, and electing, under Section 83(b) of the IRS Code, to immediately pay tax on the difference between the fair market value at the time of grant and the amount you paid for your stock. Usually this tax is a small amount, even zero if the company has recently been formed. When you use this election procedure, any future appreciation will be taxed not when the restrictions lapse (i.e., you become vested), but when you dispose of the stock. Note that there is a distinction between selling stock and disposing of it. Disposition includes gifting it to someone else. Before the Tax Reform Act of 1986 (TRA-86) took effect, you only needed to pay the lower long-term capital gain rates. Tax laws change continuously, though; by the time you decide to sell your shares, the tax laws will probably have had, and lost and gained again, a significant long-term capital gains tax preference. In fact, TRA-86 kept intact the concept of long-term capital gains, it just did not give them preferable tax rates. It is important to work with your lawyer and a tax advisor in this matter.

In summary, by taking the Section 83(b) election, you might pay a small tax up front, but in return you will postpone payment of significant future taxes. The one drawback to a Section 83(b) election is that if you lose the stock by selling it back to the company under a forfeiture (repurchase) provision, you will not be able to offset any income recognized when you made the Section 83(b) election. Even here, though, there seems to be a loophole. IRS private ruling 9104039 indicates that employees can undo Section 83(b) elections without IRS consent by getting employers to rescind awards. The practical question is whether it will cost you more to work with a lawyer on these issues than it could be worth to you in tax savings.

While perhaps not as common, the 83(b) election can just as easily be taken as a preventive tax measure to reduce risk of paying taxes earlier than necessary for nonqualified stock options (NQSOs), which are discussed in Chapter 15. In this case, upon exercise of the option, if the stock purchased is still subject to a substantial risk of forfeiture (this is not usual), you can similarly make an 83(b) election within 30 days of exercise to recognize the compensation at the date of exercise rather than at the time the risk lapses. When the fair market value of the stock is expected to rise during the risk period and you expect to hold the stock after the risk lapses, making the election may be advisable since it could minimize the amount of compensation received. This is particularly true if the risk will expire during the same taxable year in which the option is exercised. For more details and current tax law information, ask your local Price Waterhouse office for its latest free pamphlet (published yearly) entitled *Executive Compensation: TIPS Tax Information Planning Services.*

To reduce the perceived mystery of taking the 83(b) election, reproduced in Figure 14-3 is a typical form letter for the state of California, which your company's lawyer will complete for you. Solicit the services of your company's lawyer to ensure proper execution of this critical document. Within 30 days of receipt of your shares, this letter must be mailed to the IRS and your state tax board. Send it to the same addresses to which you sent your last year's tax returns. Also, attach a copy of this letter to your next year's federal and state tax returns (thus explaining the gain you chose to recognize by the purchase of your founder's stock or exercise of your controlled NQSOs).

Transferable Shares

Transferable shares are those without transfer restrictions as discussed previously. You own them free and clear, and they could be sold the next day if a suitable buyer could be found, provided the seller complies with the applicable state and federal securities laws. Of course, when you incorporate your business, you could grant to yourself all the transferable shares you want up to the limit of the number of shares you authorized the business to issue. However, when investors, cofounders, or knowledgeable key employees join the game, they will want you to change the rules. They will want you to vest your shares also, probably over a four- to five-year period. A four-year (or even a three-year) vesting period is more popular on the West Coast, while five-year vesting is frequently encountered on the East Coast.

<u>Election Under Section 83(b)</u>
<u>of the Internal Revenue Code of 1954</u>
<u>and Section 17122.7 of the California Revenue and Taxation Code</u>
The undersigned taxpayer hereby elects, pursuant to the above-referenced Federal and California Tax Codes, to include in his gross income for the current taxable year, the amount of any compensation taxable to him in connection with his receipt of the property described below:

1. The name, address, taxpayer identification number and the taxable year of the undersigned are as follows:
   NAME: TAXPAYER: _____ SPOUSE: _____
   ADDRESS: _____
   I.D. No.: TAXPAYER: _____ SPOUSE: _____
   TAXABLE YEAR: _____

2. The property with respect to which the election is made is described as follows:
   _____ shares of _____

3. The date on which the property was transferred is: _____

4. The property is subject to the following restrictions:

   The shares are subject to restriction set forth in an agreement between the Corporation and the registered holder, a copy of which is on file at the principal office of the Corporation.

5. The fair market value at the time of transfer, determined without regard to any restriction other than a restriction which by its terms will never lapse, of such property is: $ _____

6. The amount (if any) paid for such property is: $ _____

The undersigned has submitted a copy of this statement to the person for whom the services were performed in connection with the undersigned's receipt of the above-mentioned property. The transferee of such property is the person performing the services in connection with the transfer of said property.

<u>The undersigned understands that the foregoing election may not</u>
<u>be revoked except with the consent of the commissioner.</u>
Dated: _____ Taxpayer: _____
The undersigned spouse of Taxpayer joins in this election.
Date: _____ Spouse: _____

Figure 14-3 83(b) Election Form Letter

There is not much reason for a start-up company to give any employee a stock grant free of restrictions. If you did, the employee would be free to move on to another job, and sell the shares later for a handsome profit.

The preferred shares that you sell to your investors will, of course, be transferable since they are giving you full consideration for them. Sometimes intellectual property rights such as patents or trademarks will be exchanged for shares, and these shares, likewise, would have no reason to be ownership restricted. Similarly, you may try to conserve funds by paying some of your service providers shares instead of cash. It would serve no purpose to have these shares subject to repurchase either.

In the event that you receive transferable shares, any difference between the fair market value and the purchase price of such shares would be taxed as ordinary income (e.g., as compensation for service), as would seem fair.

Make sure you execute your stock grants properly with a lawyer. Otherwise, an irregularity may, in the future, force you to sell your founder's stock back to the company at your original cost of almost nothing. This happened in 1980 to some of the founders of Genentech, Inc., a very successful biotechnology company that raised $35 million in its initial public offering. Two sidebar stories in this chapter and the next illustrate the importance of your understanding the nature of vesting and other conditions involved in acquiring value from stock and options.

Venture Capital Ratchets

This subject has rarely, if ever, been mentioned in a book. If you have ever been with a start-up, you are probably aware of venture capital ratchets, but the uninitiated would not have any idea that this is a common practice.

Be aware of some very powerful and sophisticated techniques in the venture capital community. Professional investors often attach special warrants or other vehicles to their stock investments. These often-invisible warrants and vehicles are a kind of option to buy/convert stock. They can be structured so that if any future investor ever pays a lower price per share, the holder of the original warrants or vehicle multiplies his or her original conversion ratio to prevent any dilution (investors often call this full ratchet down protection). A ratchet provides significant financial advantage to the investor and its implications should be recognized explicitly up front. Plummer (1987) reports that warrants are involved in about 30% of venture capital deals, and antidilution ratchets are involved in about 70% of deals. Sometimes, however, ratchets are good for the start-up entrepreneur in that the syndicate or group of initial investors will build a ratchet to all but guarantee that the entire group must continue to put funds into the company on a pro rata basis if needed. Otherwise, the nonparticipating investors would suffer the blow of the ratchet.

Following is a simplified, fictitious example of how a ratchet could work against you and your second-round investors. To emphasize the power of ratchets, this example is extreme. The ratchet technique is so powerful that knowledgeable second-round investors may avoid such deals altogether, or will at least negotiate with the first-round investor to change terms before investing. While investor #1 and investor #2 may work something out, you and your management team will likely remain disadvantaged. Also, keep in mind that this example concerns a nonperforming management team—perhaps one that deserves to be penalized.

Investor #1 purchases 1 million shares of series A preferred stock for $1.00 per share, with the stipulation that these series A shares will be converted one-to-one into common shares at some point in the future. However, if shares (of any preferred series X) are ever sold for a lower price (P_x), the conversion ratio will be changed from one-to-one to one-to-N, where $N = \$1.00/\$P_x$. For the purposes of this example, it is assumed that management has retained 500,000 founders' shares (or one-third of the company).

The company runs out of cash, falls behind schedule, and takes the only deal to be found. In a very minor second round, investor #2 purchases 200,000 shares of series B preferred stock for $0.10 per share, for a total cash infusion of $20,000. Investor #1, because of the ratchet, now has future rights to convert one series A preferred share into 10 common shares ($N = 10 = \$1.00/\$0.10$).

If these two investors were the only capital sources for the business, $1,020,000 would have been invested, and the future ownership picture would show substantial dilution for the business founders and the second-round investor, as shown in Figure 14-4.

	Shares Before Ratchet	Perceived Percent Owner-ship	Shares After Ratchet	Effective Percent Owner-ship
management	500,000	29.41%	500,000	4.67%
investor #1	1,000,000	58.82%	10,000,000	93.46%
investor #2	200,000	11.76%	200,000	1.87%
total	1,700,000	100.00%	10,700,000	100.00%

You can see from this extreme example the power of the ratchet. Management's initial one-third ownership interest would drop to under 5%, while the initial

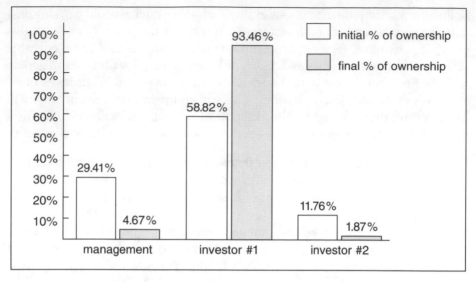

Figure 14-4   Consequences of Antidilution Ratchet

investor's interest would increase from less than 60% to over 90% at no additional cost. No rational, sophisticated second-round investor would play this game. It is frightening to think, however, that the first-round investor may have some indirect influence on the behavior of the second-round investor through whatever relationships and obligations exist in the world of finance. But this is a much too sinister and undeserved thought. What may be worse, and even more likely to be fact, is that the ratchet could be written to be applied even if the second-round investor is the same entity as the first-round investor.

If the price per share of the current round of investment is less than the previous round, it is called a *down round*. You can see that a small down round would be a fast, cheap way to wipe out the management team.

A down round puts the company into a position where it is usually called a *restart*. Restarts usually mean bad news for some stockholders. *Turnarounds* are a bit different. In a turnaround, one attempts to rejuvenate a thwarted or stalled start-up without lowering the price (or diluting stockholders) in the process.

This behavior would never happen unjustifiably in practice, it would be illegal, and it would remove all motivation from a performing management team (non-performing management teams may deserve what they get). But at least now you see why the term *punitive financing* needs to be well understood.

It is a bit more likely, however, that you will encounter a (usually) less severe antidilution clause that enforces a type of weighted-average method for computing the impact of the ratchet, often called a *California ratchet*. This weighted-average method takes into consideration:

1. the cost per share in each round
2. the amount of money invested in each round
3. the number of founders' shares held

There are a number of variations of the weighted-average method, and surprisingly, the formulas most frequently used are not very intuitive. The method illustrated here is reported to be most commonly used. It has the interesting (but not widely publicized) side effect of substantially diluting the founders even more than a full ratchet would in certain cases (e.g., where the founders hold a large percentage of the stock).

The intent of the weighted-average method is to lessen the impact of the ratchet if the number of new shares purchased is small. Selling only one share at a drastically lower price, for example, should not entitle the first-round investor to severely dilute founders or other nonparticipating investors. *Burnout financing* is venture capital jargon for severely diluting others, i.e., burning them out of the opportunity. New second-round investors will not be concerned with burnout since they will get the percentage of equity they bargained for at the specified price (as they factor in the effects of antidilution clauses).

Using the preceding extreme example, apply the weighted-average method described by Joseph W. Bartlett in *Venture Capital*. Note that this method is only an approximation to the mathematical definition of a weighted-average function.

	Money Invested	Price per Share	Number of Shares Purchased
founders	0	0	500,000
first-round investors	$1,000,000	$1.00	1,000,000
second-round investors	$20,000	$0.10	200,000
total	$1,020,000		1,700,000

With a full ratchet, recall that the first-round investors would be entitled to convert their preferred shares to common shares at an effective price of $0.10. Thus, they would enjoy a ratchet factor of 10 [the old price ($1.00) divided by the new price ($0.10)], entitling them to convert their 1,000,000 preferred shares into 10,000,000 common shares. Using Bartlett's weighted-average method, however, these first-round investors would only be entitled to convert their shares at an effective price of $0.80, enjoying a ratchet factor of 1.25 ($1.00 divided by $0.80), which entitles them to only 1,250,000 common shares upon conversion.

Here is how to compute the ratchet effect using Bartlett's weighted-average method:

A = total number of shares outstanding before second-round financing (includes investor's and founders' shares)

B = total number of shares outstanding after second-round financing

C = number of shares second-round financing would have purchased at higher first-round price

D = number of new shares actually purchased at the lower second-round price

It follows that

$$B = A + D$$

The number of shares before and after and price before and after (expressed in number of shares) leads to the following formula used in computing the first-round investor's new conversion price:

$$F = \frac{A + C}{B + D}$$

$$= \frac{A + C}{A + D + D} = \frac{A + C}{A + (2 \times D)}$$

The pseudo-fraction A over B takes into account the number of shares (small or large) issued in the dilutive financing.

The pseudo-fraction C over D takes into account the drop in price.

F is the fraction (≤ 1) used to multiply the old conversion price (the original first-round price) to get the first-round investor's new conversion price.

$$\text{new conversion price} = F \times \text{first-round price}$$

Understanding the logic of Bartlett's weighted-average method is frustrating, since it is a heuristic and is not really a weighted-average function in the mathematical sense.

The ratchet factor R, by definition, is

$$R = \frac{\text{first-round price}}{\text{new conversion price}}$$

$$= \frac{\text{first-round price}}{F \times \text{first-round price}} = \frac{1}{F}$$

In comparison, if you used traditional mathematical formulas for computing weighted averages for this example case, you would obtain the following conversion factors. (Keep in mind that details such as conversion formulas are negotiable when you and your investors draw up an investment term sheet.)

Antidilution Method Employed	New Conversion Price	Ratchet Factor $R = \dfrac{1}{\text{new conversion price}}$
full ratchet	$0.10	10
Bartlett's weighted-average	$0.80	1.25
weighted-average by number of shares (excluding founders' shares)	$0.85	1.176471
weighted-average by number of shares (including founders' shares)	$0.60	1.666667
weighted-average by dollars invested (assumes founders contribute $0)	$0.982353	1.017964

You could easily construct a computer spreadsheet for further analysis. Keep in mind that this case represents the simple situation where there are neither multiple financing rounds nor multiple investors involved, which would be usual. It is beyond the scope of this book to address those cases.

Punitive Financing

Imagine a scenario like the preceding one, where a nonperforming management team, fully vested in its founders' stock, has been replaced (a frequent occurrence when performance falls off). A new management team comes in, and it needs stock. Where do the investors get it without diluting their holdings? If they have a ratchet clause, and if the value of their shares really is one-tenth of what it was, the previous scenarios could legally and ethically be played out.

It is illegal to price shares below fair market value to exploit a ratchet, and it would be highly unusual for a venture capitalist to knowingly break the law. However, what determines fair market value is not always straightforward. What you do need to know is that ratchet downs are appropriate (and they do take place) to penalize early investors and founders who are no longer in the game when valuations drop and the business has to be reenergized.

Your best protection against ratchets is to give realistic plans and then meet or come close to meeting them. Be a performing team and you will not be penalized. If you underperform, you will feel the effects of the ratchet.

When and How Often to Grant Stock

To your cofounders and key employees you will want to provide as much motivation and express as much confidence and expectation as you can up front. On day one, grant to yourself and your key employees and founders as much stock as you think will be fair, assuming they will perform as projected in your business plan. This is all the better reason to assemble the team first and then write the plan, as opposed to writing a plan and then looking for a team. That way (as discussed in Chapter 11) everyone will have bought into the performance objectives in advance. Then, if employees exceed expectations or the plan, consider granting more shares in the future, but in the form of options (as explained in Chapter 15).

One case where the model of front-loading stock grants fails is when you have a strong technical person in whom you are entrusting unproven management responsibility, someone who may not work out as a manager, but could remain as a strong technical contributor. In such a case, grant 75% of the stock you had in mind on day one, and plan to enhance that with options equal to the remaining 25% if he or she proves worth your trust. Resist the temptation to restrict vesting in founder's stock contingent on an individual's occupying a certain position at a future point in time. Things will change too rapidly to see that far ahead, and vesting based on anything other than time will likely serve to misdirect energy and focus. On the other hand, people in key profit and loss positions can be promised stock or stock option bonuses if they meet or exceed profit and revenue goals. This is a better form of vesting. It is important to review stock positions at least annually to preserve equity and maintain motivation. You started your business because you had a passion and motivation, and you need those same feelings instilled in every one of your employees.

On rare occasions you may be tempted to consider accelerating the vesting period on options for some of your key employees as an additional reward. This is generally advised against since you want to keep the pressure on, and minimize potential dilution. If you try to be fair, you will make the right decision. Never burn a bridge; you will likely be working in some relationship with your associates and investors again in the future.

Playing on Employee Desire for Stock Grants

In one start-up that I was involved in, two of us were having dinner, discussing the fortunes each of us was to make if the company's predicted sales were met that year. Our stock would soar in value for sure!

My friend was from Australia and did not really understand how U.S. securities laws, tax laws, and other such esoterica operated. He was confident, however, that he owned a good piece of the pie, and that he would share in the goodies. After all, the president had told him that he was a partner in the company. Well, the enterprise was not legally a partnership, it was a corporation, so that term lacked substantive meaning. However, it sounded good to my friend.

Upon further discussion, it became obvious to me that this gentleman had been granted not founder's stock but stock options (he did not own stock in the company as he had assumed), and he certainly had no idea when he would be eligible to buy the stock, for how long he would be eligible, and at what price he could purchase it.

15

Stock Option and Stock Option Grant Practices for Your Start-Up

"May fortune favor the foolish."
— Kirk (Star Trek IV)

Stock Option Grants versus Stock Grants

What is the difference between stock and stock options? Stock is printed on fancy paper that feels and looks like money, while stock options are typed on cheap 20-pound office stationery. Beyond that, stock options (an agreement to allow, but not obligate, one to purchase some shares in the future at a specified price, under very restricted conditions) are inherently inferior, because they only provide the individual with the opportunity to realize significant financial gains if the company does remarkably well and if timing works out just right. Stock, on the other hand, while it may entail some tax liability if granted at a discounted price, has long-term potential value that is easier to realize. Obviously, if the company performs poorly, stock is just as bad as an option. It may even be worse, because the employee/investor loses real dollars. The message in this section is that too many stock options are never exercised (and thus are lost forever) because they are under water at the end of their exercise period. Stock, on the other hand, always has the potential to recover, and once you are fully vested in a stock grant, it can never go away. This is not to say you will not be substantially diluted at some point in the future, however.

Stock options are the most widely used and most popular mechanism by which employers make it possible for employees to participate in the future increased valuation of the company. The number of shares you will grant to an individual in your stock option plan will reflect that person's perceived importance and potential contribution to your enterprise. Vesting schedules will be established so that as time passes (four or five years typically), and perhaps also when performance targets (profitability, personal objectives, etc.) are met, the employee becomes eligible to exercise his or her options.

Table 14-1 provides a convenient overview of the basics of stock and stock option grants.

When to Grant Stock Options

Chapter 14 dealt with the issue of stock ownership: primarily when and how to grant founders' stock to yourself, your start-up founders, and your first key employees. It was established that a stock grant is an appropriate vehicle to motivate and reward an individual contributor before substantial capitalization of the business. Chapter 14 also showed that after the business is substantially capitalized, cheap stock is more difficult to grant without encountering adverse tax consequences. Thus, it was suggested that stock options would be a more appropriate vehicle for motivating individual contributors after funding. In this chapter you will learn about the kinds of stock options available, and how and when to grant them. As with stock grants, important concepts such as vesting and tax consequences are also covered.

How Often to Grant Stock Options

Usually, the options you will grant to an employee upon employment are the only options you will grant to that individual unless his or her responsibility increases. Some people think of stock options as a kind of yearly bonus. They are not too far off, since at many larger, more established companies, key employees and executives are often granted small amounts of stock annually as a reward for a job done well and as an incentive to stay with the company for a few more years. You can do this also, but at most start-ups, larger amounts of stock are usually granted upon employment, and then little or none are granted after that.

In start-up companies where options are granted yearly, proportionally fewer options should be granted annually, and the primary effect is to extend an employee's vesting period. This approach is not as effective, though, since the potential to make a financial killing is not as obvious to the employee in the earliest days when the need to motivate your people is at its highest. Other start-up entrepreneurs like the incremental grant approach because it allows rewards to track more closely changes in the perception of an employee's importance and contribution to the company over time. Enlightened management regularly reviews the amounts of stock options issued to employees and makes adjustments based on perceived inequities.

On How Many Shares Do You Grant Options?

This is a very negotiable issue. The more an employee knows about options and business valuations, the more you will likely have to grant to satisfy that individual.

It is important that you start off with a pool of shares for all founders, employees, and future hires. Then, work out a one- or two-year plan showing the average number of shares to be granted per employee, declining over time as the price per share goes up (see Table 17-2 for share price changes to be expected). Be a little stingy as you have a very fixed pool to work with. Worry about relative number of shares per key employee; percentage ownership is only part of the picture. It may not be fair, but tradition has it that percentage share ownership decreases almost by a factor of 10 from each level from the top to the bottom. In relative numbers, then, if the CEO gets 1 million shares, a vice president might get 100,000, an engineering manager might get 10,000, and a programmer might get 1,000, leaving 100 shares for a support staff member. For employees clearly in the same level in the organization (for example, all of your senior computer programmers) you might consider granting stock options proportional to salary to build some equitable treatment into your compensation structure.

For a key employee, someone on whom you are betting the future of your company, one rule of thumb is that you should grant stock options whose fair market value is equal to one year's salary. In calculating the fair market value of one share of stock, it is important to use the latest preferred share price, even though you will be granting options on common shares. This takes into consideration the fact that the preferred will convert to common someday if the business is successful. The employee thus hopes to multiply this value by 10 just as the investors hope to multiply by 10 the value of their preferred stock investments if your company is one of their few home runs of the season. Thus, a $50,000 salary level employee can clearly see $500,000 on the horizon, and your $100,000 vice presidents can see their million dollars.

To summarize, look at employee positions, levels of responsibility, and individual abilities to contribute to the future increased valuation of your company when deciding the number of shares upon which options will be granted.

Once in a while a rare, knowledgeable employee will be able to do his or her own due diligence on your start-up (much like an investor would) and might be in the position to reasonably argue for a much larger grant based on a different view of the future. Is not a five times return on investment more realistic for your business? In such situations you can grant the employee more stock if you think he or she can help you achieve your goals. The more knowledgeable employees are of valuation methods and option practices, the more practiced they may be in start-ups, and thus the more valuable they may be to you.

Robert Carr, who heads software development at GO Corporation, suggests that staff members should receive stock equal to half their salaries. Applying this or a similar rule of thumb may build credibility for you if it results in your compensation structure being perceived as fair by most of your employees. If you have some sort of a defensible formula, you will avoid dissension in the ranks. An engineer who makes 10% more salary than another might not need to have exactly 10% more stock, but he or she had better not have less stock unless you have a pretty good reason! Follow the advice of your board of directors, which presumably is experienced in this area. It has been said that you can never win the remuneration game, so do the best you can and be sensitive to the needs and perceptions of others. You are not a *Fortune* 500 company, so you do not have to have policy manuals and formulas to guide your every move. Find out who the key players and contributors are, understand what motivates them, and dispense the appropriate rewards as needed.

The bounding parameter in granting stock options is the rule of thumb that was previously mentioned, which is that after the last financing round, management and employees should own or have claim to between 25–30% of the business. There is an unfortunate trend these days, however, that moves the 25–30% target level to only 20%.

If you keep in mind the preceding basic ideas, it will soon become obvious how many options to grant to your employees. It is recommended that you be as generous as you can with your associates, but be realistic. Start out low for most employees, and leave room to give more to performers who do exceptionally well. You alone are not going to make your business worth $100 million. Many entrepreneurs hold tightly onto control, never giving anyone else a piece of the action. While some succeed in this stinginess, most would come out further ahead if they were more generous.

Two Kinds of Stock Options

There are two kinds of stock option plans you need to be familiar with: incentive stock options (ISOs) and nonqualified stock options (NQSOs). Most common for employees are ISOs, but you need to understand clearly the ins and outs of each in order to avoid any serious mistakes. With recent changes in capital gains taxes, NQSOs have become more popular over the past few years. Also, there are situations where ISOs simply cannot be granted (e.g., to consultants, board members, and other nonemployees). This section will review each.

Incentive Stock Options (ISOs)

Under an ISO plan, one is granted the option (but has no obligation) to purchase shares in the future at a given price, usually the fair market value of the stock on the date of grant (established by the board of directors, if there is no market). ISOs were especially attractive before the Tax Reform Act of 1986 (TRA-86). (See IRS Publication 525, *Taxable and Nontaxable Income*, for current guidelines.) The following are some salient features of ISOs:

- No ordinary income is reportable on grant or exercise. (Nonqualified options, though, can be taxed upon the date of grant, and are taxed when the option is exercised, even if the stock is not sold at that time.) ISOs are taxed only when the shares are sold or otherwise disposed of.

- If requirements were met, gain on the sale was a long-term capital gain. (The Tax Reform Act of 1986 largely eliminated the advantage of a long-term capital gains tax preference. However, with the 1990 act, Congress did reinstate a small tax benefit for long-term capital gains. In theory, the individual now pays a maximum tax rate of 28% on long-term capital gains, versus 31% before.) However, to qualify for ISO treatment, all the following requirements must be met.

  The option price must equal or exceed the fair market value of the stock at the time the option is granted. Also, an employee who owns more than 10% of the outstanding voting stock is not eligible to receive an ISO unless the option price is at least 110% of the stock's fair market value at the time the option is granted, and the option is not exercisable later than five years from the grant date.

  The option, by its terms, must not be exercisable later than 10 years following the date of grant.

  The option must be exercised while the grantee is an employee, or within three months after termination (one year if you are disabled). There have been cases where individuals, in good favor with past employers, have arranged to be employed (albeit on a very part-time basis) in order to retain their incentive stock option rights, while moving on to other full-time employment. Obviously, this is something you might want to consider as part of your severance agreement before you join. Again, the advice of legal counsel in formulating a valid plan is essential. (You can see from this that ISO exercise schedules cannot be negotiated for the most important period—that following employment. You could negotiate for a maximum exercise schedule of 10 years for those years in which you are employed.

In the past, an ISO could not be exercised whenever previously granted ISOs were still outstanding. TRA-86 favored ISOs by eliminating this restriction. Options may now be exercised in any order desired. In the past, this prevented the exercise of lower-priced ISOs that were predated by higher-priced ISOs. In start-ups where stock options were granted yearly and the price of the stock had risen and then fallen, a severe penalty could have been imposed. One could have actually lost some money by having to exercise options on older ISO shares, now priced above market value, to get to the newer lower-priced options.

The maximum value of shares that an employee may be granted in any calendar year is $100,000 in fair market value of the stock at the time the options are granted. However, if you are granted less than $100,000 in any year, a partial carryover may be utilized in subsequent years.

The stock must not be disposed of within two years after the option is granted, or within one year after it is exercised. If the shares are sold prior to the end of these time periods, a disqualifying disposition occurs so that the options are then treated as nonqualified options. The amount by which the fair market value on the date of exercise exceeds the price paid is then deemed to be (ordinary) income. This may or may not be important, depending on the current state of the capital gains tax.

ISOs had been the staple of key employee compensation since the Tax Reform Act of 1981 made this device attractive to employees by reducing the tax rate on capital gains. No taxes needed to be paid until one disposed of the stock, and one received favorable long-term capital gains treatment if the stock was held for one year after being obtained through exercise of the option. As a recipient of the option, one had to wait two years from the date of grant before disposing of shares to avoid losing the favorable ISO tax treatment. Also, the option could not be exercised later than three months after one ceased active employment with the company. It was also important that, while one may have been able to exercise an option to acquire stock when the market price was high, one also had to wait one more year to sell to get the long-term benefits of those capital gains. The market must have at least remained level for these shares to really pay off. Getting the money to exercise the options could have been a problem, too.

Nonqualified Stock Options (NQSOs)

Stock options are called *nonqualified* if ISO provisions are not specified in the stock option plan, and any profit on a NQSO transaction is taxable as ordinary income. The value of nonqualified options is considered taxable income on the date exercised. In addition, the granting of NQSOs itself can trigger a taxable event if the fair market value of the underlying stock exceeds the stated exercise price (which is not the usual case) and there is no risk of forfeiture (which, again, is not the usual case). Furthermore, if the NQSO has an ascertainable fair market value, the value of the option less any amount paid by the employee is taxable as ordinary income in the first year that the employee's right to the option is freely transferable or is not subject to a substantial risk of forfeiture. In contrast, recall that ISOs generate taxable income only when the shares are disposed of. This subject gets so incredibly complex that even experienced tax lawyers trip up here and need to go back to original source materials to answer individual questions. Do not try to figure it all out by yourself. Consider this chapter to be only an introduction. Refer to IRS Publication 525 or Treasury Regulation Section 1.83-7 for further details.

As noted, TRA-86 largely eliminated the distinction between ordinary income and long-term capital gains. Therefore, ISOs no longer have so many significant advantages over nonqualified options. From an employee's point of view, the risk of losing incentive stock options (due to restrictions on when and for how long they can be exercised) can outweigh the disadvantage of paying taxes upon the grant or exercise of nonqualified options. Unfortunately, many key employees who make a business successful will leave that business after five faithful and fruitful years and not realize one penny beyond their salary for their efforts. That is because they will have been granted not stock (or nonqualified options with negotiated extended exercise periods) but incentive stock options, which they must exercise or lose within three months after leaving the company. Quite likely, the company stock will not yet be worth the price to make the exercise pay. Yet in a few more years, due largely to the original key employees' contributions, the company may make it big. To exploit this potential longer-term value of NQSOs, you must negotiate in advance for extended exercise periods for your NQSOs. If you are granted NQSOs with the same exercise terms as ISOs, the advantages evaporate rapidly. Also, a company can always effectively convert your ISOs into NQSOs by agreeing to extend your exercise period after you leave, for example.

Make sure to review Section 83(b) Election in Chapter 14 to see if you need to take preventive tax liability action for your NQSOs as well as your founder's stock.

Option Vesting and Exercise Schedules

Like stock grants, vesting schedules for stock options are negotiable. Also, exercise schedules are negotiable for the period following employment for non-qualified options.

Most of your new key employees will be told what the plan calls for and will simply accept those terms. Indeed, most employees do not even know that they have to vest in their options or that they will have limited time periods to exercise options.

In vesting options, like in vesting stock, the same rules of thumb apply. For example, on the East Coast, many employees will vest 20% after one year, and 20% each year after that for four more years; on the West Coast, one typically vests 25% after one year, and 2% a month after that until fully vested.

Exercising Options

Here is an interesting note. Even if one had options on cheap stock, exercising those options could inject much-needed capital into a company—more than reflected by just the exercise price of the stock. One interesting case involved a Fortis Corporation's CEO who had an opportunity to exercise nonqualified stock options on 750,000 shares for one-hundredth of a cent per share. A $75 investment would bring him about a $7.5 million gain at a current market price of $10 a share. The company would benefit because exercised options become part of the company's compensation costs, reducing taxable profits. So, even though the company does not sell the exercised shares at market value, it still benefits, thanks to the tax code.

The Future of Stock Options

The effect of the Tax Reform Act of 1986 on stock options was clear for major corporations. Many of them eliminated incentive stock options, or in the case where both incentive and nonqualified options were offered, they dropped the incentive options. However, other companies figured the preferential tax rate on capital gains would come and go, making incentive stock options attractive again. In addition, because the need for cash to pay tax on nonqualified options at the point of exercise often encourages executives to sell their stock quickly, public companies that want to encourage executives to hold stock for long periods of time will tend to stay with incentive stock options. Some larger companies are de-emphasizing options entirely in favor of more cash. Other companies still want executives to identify with the stock, and thus discussions of cash incentive plans are commonly linked to stock performance.

ISOs are still popular in Silicon Valley, especially in start-ups and start-ups recently gone public. This is in part due to the elimination of the one big drawback where ISOs had to be exercised in the order they were received. Also, the trend toward larger salaries for executives and key employees has already been noted. Stock options will continue to play a major role in young companies, distinguishing them further from the *Fortune* 500 kind of existence.

A Comparison of Tax and Accounting Effects on ISOs and NQSOs

Tables 15-1 and 15-2 present an adaptation of an excellent summary of the salient tax and accounting effects of ISO and NQSO grants on the company and on the employee. This summary information was placed into the public domain at a California Bar Association seminar in 1991.

Table 15-1   Tax Effect on Company

Type of Stock Option	Tax Effect on Company upon:		
	Grant	Exercise	Sale of Stock
NQSO (No reverse vesting, i.e., shares fully vested at exercise.)	No tax effect (in general).	Employer may deduct amount of ordinary income recognized by optionee, i.e., the difference between fair market value (f.m.v.) at exercise and exercise price. The employer is required to withhold taxes on the amount of ordinary income recognized in order to take the deduction.	No tax effect.

Table 15-1   Tax Effect on Company (continued)

Type of Stock Option	Tax Effect on Company upon:		
	Grant	Exercise	Sale of Stock
ISO	No tax effect.	No tax effect.	Employer may deduct amount of ordinary income (if any) recognized by optionee. No withholding tax is required. If sale occurs within two years from grant or within one year from exercise, employer may deduct ordinary income equal to spread that existed at exercise. No deduction if sale occurs more than two years from grant and more than one year from exercise.

Table 15-2   Tax Effect on Employee

Type of Stock Option	Tax Effect on Employee upon:		
	Grant	Exercise	Sale of Stock
NQSO (No reverse vesting, i.e. shares fully vested at exercise.)	No tax effect (in general).	Taxable on ordinary income equal to spread at exercise, i.e., difference between f.m.v. of stock at exercise and exercise price. This amount is subject to withholding.	Taxable on capital gain equal to difference between sale price and f.m.v. of stock at exercise.
ISO ▪ Optionee must be employee (as opposed to director or other independent contractor) continuously from grant to the date three months before exercise (12 months in case of disability). ▪ Plan must be approved by shareholders. ▪ Maximum option term is 10 years (five years if optionee owns more than 10% of total combined voting power of all classes of stock).	No tax effect.	No tax effect, except for possible alternative minimum tax on spread. A tax advisor should be consulted for alternative minimum tax consequences.	If sale occurs within two years from grant or within one year from exercise, then taxable on ordinary income equal to spread that existed at exercise plus capital gain equal to difference between sale price and f.m.v. at exercise. No withholding is required. In general, ordinary income will not exceed amount of gain realized (sale price minus basis).

Table 15-2 Tax Effect on Employee (continued)

Type of Stock Option	Tax Effect on Employee upon:		
	Grant	Exercise	Sale of Stock
▪ Option price is at least 100% of f.m.v. at grant (110% if optionee owns more than 10% of stock). ▪ Of all options held by an optionee that vest in the same year, only the options covering the first $100,000 worth of stock qualify for ISO treatment. The value of the stock is measured for this purpose at grant.			If sale occurs more than two years from grant and more than one year from exercise, then taxable on long-term capital gain equal to difference between sale price and exercise price.

Note on accounting effect: The accounting effect on the company is the same for NQSO as it is for ISO. Options with an exercise price equal to at least 100% of f.m.v. of stock at the time of the grant generally produce no compensation cost at any time. However, options with performance-based vesting (as opposed to service-based vesting) may be subject to accounting treatment as stock appreciation rights (SARs), with the result that increases in stock f.m.v must be expensed in each reporting period while the option is outstanding. An accountant should be consulted on this issue. Options with an exercise price below 100% of f.m.v. on the date of the grant produce compensation cost equal to the discount, which can be amortized over the vesting period for each option.

Exploiting Employee Desire for Stock Options

One well-established post-start-up made a point of advertising that the company was owned entirely by its employees. Every job offer was accompanied with a grant of options on thousands or tens of thousands of shares of stock, each of which was valued at several dollars a share. Imagine, if the stock ever doubled one would have a very nice nest egg. But, upon reading the fine print of the stock option plan one could see that it was a ruse to raise capital for the company. The employee not only became fully vested in just two years (which is very good; it usually takes four to five years), but had to exercise the option (buy the stock with his or her own money) within three years (which is bad; it usually is good for 10 years as long as one is employed), or lose the option as it expired. Since the option was granted to buy stock at 110% of fair market value, the company had to increase significantly in value to represent a good investment. Also, the shares bought were transfer restricted; that is, there was no market for them—no way to sell them and get one's money back out. The board of directors did claim that they would make a market for any employee wanting to sell shares, but they were under no obligation to do so. Employees were investing for the long term on very short options.

This plan was such a cash generator for the enterprise (which, by the way, was not a product-oriented growth company—it sold the professional services of its employees) that management usually offered a potential employee options on double the number of shares if he or she would exercise them immediately. In reality, that is just selling stock in the company. Where is the leverage and the risk-free potential for great financial returns that a hardworking founder or key employee is looking for? In this particular business, the really important key employees knew what they were doing and managed to negotiate for no interest, low interest, or forgivable interest loans, and partially or wholly forgivable principal loans from the company to exercise their options. They also negotiated for extended stock option exercise schedules—up to 10 and 15 years in some cases.

When you negotiate for your (incentive) stock options or set up an option plan for your employees, make sure the incentive does not evaporate and turn into a liability.

16

Other Equity and Wealth-Building Vehicles

"The future will not just happen if one wishes hard enough.
It requires decision—now. It imposes risk—now.
It requires action—now. It demands allocation of
resources, and above all, human resources—now."
— Peter F. Drucker

To this point it has been established that you, as the founder of your own business, will have a significant stock ownership in your business through a founder's stock grant. In addition, it is likely that you and your board will have granted you additional options on stock contingent upon meeting performance objectives.

This section will explore other vehicles for building wealth as your business grows and prospers. You will want to consider some of these vehicles for your key employees and fellow management team members as well. Many of the vehicles described here are especially well suited for rewarding key players who are not founders.

Unrelated Stock Purchase

You always have the option of buying into your business just like one of your investors. Some entrepreneurs decide against this option, preferring not to put all their eggs into one basket; that is your choice. But consider how infrequently an excellent investment opportunity comes along in which you really believe, in which you have deep, inside knowledge of the situation, and which can be highly leveraged. If this is a good deal for your investors, it should be a good deal for you too. In fairness, however, it should be noted that your investors have the safety of diversification, where you would not. If you do not feel that confident about your proposed business, why start it? Instead go back to the drawing board until you have it figured out. Launching a successful company is difficult enough; do not compound your problems by starting something you do not believe in 100%.

If you like the idea of investing in your own company but are short on cash, consider setting up a stock purchase plan for yourself and your employees. It will help the cash flow of the business and allow everyone to increase their ownership without sacrificing precious savings.

Even before establishing a full-blown stock purchase plan for all employees, you can set up a special deal for yourself to acquire more stock in your new company. You will have to negotiate with your board of directors since the board establishes remuneration policy for the officers of your company, which includes yourself. As part of your compensation package, obtain the right to buy preferred shares of stock in your company at fair market value (just like any investor). This stock can be issued monthly or quarterly and effectively deducted from your paycheck. You may need to be paid a higher salary, or eat into your savings a bit, to keep making your mortgage payment. But where else can you invest relatively small amounts of money in a start-up company that you obviously have a lot of confidence in, especially if you are not a sophisticated investor, as is required in most states? As a founding employee, you should be legally entitled to purchase stock in your company if the company is willing to sell it. Keep in mind that venture capital investors legitimately like to keep the number of preferred stockholders to a minimum to avoid complications in subsequent rounds of financing.

How much stock should you purchase? Assume that you want to accumulate additional stock that will one day make you worth an extra $0.5 million. Since you are betting that the stock price will increase by a factor of 10 over the next five years (as are your investors), you need to acquire about $50,000 worth of stock in the next two or three years. Thus, you might purchase $2,000 worth of stock each month for the next two years. You may be able to pay yourself the $2,000 extra in salary to make this relatively painless, but how could the company possibly afford that? Because the cash flows directly back into the company as you pay for your stock, all the company suffers is dilution.

Professional Publications, Inc. ▪ Belmont, CA

Even if your board of directors does not agree to raise your salary, you could also try to live on $2,000 less. Purchasing stock in your company is worthwhile. You will have the stock cleanly in your pocket (without any risk of losing it) because, like an investor's preferred stock, there is no vesting. Beware that most investors will want to pay you what they consider to be a fair salary and have you reinvest part of that. Therefore, it is up to you to negotiate what is fair these days. See Chapter 13 for more information on remuneration practices for start-ups.

If you have a board of directors that looks unfavorably on increasing your salary, there are other options. If you do not have any additional savings that you can invest, get creative. How about taking out a loan from your own company? Do anything to buy an additional block of stock now to hold free and clear. The private placement memorandums and footnotes to financial documents of the small start-up companies in this country are littered with sweetheart deals. If you do not act, do not ask, and do not try, all you will have is your vested founder's stock and you probably deserve more.

Tax-Free Exchange of Intellectual Property for Stock

The technique addressed in this section is fairly commonly practiced. One way to avoid paying any tax at the time you obtain shares, whether they are restricted or transferable (and, prior to TRA-86, to have received favorable long-term capital gains tax treatment for the future), is to exchange intellectual or other property (technology, business plans, patents, etc.) for stock in a tax-free exchange. This method often works only during a new, fresh, tax-free incorporation.

For example, the intellectual property assets of a sole proprietorship may be exchanged tax-free for stock in a new company, at fair market value; then the new stock can be held for later sale. Your basis for the value of your assets must be realistic, and you may realize a taxable gain here! This is a complex issue requiring the assistance of a tax attorney. Many founders and key employees of a start-up will have some property of true value, which can be transferred to the company in exchange for stock of equal value. If you are not launching your start-up today, consider obtaining some legitimate and valuable patents now, on your own, to exchange for stock in the future. It is again emphasized that you work with a lawyer and a tax advisor to make sure that what you propose is legal and will accomplish the desired tax consequences.

Investment Through the Provision of Real Property

In theory, you should think of yourself as an investor in your start-up, even if you are not providing significant financial backing. Through the provision of real property (or intellectual property as described in the preceding section), you can obtain the ownership you need on advantageous terms.

If you find yourself in the position of having to provide your own seed capital, consider providing property instead of cash. If you decide to invest property to obtain a piece of your company, follow the professional investor's example. If you have property or could buy some that the start-up needs, do not trade it outright for stock (never for common, perhaps for preferred). Instead, lease the property to the start-up in exchange for a consideration that will include an ability to acquire a future interest (stock) in the company. This is preferable to lending the company the money and then worrying about security on the loan, or purchasing stock and worrying about it becoming worthless. If the company needs to use your money or other property for developing a new process, have rights to the process assigned to you, and give back conditional rights to use the process for future stock in the company. The difference between the preceding arrangement and simply investing in the company will become apparent if the company runs into financial trouble. Having unencumbered title to tangible assets will provide you protection. Through careful analysis of how you are going to invest in your start-up, you may find yourself very comfortably positioned; indeed, you will be a true owner of this business.

To execute such an elaborate plan, you must think and act like a venture capitalist, perhaps with the assistance of an experienced venture capital lawyer. Expect to meet some resistance from the sophisticated investors on your board of directors, who do not receive these demands from every entrepreneur they run across. Enjoy the process, and learn from it. Otherwise, you may find yourself feeling less like a founder and more like an employee by the end of the year.

Warrants and Stock Purchase Plans

This section briefly outlines a few other related equity and wealth-building vehicles to insure your complete familiarity with the subject. Many of these vehicles are associated primarily with larger and more mature companies, but you should be familiar with the terminology and try to be creative in adapting these vehicles to your start-up where appropriate.

Warrants

Warrants are certificates, usually issued by the company, that give the holder the right (but not the obligation) to buy a specific number of shares of a company's stock at a stipulated price within a certain time limit or in perpetuity. Typically, warrants are issued in conjunction with rounds of financing, as leverage and protection mechanisms for the investor and as assured future sources of capital for the company. Warrants are also used frequently by penny stock underwriters to motivate the market-makers to keep the stock's price up. They are not usually used as a form of employee incentive or compensation. Warrants are also more easily sold or transferred between individuals since usually there are no vesting conditions or repurchase agreements associated with them. The financial reporting documents of many high-tech companies are littered with footnotes describing special investment situations where warrants were attached. If you have the opportunity, be creative in this area.

Rights and Plans

- Stock Appreciation Rights (SARs): a company grants an employee the right to appreciation in the underlying stock over time

- Phantom Stock Plan: an employee receives units analogous to company shares and, at some point in the future, receives the value of the stock appreciation plus dividends

- Performance Unit Plan: an employee earns specially valued units at no cost based on achievement of predetermined performance targets

- Performance Share Plan: an employee receives shares of stock based on achievement of predetermined performance targets

- Formula Value Stock Plan: an employee earns rights to a special class of stock (not publicly traded) that is valued according to a formula such as book value

Employee Stock Purchase Plan

An employee stock purchase plan is actually a kind of stock option plan and is most frequently used with public companies.

Under the Internal Revenue Code, such a plan is designed to permit employees to buy stock of their employer corporation, usually at a discount. The plan must be nondiscriminatory and include almost all employees. Therefore, this is not a good vehicle to reward key employees for performance. A plan may provide that the grant of options will be based on a uniform relationship to pay. The option must be issued under a stock purchase plan approved by the company's stockholders.

- amount of purchase: All employees granted options must be given the same rights and privileges. The amount of stock you may buy may be limited to a percentage of your pay. The terms of the plan must provide that you may not buy more than $25,000 of stock in one year based on the fair market value of the option at the time of grant.

- price: The option price to you cannot be less than 85% of the fair market value of the stock at the time the option is granted, or 85% of the fair market value of the stock at the time you exercise the option, whichever is less. Typically, the employee gets to buy stock at the lower of the two prices during a six-month period.

- time of exercise: If the price you pay is solely in terms of percentage, you must exercise the option within five years from the date it is granted to you. If the price you pay is not determined solely in this way, you must exercise the option within 27 months.

- tax treatment: You do not realize any reportable income as a result of the grant or exercise of the option. To have received maximum tax benefits (prior to passage of TRA-86), more than two years must have passed from the time the stock option was granted to you to the time you disposed of your shares, and you must have held the shares for more than six months. If you sell the stock for less than the option price, your loss is deductible as a capital loss.

Founder Retains Control Through Foresight

A small model-building company in Silicon Valley owes its livelihood in large part to the special machinery it uses to produce certain essential components. Neither the machinery nor the components can be easily procured on the outside. The founder of this company had first considered the traditional method of financing the acquisition of this machinery by the company: using the $20,000 seed capital he would inject into the company. Instead, though, he crafted an agreement between himself and the company, which said, in effect, the following:

> I, the founder, will buy this machinery with my own money, and I will lease this machinery to the company for a period of five years, for a cash consideration (which roughly equals the time-value of the money), and, the consideration of the right for me, the founder, to exchange my ownership rights in the machinery for 100,000 shares in the company at any time during the term of the lease. At the end of the five-year lease, if I have not exercised my exchange rights, the company will have right of first refusal to purchase the machinery from me at fair market value.

In this way, should the company prosper, the founder would gladly relinquish ownership rights to the machinery in exchange for the more valuable stock. On the other hand, should the company encounter financial difficulty and face liquidation, the founder would at least have unencumbered title to the machinery, which he could claim as his, and liquidate to help recover his initial investment.

17

Valuing Your Equity Position

*"When you can measure what you are speaking about,
and express it in numbers, you know something about it."*
—Lord Kelvin (1824–1907)

Your stock's future value may easily equal five, ten, or even twenty to one hundred times its present value if your business is successful. But, do you even know your stock's present value? Businesses are valued all the time by investors, and prices are put on shares. Common shares are always worth some fraction of the preferred shares. You and your board of directors will establish the fair market value of common shares when you declare the exercise price for options on these shares. However, this number means little. If the company succeeds, the value of the common shares will step up to that of the preferred shares. If the company fails, the common shares will likely be worthless. Since the usual presumption is that all preferred shares will convert into common shares at some point in the future, it is common to value a company based on the total number of common and preferred shares outstanding. In the simplest case, after a round of financing, a company's value can be stated to be the multiple of the latest price paid (ideally this is also the highest price paid) for a preferred share, times the total number of common and preferred shares outstanding. However, this still does not answer the question regarding the value of your company prior to initial funding or just before you need a new round of funding.

Company valuations at different periods of time are interesting to consider. For example, you might want to compute value:

- at launch
- at capitalization, when you first start to sell preferred stock to investors and when it is perhaps more important
- at a number of years further out in the future when those investors exercise their exit strategy

Terminology

Two terms you will hear frequently need to be clearly understood before you negotiate for funding.

Pre-Money Valuation

The value of an enterprise before new money is injected is called its *pre-money valuation*. For example, suppose that after your first year your company has 1 million shares outstanding. Of those, 300,000 (common) shares were sold on day one for $0.01 a share as cheap founder's stock, and immediately thereafter 700,000 (preferred) shares were sold for $1.00 a share to a first-round investor. The total paid-in equity is only $3,000 plus $700,000, or $703,000, but the current (pre-second-round financing) valuation will be computed to be equal to the total number of shares outstanding times the stated value of one share today (which should be greater than the $1.00 price paid a year ago). If the current stockholders are only willing to sell new shares to the next-round investor at, for example, $2.00 a share, then the company is valued by the stockholders at $2 million (based on 1 million shares, each now worth $2.00). If, in fact, the company's performance supported it, the current valuation could arguably be much higher. Likewise, if the company wasted its first-round cash, its current valuation could arguably be much lower. Whatever value is placed on one share of stock at this time by either the stockholders or potential investors, the pre-money valuation is determined by multiplying that share value times the total number of shares outstanding (before the next financing round is completed).

Post-Money Valuation

In the preceding example, assume that both current shareholders and new investors agree that pre-money valuation for this company should be $2 million (based on a current share worth of $2.00). If the new investors buy 1 million additional shares, they will contribute an additional $2 million, for a total paid-in equity of $2,703,000. Now, what is the post-money valuation? The answer is simple; it is the total number of shares outstanding after the second round is funded (2 million shares) times the current per-share valuation ($2.00), or $4 million.

Another approach to computing this post-money valuation is to impute value based on the percentage of equity purchased and the total amount paid for it. This imputed value is equal to the amount invested divided by the percentage of the venture purchased for that amount. In this example, the new investors bought 1 million shares (50% of the company) at $2.00 per share (for $2 million total), so post-money valuation would equal $2 million divided by 0.50, or $4 million. It follows that pre-money valuation is calculated by subtracting the amount of new capital invested ($2 million) from the post-money valuation ($4 million). (In this case, $4 million minus $2 million equals a pre-money valuation of $2 million.)

It is obvious that a new $2 million investment might make a $2 million company worth $4 million. Reasoning by extremes, however, if the new investors only bought one new share at $2.00, the post-money valuation would then be 1,000,001 shares times $2.00, or $2,000,002. So you can see that a small amount of new money does little to increase post-money valuation, while a substantial injection of funds can double a post-money valuation. This is why, if you tell investors that the company is worth $2 million, they will be tempted to ask, "Is that before or after we put in our $2 million?" However, they will not usually spell the question out; they will simply ask, "Is that pre- or post-money?" These terms are simple, intuitive, and logical, but lots of entrepreneurs stumble over them, only to destroy their negotiating positions.

Valuation at Launch

The value of your company on the day it is formed is highly subjective. While your potential is enormous, your market value is nil. However, your stock obviously has some value because you will not sell as many shares as each of your cofounders wants to buy (at the nominal penny per share or whatever). What your stock is worth at this time is a futures game. When you buy founder's stock, you are buying futures. Actually it is more like options on futures—it is pretty speculative.

The valuation of the company at launch might be said to be equal to the total number of shares sold to date (i.e., your founder's shares), times a price all of you would agree would be a fair price for one more share to be sold to an outside investor. The value of this one new share can and indeed should be equal to more than the price paid for founder's shares, since it represents all the potential future worth of your company as reflected by your abilities and impending contributions.

Valuation at Capitalization

Your company probably will not be substantially capitalized at the time of distribution of founder's stock (depending upon whether a significant price was placed on the founder's stock). Typically, each founder will contribute a token amount (perhaps $2,000 to $20,000) to pay for his or her founder's stock. Whether the sum of such contributions constitutes a substantial capitalization depends on the particular business. Many businesses are founded, incorporated, and distribute founder's stock, and have only a few hundred dollars in the bank. While this is discouraged for a variety of practical and financial liability reasons, it is common.

Investors can reasonably aim for future valuations equal to 10 times their original investments in preferred stock. They will work backward from estimated future values of your company, factoring in risk, to determine today's appropriate investment value. Your common stock returns can easily be orders of a magnitude higher (a 100–1000 times return or more). What really counts, however, is not how much cash you put into the business, but how many shares you can acquire and hold onto. It is precisely this dividing up of stock ownership that is most controversial and that establishes how much equity ownership you have to give up to investors for the cash you need. While highly subjective, there exist various well-defined methods venture capitalists use.

In conclusion, if your business is successful, you might well expect to turn a small founder's contribution of a few thousand dollars into several million dollars. As your investors will do, you too can work some interesting numbers on the future value of your founder's stock by attempting to predict your future per-share stock value based on projected sales, profit margin, and stock dilution. All the information needed to do this should be found in your company's business plan (although that may represent your best-case scenario).

The Effect of Founder's Cash on Company Valuation

It would seem obvious that a founder who invested a substantial amount of capital in the seed stage could realize much higher valuations in start-up and later stage financing rounds. This is usually (but not always) the case. The valuation that investors will put on your company can vary dramatically.

Some investors almost do not seem to care if or how much cash you personally have invested. Some do not want you to be preoccupied with losing your house, and they will pay the fair price for your business opportunity. These investors generally figure they will own about 75–80% of your business regardless of its financing history. They also figure that management and employees need about 20–25% of the pie to be properly motivated; you need not pay much for your slice in their eyes.

Other investors, however, will put a high value on your sacrifice and hard-earned invested cash. It really pays to do your due diligence on your prospective investors to ensure optimizing your investment.

Future Value of the Start-Up as a Multiple of Sales

Before settling upon any assumptions regarding the future annual sales of your company, look at your competition: could your assumption be realistic in your market? If your competitors are public companies, their sales information is available. The market value of a company might then be two to three times its sales, but this is highly dependent upon your industry segment. You need to get exact numbers for these calculations. This information is readily available from any stockbroker (or from your library) through Standard & Poor's Corporation, Value Line, and many other financial reports.

First find a public company that typifies your start-up. For example, if your start-up makes personal computers, look at Apple Computer, Inc. For illustration purposes, this section examines Apple Computer at the end of 1987 (because Apple was still an entrepreneurial company then). To estimate its value, multiply the number of Apple shares outstanding (roughly 125 million shares) by the market price of Apple's stock (roughly $40 per share). Apple Computer was said to have a market cap or market capitalization of approximately $5 billion. Apple's annualized sales were roughly $2.5 billion. Thus, the value of a successful personal computer company can be estimated to be equal to about twice its sales. Each industry, and segment within an industry, will differ. Software companies, for example, with high gross margins are often valued at four times sales. Many high-growth, high-margin software companies have recently gone public at valuations of seven to eleven times sales. Other less explosive software companies are valued at only one to two times sales. However, you should not even have to go through these calculations if you look hard enough; many financial reports list market capitalization as a percentage or multiple of sales.

Future Value of a Company by Miscellaneous Multiples

Table 17-1 suggests popular methods of valuation for different kinds of engineering-oriented companies. You might use this as a rough guide to see if you are in the ballpark. These are valuations for established public companies. To apply these ratios to a start-up, you need to use anticipated sales, income, etc., for at least one to two years out. In many companies, at the time of an initial public offering, you can realize sales multiples of up to 10 times what is shown in Table 17-1.

Table 17-1 Popular Methods of Valuation

Business	Method of Valuation	Multiple
aerospace: products	sales	0.7
aerospace: systems	sales	2.0
automobile parts	free cash flow	12.0
chemicals	operating income	10.0
computer: mainframe and mini	sales	1.0
computer: peripherals	sales	0.9
computer: systems and software	sales	0.6
defense products	sales	0.6
electrical equipment	free cash flow	7.2
electronics: parts	sales	1.0
electronics: services	operating income	5.0
electronics: systems	sales	0.7
plastic products	operating income	4.9
precision instruments	operating income	5.9
semiconductors	sales	0.9
telecommunications products	sales	1.7

Source: Excerpts from *Financial World*, October 30, 1990, p. 33.

Future Value of the Start-Up as a Function of Sales, Profit Margin, and Price-Earnings Ratio

Another way to estimate a company's value is to estimate its future sales, and then apply industry standards for expected *profit margin* (PM), which is profit as a percentage of sales, and expected *price-earnings ratio* (PE), which is price per share divided by earnings per share or price (value) of the company divided by the earnings of the company. In the case of Apple, its profits or earnings after taxes were about $200 million; thus its profit margin was about $200 million earnings divided by $2.5 billion sales, or 8% of sales.

The daily newspaper stock listings tell us that the stock sells for about 25 times earnings (profit) per share. Thus, Apple's worth (price), W, in 1987 also could be calculated as:

$$W = \text{sales} \times \frac{\text{earnings}}{\text{sales}} \times \frac{\text{price}}{\text{earnings}}$$

$$= \text{sales} \times \text{PM} \times \text{PE}$$

$$= \$2.5 \text{ billion} \times 0.08 \times 25 = \$5 \text{ billion}$$

Again, the value of Apple is found to equal about twice its annual sales.

To take your start-up's example again, assuming you are in the same industry as Apple Computer and that your business will someday do $100 million annually in sales (if that is what the business plan projects), your company's future value can be estimated to be:

$$W = \text{sales} \times \text{PM} \times \text{PE}$$

$$= \$100 \text{ million} \times 0.08 \times 25$$

$$= \$200 \text{ million}$$

What Percentage of the Company Value is Yours?

It is important to estimate what percentage of the total company value, W, will be yours. To do this, you need to estimate the number of shares that will be outstanding at the time your company goes public or is sold (five to ten years in the future), and then calculate your percentage. Your business plan should tell you approximately how many more shares of stock must be sold (and at what price) before the business is self-sustaining (review your financial pro formas). Remember, this is just a plan; the actual results can be off by an order of magnitude. First, compute the dilution factor. Let N be the total number of new or future shares to be sold and let O be the total number of shares currently outstanding. Then the dilution factor will be:

$$D = \frac{O}{N + O}$$

You can calculate your future percentage ownership, FP, as your current percentage, CP, multiplied by the dilution factor, D.

$$FP = CP \times D$$

Then multiply your estimated FP times the market value, W, of the company (estimated above) and you have your fortune.

$$\text{fortune} = FP \times W$$

In other words, if you obtained stock or options on 5% of the company when you founded it, CP = 0.05, and if $D = \frac{1}{5}$ (in this case we are assuming that dilution is a factor of 5, e.g., 1 million shares were issued by the time you received yours, and an additional 4 million new shares were issued afterwards), your future percentage is:

$$FP = 0.05 \times \tfrac{1}{5} = 0.01 = 1\%$$

Your future worth is:

$$FP \times W = 0.01 \times \$200,000,000 = \$2,000,000$$

It is highly unlikely that you could achieve this wealth as an employee in someone else's start-up, which is why you want to start your own company.

Alpha Partners Capitalization Model

Quoted material in this section is excerpted from *Partnering with Entrepreneurs*, Alpha Partners, courtesy of Brian J. Grossi, general partner.

> Alpha Partners is an investment firm [in Silicon Valley] specializing in venture capital seed investments in high-growth markets in which applied technology leverages market penetration and provides competitive barriers to entry. The term *venture capital seed financing* covers the time period, the effort, and the money required to develop a company from an idea to an operating organization with a presence in the chosen marketplace.
>
> It is of critical importance to plan potential sources of capital beyond the seed commitment which would sustain the company growth through liquidity. Alpha uses this information in planning a viable investment scenario which balances the financial expectations and desires of the founders and management, the internal-rate-of-return criteria for Alpha, and expected internal-rate-of-return criteria for investors participating in later rounds.

An example of such an investment plan is presented in the capitalization model shown in Table 17-2 to help you understand the capital formation requirements of your business.

Von Gehr & Tan Model

In addition to looking at a standard model, you can predict your company's equity value and your personal equity share value by comparing your forecasted business performance against that of other model businesses. The key comparison parameters are:

- after-tax margins
- three-year compounded annual growth rate
- return on equity

From these, you can predict your company's revenue multiplier and its price-earnings ratio.

Table 17-2 Alpha Partners Capitalization Model

	Seed (Building Value)				Expansion	Liquidity	
	Phase I 6 Months	Phase II 6 Months	Phase III 9 Months	Phase IV 12 Months	27 Months	60 Months	
capitalized value	$0.50M	$1.26M	$2.93M	$7.06M	$17.9M	$60.0M	
annualized revenue			$0.35M	$2.21M	$7.15M	$30.0M	
value/ revenue (revenue multiplier)			8.37	3.19	2.5	2.0	
$ raised	$0.20M	$0.50M	$1.20M	$1.20M	$5.50M		
$ share	$0.50	$0.90	$1.50	$2.56	$5.74	$13.40	
cumulative $ raised	$0.20M	$0.70M	$1.90M	$3.10M	$8.60M		
total shares	1.40M	1.96M	2.76M	3.27M	4.48M		
% ownership:						value	
founders	25.0%	17.9%	12.7%	10.7%	7.8%	$4.7M	
CEO	17.9%	12.8%	9.1%	7.6%	5.6%	$3.3M	
management	14.3%	10.2%	7.3%	6.1%	4.5%	$2.7M	
options	14.3%	10.2%	7.3%	7.5%	10.0%	$6.0M	
Alpha Partners $ ownership % ownership	$0.20M 28.6%	$0.50M 48.9%	$0.60M 49.2%	$0.60M 48.6%	$0.50M 37.5%	$22.5M	IRR 87%
investors 1 % ownership			$0.60M 14.5%	$0.60M 19.40%	$1.00M 18.20%	$10.9M	72%
investors 2 % ownership					$4.00M 16.3%	$9.8M	50%

Excerpted from *Partnering with Entrepreneurs*, Alpha Partners,
courtesy of Brian J. Grossi, general partner.

By definition, the value of your company is equal to your revenue multiplier times your annual revenue. As you will see, for lower performing companies, company value can equal less than annual sales. For higher performing companies, however, company value is often equal to 10 times annual sales. The performance of your company, measured in terms of profits and growth, will determine the value the market puts on your equity.

The valuation assessment table shown in Table 17-3 shows three cases of businesses with varying degrees of success.

Table 17-3   Valuation Assessment Table by Von Gehr & Tan

Parameters	Value		
	High	Medium	Low
after-tax margins	20.5%	16.6%	4.5%
three-year compounded annual growth rate	91.4%	88.7%	46.8%
return on equity	36.3%	26.9%	12.1%
expected revenue multiplier	6.1	3.5	0.9
expected price earnings ratio	30.2	21.8	21.4

Adapted, with permission, from Von Gehr, George,
"Valuation Assessment of Emerging Companies: A Universal Approach."
Presentation at the September 1991 meeting of the Northern California Venture
Capital Association, Palo Alto, CA.

Will your company's revenue multiplier be 0.9 or 6.1? That will depend upon your start-up track record: how fast and to what extent you become profitable, and how fast you grow.

Q.E.D.'s Valuation Methods

Dr. Jim Plummer, president of QED Research, Inc., in Palo Alto, CA, has compiled a comprehensive book on the subject of venture capital valuation techniques, based on his exhaustive survey of valuation methods used by almost 300 venture capitalists. You should refer to his *QED Report on Venture Capital Financial Analysis* for essential details. The essence of many of the valuation methods reported is based on the time-value of money: that is, some sort of discounted cash flow analysis. Since Chapter 11 covered these valuation basics, the following are highlights of several of the more interesting variations reported by Plummer.

Adjusted Net Worth

If one simply takes the net worth of a business and makes adjustments for intangibles such as patents and goodwill, a valuation can be obtained that may be useful for businesses where fixed assets are the most important component of value. However, unless your start-up just built a $200 million semiconductor wafer fabrication facility, investors are unlikely to use this method to value your new venture.

IRS Excess Earnings Method of Valuing Intangibles

The IRS has a valuation method based on excess earnings. Your excess earnings (i.e., a rate of return realized beyond what is normal for a business of comparable risk) are used to compute the capitalized value of your assets (tangible and intangible). Again, since your new start-up will likely have no earnings, this valuation method will not be relevant for your seed and start-up rounds.

Rule-of-Thumb Ratios Applied to Before-Tax Earnings

For normal-growth, closely held companies, this is a before-tax form of the common price-earnings ratio method. It is used because it is less subject to manipulation by owners. Again, because your new start-up will likely have no earnings, this valuation method will not be relevant.

Present Discounted Value of Future Earnings Stream

By computing the present value (see Chapter 11) of the estimated future earnings stream from a business, you can arrive at a total present value of future earnings. Add to this the present value of the ending value of a company and you can compute the value of a company today. This method seems more practical than the others mentioned for a start-up, but it is based on uncertain estimates. If anyone believed the numbers in your business plan, this present-value approach could easily be computed.

The *QED Report on Venture Capital Financial Analysis* contains the desired returns used by venture capitalists for various stages of investments. The size of the discount rate used falls dramatically from the more risky early-stage investments to less risky later-stage investments.

Price-Earnings Ratios of Comparable Public Companies with Adjustments for Liquidity

It is tempting to look at the market value (prices) of public companies with similar earnings to estimate the value of larger normal-growth, closely held companies. The error in doing so is that private companies are less liquid and thus typically have values of 15–50% lower. On the other hand, younger, higher-growth companies can have price-earning ratios (PE) exceeding those of public companies. It is not unusual to see a high-growth company emerge at an IPO with a PE ratio of 30, while comparable older and slower-growth companies might reflect a PE ratio of 10.

Revenue Multipliers for Professional Practices

Companies with few assets (especially service companies, where owners can take out most earnings) are often valued on the basis of revenue. What has evolved is a set of ranges of revenue multipliers for estimating the goodwill value of professional practices. For engineering and other consulting practices with weak repeat business patterns, the revenue multiplier is often 15–25%. To this goodwill value must be added the adjusted net worth of the company, which includes accounts receivable and fixed assets. This multiplier must be adjusted upward for businesses with high growth rates.

The Conventional Venture Capital Valuation Method

The conventional method is a simple present-value computation (again, refer to Chapter 11 for the basic calculations). This computation is based on an investor's estimate (probably discounted from the numbers presented in your business plan) of:

- your current revenue, R
- your expected annual rate of growth of revenue, r
- the number of years to liquidity, n
- the expected after-tax profit margin at the time of liquidity, a
- the expected price-earnings ratio as of the liquidity date, P
- a discount rate appropriate for the investment stage, risk, and illiquidity, d

It can easily be shown that the present value, V, is computed as:

$$V = \frac{R \times (1 + r)^n \times a \times P}{(1 + d)^n}$$

You will find that P, the expected price-earnings ratio as of the liquidity date, is likely to be much higher if liquidity is associated with an IPO versus an acquisition or management buyout (MBO). It is important to note that investors using the term *rate-of-return* (ROR) are in fact talking about the conventional VC method. This bit of information might be worth a lot to you when you enter your negotiations with a venture capitalist and the subject of valuation methods comes up.

The First Chicago Method—Alternative Scenarios

The First Chicago method employs the same analysis techniques as the conventional venture capital method, except that three different outcome scenarios are considered and given probability weightings. The First Chicago method was originated by Stanley Golder of First Chicago Corporation. The three scenarios are success, sideways survival, and failure. For example, if your company is predicted to have the present values and associated probabilities shown in Table 17-4, your First Chicago method present value will be the sum of weighted present values as shown.

Table 17-4 First Chicago Method for Valuation

	Success Scenario	Sideways Survival Scenario	Failure Scenario
expected present value	$10 million	$1 million	$0.5 million
probability of scenario	50%	30%	20%
weighted present value	$5 million	$0.3 million	$0.1 million
First Chicago method valuation (sum of weighted present values)	$5.4 million		

The First Chicago method is a very powerful and intuitive technique for explicitly accounting for the risks associated with a venture investment.

The Fundamental Method—Present Value of the Future Earnings Stream

The conventional venture capital method and the First Chicago method both focus on one point in time in the future: the liquidity date. The fundamental method, in contrast, looks at multiple years in the future, both before and after liquidity. The total present value of the company is the sum of the stream of after-tax earnings during, for example, the first 10 years, plus the present value of the estimated residual value of the earnings stream beyond year 10, when your growth rate levels out. This forces the investor to look at a more complete story of your company's future. For this method to be valid, it cannot be used for short streams of earnings; the analysis should be carried out beyond the period of assumed supernormal growth.

Revenue Multipliers (Value-to-Revenue Ratios)

A revenue multiplier is a factor that can be multiplied by the revenue of a company to obtain a rough estimate of the value of the company. Revenue multipliers are used because their simplicity allows them to be applied quickly.

Revenue multipliers vary tremendously depending on:

- the annualized rate of growth of the company

- the investment stage the company has reached

- the product sector it is in

- whether revenue is being measured on a leading basis (the next 12 months) or on a trailing basis (the last 12 months)

The *QED Report* contains 40 QED curves that adjust the size of the revenue multipliers for each of these factors.

The revenue multiplier method is widely used, despite its weakness of not taking into account variations across industries in such factors as profit margins, required capital intensity, R&D required, and differing lead times for R&D, marketing, and production. Plummer presents additional quantitative feedback from venture capitalists about how revenue multipliers are used in practice.

Table 17-5 summarizes the popularity of the principal valuation methods described in this section.

Table 17-5   Popularity of Principal Valuation Methods

	Primary Method	Secondary Method	Seldom Used	Not Used
conventional VC method	68%	20%	5%	7%
fundamental method	6%	25%	28%	41%
First Chicago method	16%	28%	18%	38%
revenue multiplier method	11%	29%	31%	29%

Plummer reports that revenue multipliers are used as a primary valuation method more in early stages of investment. This method may be appropriate for your start-up. Since start-up companies have little, if any, profit margins, it is natural to look at valuation techniques based on estimates of revenue. As your company matures, it will be more natural to measure its value based on earnings-oriented methods.

Valuation Benchmarks from VentureOne Study

VentureOne is a research firm founded by David Gleba that tracks activities in venture capital and private company financings. In 1991, Gleba completed a valuation study using pricing data from 1000 private equity rounds concluded since 1987. His study was reported in *Upside*, November 1991.

From his study, important valuation benchmarks were obtained in terms of:

- source of capital
- stage of company development
- company industry

You can use these benchmarks as a sanity check to see whether the size of the investment you are looking for and the pre-money valuation you place on your start-up are consistent with averages in your industry for the source of capital you are soliciting.

For rounds of more than $1 million, Gleba found that venture capital was twice as expensive as corporate cash and corporate cash was at least twice as expensive as capital raised from an IPO. Table 17-6 shows the percentage of equity relinquished for a $1 million investment. Keep in mind that post-start-up companies will more easily attract corporate cash, and only the more mature companies will be able to do an IPO. The earlier the stage of your company, the more expensive will be your source of capital. To translate, early stage companies have lower valuations. Not a big surprise perhaps, but Gleba's study also showed that for companies at the same stage of development, corporate investors still paid two to five times the average venture capital valuation because of the strategic value to the investing corporation. Corporate cash will be out of reach for your seed-level start-up, but you will want to keep it in mind for future financing.

Table 17-6   Equity Relinquished versus Source of Capital

Capital Source	Venture Capital	Corporate Cash	IPO
percent of equity given up	10.8%	4.4%	1.7%

Analysis of venture-funded seed rounds where less than $1 million was raised showed that the average seed-stage company gave up 7.6% of its equity for every $100,000 raised. Equivalently, the average seed-stage company valuation is $1,315,789.

Now you have your first guideline. If your start-up is an average seed-stage deal, do not plan to raise anything near $1,315,789. Reasoning by extremes and using the preceding guideline, you see that you would have to give up all of your equity.

$$\frac{\$1,315,789}{\$100,000} = 13.16$$

$$13.16 \times 7.6\% = 100\%$$

Figure 17-1 summarizes the VentureOne study, plotting the average deal size and average pre-money valuation (not weighted by industry) versus stage of company development for all industries surveyed (computer hardware, computer software, telecommunications, health care, industrial equipment, and semiconductors). Variations from industry to industry are not insignificant. Software companies, for example, have higher valuations at start-up and lower valuations at profitability. Gleba's advice to entrepreneurs follows from the preceding data, "Secure seed capital from individuals; seek a corporate partner early; get profitable quickly; and avoid restart [down] rounds."

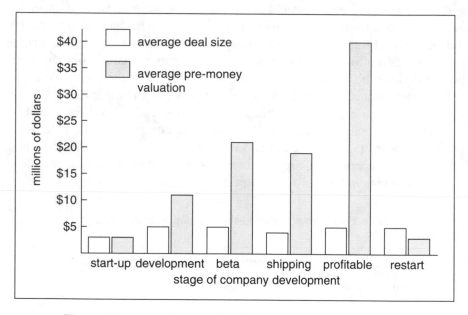

Figure 17-1   Deal Size and Pre-Money Valuation versus Stage
of Company Development

18

Other Compensation and Start-Up Employment Considerations

*"The engine which drives enterprise
is not thrift, but profit."*
—John Maynard Keynes

Entrepreneurs Need Insurance

You may be accustomed to big company fringe benefits at minimal or no cost to you, such as medical, dental, and vision insurances, long- and short-term disability insurances, and life insurance.

When you decide to launch your own business, do not overlook how new insurance premiums or the lack of insurance might affect your personal finances. If you became seriously ill or died, the consequences would be grave to you and your family. While you can survive without dental and vision care insurance benefits, you will need basic medical and life insurance coverage.

Insurances—Individual or Group?

On the first day you start business or leave an old employer, you will want to be covered for your basic insurance needs. This chapter discusses what you as an individual founder need to consider for your own short-term protection. Later, you will want to consider putting group insurance plans into place for yourself and your employees. A July 1991 Labor Department survey found that 69% of small businesses provided medical care benefits for full-time workers in 1990; an earlier poll found that in 1989, 92% of large businesses did so. However, before you work on group plans, it is important to take care of your own short-term needs. That is primarily what this chapter is all about.

Life Insurance

Some forms of protection, such as proper medical and life insurance, are almost routine.

You probably already own some life insurance. Review your policies and purchase some additional term insurance if needed to cover the coming several years. If you are in good health, this insurance is cheap and comforting. Inexpensive term insurance is available through the IEEE (Institute for Electrical and Electronic Engineers) and many other professional organizations.

Most group term life insurance policies from previous employers can be converted into individual whole life policies after termination of employment, but this whole life is often extremely expensive and the rates offered are usually not at all competitive. The rule of thumb is to take advantage of group term conversion options only if you are totally uninsurable. Shop around.

Key Person Life Insurance

You have probably read about companies that have key man or key person life insurance for their key executives. Investors, who are the beneficiaries, often require this insurance to make sure they get their money back if you expire. This will not be of much help to your family. Some of these key insurance policies do, however, include some payment to your spouse, which is something to keep in mind in your negotiations with investors.

Medical Insurance

If you are not covered by a spouse's group medical plan, you should shop for competitive medical insurance.

An excellent temporary solution for many is provided by the Consolidated Omnibus Budget Reconciliation Act of 1986. Commonly known as COBRA, this law requires most employers (those with at least 20 employees) sponsoring group health plans to extend to previous employees certain existing group plan insurance benefits for 18 months (even if the employee quits) at a cost of just a few percentage points above group plan rates. Even after the allotted time, the plan can be converted to an individual rather than a group rate, but it may be cheaper to shop around. COBRA may provide a much-needed temporary solution to your medical health insurance needs, especially if you have an uninsurable prior condition. Be aware, though, that many companies have been negligent in properly implementing their obligations under the law. Also, when one becomes covered by any another group health plan, no matter how poor the new benefits may be, COBRA coverage could be cut short.

Asset Protection Maneuvers

The area of asset protection also needs your consideration. You probably should visit an estate planner to determine the best way for your family's assets to be held. To prevent your family from being economically wiped out if the business fails, it might be advisable to put certain assets in trust for your spouse or to make them separate property. Furthermore, should the business succeed, it might make sense to put some of your new company stock in trust funds for your children.

Disability Insurance

People 45 or younger are three times more likely to become disabled than to die, yet almost everyone has some life insurance and few have disability insurance. If you die it does not cost your family much money. Financially, they just have to deal with the loss of income. If you are disabled and sick, additional expenses will be incurred.

Disability insurance normally pays no more than 60% of what an individual earned before he or she became ill, and does not take effect for 60 to 120 days, depending on the policy. In many cases these insurance proceeds are not even treated as taxable income. The shorter the lag before the insurance takes effect, the more the insurance costs. Look for a policy that pays if you cannot work in the same capacity as you did before an illness. While disabilities do not occur frequently, they can be devastating. If you are healthy, disability insurance is not expensive, and you should buy it to protect your family.

Retirement Plans

When you first launch your start-up you probably will not have a good retirement plan in place.

Because IRS rules are constantly changing, you will need to supplement the comments in this section with up-to-date information from the following pamphlets, available free from the IRS:

- Publication 17, *Your Federal Income Tax for Individuals*

- Publication 590, *Individual Retirement Arrangements* (IRAs)

- Publication 560, *Retirement Plans for the Self-Employed*, for payments to a Keogh retirement plan or self-employed simplified employee pension (SEP)

Kinds of IRAs

Your IRA can be an individual retirement account or annuity. It can be either a part of a simplified employee pension or part of an employer or employee association trust account.

You will soon want to investigate setting up an SEP, which is a type of IRA. The SEP is a written plan that allows an employer to make contributions toward his or her own (if a self-employed individual) and the employees' retirement without becoming involved in more complex retirement plans.

The SEP rules generally permit an employer to contribute each year to each participating employee's SEP-IRA up to 15% of the employee's compensation or $30,000, whichever is less. The contributions are funded by the employer. See the previously mentioned IRS publications for details on contribution limits.

If you are in transition from employment with a larger company to your yet-to-be-incorporated start-up, you may find yourself self-employed. As a self-employed individual, you may still contribute to your own SEP-IRA, and special rules apply when figuring your maximum deduction for these contributions.

An SEP may include a salary reduction arrangement. Under this arrangement, you can elect to have your employer contribute part of your pay to your SEP-IRA also. Only the remaining part of your pay is currently taxable. The tax on the contribution is deferred. This election is called an elective deferral.

Many of you will already have a Keogh plan in place. A Keogh is a tax-deferred pension account designed for employees of unincorporated businesses or for persons who are self-employed, either full-time or part-time. A Keogh may be ideal for you during the planning stages of your business, but if your start-up incorporates soon, you can establish a broader retirement plan for yourself and your employees, such as the SEP discussed previously or the popular 401(k) elective deferral plan. You will want to discuss your options with your CPA or other qualified individual when the time comes. This section is meant to give you just the briefest overview.

Employment Contract

See Chapter 13 for comments on employment contracts for others in your company. This chapter is primarily about you. As you employ yourself in your new business, you will want to create some form of simple employment contract for yourself. This may sound absurd since it is, after all, your business. But if the business is to grow, you will soon be surrounded by other stakeholders such as investors (shareholders), employees, customers, and suppliers.

These individuals may assert an intense interest in your business affairs if they do not like how the business is going. Many start-up entrepreneurs are later dismissed from their own companies.

Include the following clauses in your employment contract:

- Severance pay equal to your salary will continue for 12 months after you are terminated (or you are asked to resign) without cause.

- You have the right to resign rather than be fired.

- You will continue vesting in your founder's stock and stock options during your severance period.

- You will be given an extension to the period of time during which you must exercise any outstanding incentive stock options (from the standard one to three months) to three years. (If you take advantage of this extension, your incentive stock options will convert into nonqualified stock options, but that may be preferable to exercising options when stock values are low).

- Outplacement services will be provided for one year after termination or involuntary resignation.

By the way, most investors will review and, if necessary, renegotiate all employment contracts prior to committing funds, so keep your contract simple and reasonably fair.

Emotional Distress Compensation

Fortune 500 companies can have reorganizations, acquisitions, mergers, and recapitalizations that decimate their ranks, but start-ups are subject to extermination.

As founder, you can do a lot toward protecting yourself in times of future distress. In the case of bankruptcy of your start-up, the company probably cannot help you very much; however, it is not unheard of for six-figure settlements to go to ousted founders and presidents under bankruptcy proceedings (for example, Worlds of Wonder, Inc., in 1988). They called them emotional distress payments, and the payments were nontaxable because they were deemed personal-injury settlements rather than income. The architect of the perk was Palo Alto, CA attorney William Mclean, who represented the two executives.

If your business is flying high, or even not so high, and a future board dismisses you with or without cause, you may feel you deserve some help; you may not get any unless you arranged for it early on. It makes sense to create a written employment contract for yourself that will protect you if you are let go.

If terminated early, you may lose any value in your founder's stock or stock options unless your employment agreement stipulated that you would extend your vesting upon termination (e.g., without cause). If you had only ISOs (which must be exercised within a three-month period), you have lost them regardless of any accelerated vesting schedule if the company is faltering and the stock is worth less than your exercise price. However, if you have nonqualified options and you successfully negotiated to exercise them within the next three to ten years if you are let go without cause, you can go on to a new job or start a new company and possibly cash in later after the new management team turns the company around.

A couple of concepts from larger companies have recently found their way into the employment contracts of start-up companies: golden handcuffs and golden parachutes.

Golden Handcuffs—When and How to Stay

You keep good employees in part by making it financially painful for them to leave. If you arrange it so that when someone leaves early they lose deferred salary, nonvested stock options, deferred bonus payments, etc., you have placed what are known as golden handcuffs on that individual. Put handcuffs only on your key employees; avoid them for yourself. Be aware, however, that this can be a point of dissension with other sophisticated cofounders and key employees.

Golden Parachutes—When and How to Leave

If you are asked to leave your company, or if you agree that is the thing to do at some point in the future, it will be to your benefit to have already negotiated the terms of your departure. Insert in your employment contract stipulations regarding your severance and vesting rights. This will give you a cushion—a golden parachute to soften your landing.

Severance pay, if you are forced out, should equal at least three to twelve months salary. A lump-sum payment would be to your advantage, but it is more common to pay severance over time just as if it were salary. Vesting in your stock and options should continue for some period of time also, certainly during your severance payment period.

Summary

In conclusion, it is obvious that you will need a fair salary and a fair equity position as discussed in earlier chapters. However, it is also important to have needed auxiliary coverage (life insurance, medical insurance, asset protection plans, and disability insurance). Construct a fair and simple written employment contract so investors will accept it when granting the funding for your start-up.

5

DOING IT

Part Five of this book contains some final thoughts for you to consider before launching your start-up. A sidebar to Chapter 19 describes an exciting experience the author had in launching one start-up. You can learn from others' earlier mistakes.

Here also is a chance for you to reflect before making the start-up decision. This section briefly reviews the key points of the book to aid you in deciding whether engineering a start-up is the right action for you now.

■ ■ ■ ■ ■

19

Making the Start-Up Decision

"Do not follow where the path may lead.
Go instead where there is no path and leave a trail."
— Entrepreneur's creed

Mortgage the House?

More and more frequently, start-up entrepreneurs are forced to provide some of their own seed funds before attracting venture capital in today's investment climate. If you were fortunate enough to have been able to acquire a house, drawing on your own personal reserves probably means obtaining a loan (probably a second mortgage) against your house or at least using it as collateral for an equity line of credit. If you are not careful, losing your house is a very real possibility if your business fails. When corporations go bankrupt, most creditors are limited to attaching the assets of the corporation. However, if you guarantee a business loan with your house, then your house is fair play for your creditors. If you loaned your company funds obtained from a loan on your house, on the other hand, or if you purchased preferred equity, you might be in a little better position. Chapter 16 discusses sophisticated ways to best risk your own personal capital (e.g., investment through the provision of real property); it is wise to use these techniques if you decide to mortgage your house.

Leaving a Current Employer

Do not give your employer notice or let him know anything about your plans to create a start-up until everything is planned to your satisfaction and you have sufficient funds to see yourself through the concept development stage as discussed in Chapter 11.

It is important to review your obligations to your employer. If you were an officer, director, or even a manager, for example, you may have obligations not to jeopardize the company or deprive it of a business opportunity. Here are a few suggestions for you to consider when leaving your current employer to launch your start-up:

- Determine whether your start-up constitutes a corporate opportunity, which you must first offer your employer before you can pursue it (these offers are usually rejected).

- Take extreme care in hiring other employees of the company.

- Make sure that you transfer important information and knowledge of technology to others when you leave (offer to consult with them if they need you in the future).

- Make sure you do not violate a binding noncompete clause in an employment contract (while these clauses used to be very difficult to enforce in California in the 1980s, it is becoming somewhat easier in the 1990s).

David Bowen notes,

> You may want to go back to work for your old company, so make sure that you abide by the spirit of your agreements and commitments as well as the letter. If there is any way to leave on good terms, I advise you to do it. Your karma will follow you.

Following are some suggestions that you can pursue to prepare for business without actually doing business while still employed:

- lease office space and rent furniture

- reserve phone numbers

- print business cards and letterhead

- work on a business plan

You should not, however:

- order materials

- presell customers

- hire employees

- develop a product prototype (that may then belong to your employer)

To emphasize again, do not prepare your business plan at work or use your employer's resources (copy machine, secretary, telephone, etc.).

Hiring employees from your employer while still employed will also get you in a lot of trouble. James Pooley suggests,

> If approached by members of your present staff, simply thank them for their interest and explain that you cannot respond to their request until you have departed. Then note the solicitation in your records for later reference and follow-up.

If you and one or two others decide to leave the same employer to cofound a new company, you might want to talk to legal counsel to get specific advice for your situation on how to avoid a lawsuit.

Intellectual Property Protection (IPP)

Patents, trade secrets, copyrights—these are the keys to protecting your intellectual property rights. As you build your technology-based business, you will undoubtedly be creating value in intangible intellectual information. Many entrepreneurs have neglected the area of IPP only to be crushed by their competition. You must understand and take advantage of the laws created for your protection.

Copyrights

A *copyright* is protection by federal statute giving artists and authors exclusive right to publish their works or to determine who may do so. You will want your employees to assign to your company (the employer) any copyrights on material you paid them to produce. Make sure that all employees sign a document before they start working for you acknowledging their obligation to assign appropriate copyrights and patents to the company. Note that a copyright protects only the form in which an idea is expressed, not the idea itself. This distinguishes the copyright from the patent and the trade secret, which protect the substance of the invention or information, respectively. For example, by reading this book you are exposed to some original ideas, which now belong to you and anyone else who reads this book. However, if you expressed those ideas in an article or another book in the same form, using the words and phrases that appear here, you would be in violation of the copyright covering this book.

Software developers will have special concerns. The problem in interpreting copyrights is that the distinction between form and substance can become blurred. In drawings and blueprints, the form becomes the substance, since the form was most important to the creator. Similarly, in works of music, literature, and computer software, form often becomes very important in judging whether someone has stolen the fruits of creative effort. The latest debates on who owns the rights to the copyrighted look and feel of a particular windows-style graphical user-interface, for example, drive this point home. For most types of technology and business information, a copyright will not be the best form of protection. You need to protect the substance of your ideas, not just the means of expressing them. In fact, placing a copyright notice on a document often implies publication to the world, which is inconsistent with trade secret protection.

Before 1980, software was in a no-man's-land in the area of copyrights. The U.S. Copyright Office had accepted copyright registration for software since 1964, but it was not until 1980 that the U.S. copyright law was amended to specifically include software. Where mass marketing of software makes contractual trade secret impractical, copyright registration may be the best alternative. Be aware that copyrighting your source code tells the entire world exactly how you wrote a program to perform a function. Copyrights make illegal the kind of outright copying practiced by software pirates. But, just as hardware engineers reverse-engineer semiconductor designs, software developers are becoming skilled at reverse-engineering software code, thereby writing their own software that performs the same tasks without infringing on copyrights. As with patents and use of trade secrets, it is wise to get expert advice on the use of copyrights.

Because software is so easily duplicated (unlike hardware), the need for IPP is that much greater. Many attorneys suggest that developers consider protecting their software with both a copyright and either a patent or trade secret.

The term of copyright protection generally extends for the life of the author plus 50 years.

Patents

A *patent* (or patent of invention) is a grant of right to exclude others from the making or selling of an invention during a specified period of time. A patent gives its owner a legitimate monopoly. The government grants a patent to an inventor or the assignee to legally monopolize the use of a specific invention for a limited time—generally 17 years from the date of issue, except for patents on designs, which are granted for terms of $3\frac{1}{2}$, 7, or 14 years. The term of the patent can only be extended by a special act of Congress.

Software companies that in the past relied on copyrights for protection now seek patent protection as well. Whereas a copyright covers only the code or instructions for a drop-down menu, for example, a patent protects the concept of a drop-down menu itself.

Patents are granted for "new and useful processes, machines, manufactured articles, etc." The key word *useful* implies utility. But this is interpreted to mean that the invention works, not that it is commercially useful. Your invention must also be nonobvious, meaning that it is so distinct from existing practice that it is not obvious to a person skilled in your field. Business information and know-how are not patentable and are best protected by trade secrets.

Another important issue with regards to patents is timing. You must not delay; a patent application must be filed within one year of the first public use or offer for sale of the invention. Detailed records, dated and signed, of the process of creating the invention should be kept. Each employee should be issued a patent engineering workbook in which entries are made daily. These books should always remain the property of the company.

You can get plenty of good low-cost information about patents from the U.S. Department of Commerce's Patents and Trademark Office or the U.S. Superintendent of Documents. Ask for *Patents, Inventions: An Information Aid for Inventors* and *General Information Concerning Patents*.

Trade Secrets

A *trade secret* is any formula, pattern, machine, or process of manufacturing used in a business that may give the user a competitive advantage, or any plan, process, tool, mechanism, or compound known only to its owner and those of its employees to whom it is necessary to disclose it.

You should treat almost every document generated for internal use in your company as containing a potential trade secret. It is a good idea to include in the footer of the word processing template you use to generate internal memorandums words which will always appear (unless you choose to remove them) such as "CONFIDENTIAL," "PROPRIETARY," or "TRADE SECRET." The presence of such constant reminders will serve to sensitize your employees to keep company information inside the company where it belongs.

Trade secrets are defined separately by each state. In order to protect what you consider to be a trade secret, you must be specific in your claims. Courts have ruled that trade secrets can consist of things such as the Coca-Cola™ formula, customer lists, marketing plans, cost and pricing data, and employee benefit information.

Note that a trade secret (unlike a patent or copyright) need not be unique to the owner. In fact, over time, a trade secret may become a commonly known industry practice, at which time your trade secret status will be lost. An idea does not need to be patentable to receive trade secret protection, and the term covers the complete range of business practices and know-how. It is often difficult to try to protect an invention by both patent and trade secret, since a patent is public information.

Be Prepared for a Lawsuit

Although it may surprise you, your current employer may frown upon your leaving to create your start-up. After all, anyone with the qualities of a start-up entrepreneur is likely to have been a highly valued employee in most larger companies. Also, it seems that you have created a great opportunity, and you may leave behind a lot of envious people. You might very well be accused of and threatened to be sued for everything from theft of company property to denying an employer a business opportunity. Be very careful to do the reasonable and ethical things expected of you. Make sure you leave behind everything your employer owns or makes claims to, no matter how tempting they might be to take home or photocopy.

Keep a separate personal pocket calendar and notebook that you paid for (tape the cash register receipt to the first page) for documenting activities at your many start-up meetings. Be completely honest if you have an exit interview, but do not offer any more information than you are asked for. This will minimize the chances of a lawsuit for theft of trade secrets, denial of business opportunity, etc.

Stay Fit

Staying physically and emotionally fit during start-up is critical to your success. It is highly advised that you start an exercise regimen that you can maintain in the hectic days ahead. Many entrepreneurs get up early to jog or workout on an exercise machine at home. Joining a health club can be a good way to ensure getting regular exercise, and it is also an excellent way to meet people. It is vital that you take care of yourself during this time of stress and hard work. It is not an option, it is a requirement.

What if Your Start-Up Fails?

Your friends may tell you, "If you attempt to start your own business and you are a competent professional, you cannot lose anything except a little time." They reason that if your start-up fails, you will only have to get a new job, and it will probably pay more than the one you left. Meanwhile, you have gained valuable experience you could not have acquired in any other way. Unless you are close to retirement age or in poor health, this reasoning is hard to argue with.

It is worth thinking ahead about the necessity of finding new work if your start-up fails. Actually, you probably should be equally concerned with finding a new job should your current *Fortune* 500 company unexpectedly fail you. If you are unemployed, it may take you from 12 to 52 weeks to find new work. (In early 1991, the time needed for the average job search fell to 15 weeks from 20 weeks in 1990). One rule of thumb is to figure that you will be searching for work for one month for every $10,000 of salary you expect to make. Often a professional finds that next move while happily employed; these opportunities often develop over a period of months or even years.

Your decision whether to launch your start-up should be based, in part, on satisfying answers to these questions:

- Are you comfortable with the personal financial risk your start-up entails?

- Can you cleanly sever your current obligations with your employer, avoiding the possibility of a lawsuit as you launch your venture?

- Will you exploit the power of patents, trademarks, copyrights, and trade secrets to protect your new venture's intellectual property?

- Despite your determination for success, will you adequately maintain your health to endure the start-up, and are you prepared for the remote possibility of failure?

Digital Vision, Inc., and Contrex, Inc.: Schlumberger Ltd.'s Buyout of One of the Author's Start-Ups

In the early 1980s at Schlumberger's Fairchild Laboratory for Artificial Intelligence Research (FLAIR) in Palo Alto, CA, my team of research computer scientists and I built a successful prototype of a revolutionary new instrument for the automatic optical inspection of microscopic patterns on semiconductor wafers. It was one of the most exciting projects going on inside Fairchild at the time. This invention promised to vastly improve yields in semiconductor manufacturing, which could translate into savings of hundreds of millions of dollars for anyone having access to it.

To be useful, however, this prototype had to be engineered into a complete product. It would take a lot of money to develop since the machine itself was estimated to sell for $1 million. Fairchild, the renowned semiconductor company from which so many other Silicon Valley semiconductor companies had their origin, was then owned by the giant French oil company Schlumberger Ltd. Schlumberger's culture had little tolerance for entrepreneurship. Furthermore, its Fairchild subsidiary, while a potential customer for purchasing such a machine, was not in the business of developing complex and costly instrumentation. My initial plea for Schlumberger-Fairchild to exploit my invention went unheard.

Thus, the idea for a new company was born in my mind. I would call it Digital Vision, Inc. (DVI), since it used a revolutionary new technology that allowed computers to acquire digital images of objects and visually interpret them to discover killer sub-micron defects. I knew that I wanted to engineer my start-up, but I did not know exactly how to proceed. Knowing that I needed a top management team to pull this off, I first approached Dick Abraham, a semiretired and highly respected ex-senior vice president of Fairchild. Dick was quickly drawn into the scheme, and he brought along Ron Hayes, the president of Delvotec (a semiconductor instrumentation company) and an astute investor in many start-ups funded by the Hillman family via the Hillman Company venture capital fund. Ron conveyed the business idea to his Hillman connections, and venture capital funding seemed imminent as soon as we put together a suitable business plan.

Dick would be the chairman of the board, Ron would be the marketing vice president, and I would be the president. At my suggestion, we also agreed that I would drop down to the engineering vice president role if needed, either to raise additional funding or to facilitate our planned rapid growth. Recognizing up front my potential limitations to lead this company and accepting the possible need for more experienced management was very important. Bill Gates, the founder of Microsoft, willingly brought in a president to help him out when he needed it, and I was not about to try anything different. We charged on full speed after that.

Dick, Ron, and I quickly went to work writing our business plan. In order not to use my employer's resources, I spent $2,500 to buy a personal computer and printer along with word processing and spreadsheet software. My new credit card spending limit was not up to the task, so when I went to pick up the computer I had to come up with cash instead. Over the next few months I spent eight hours at work and then another six to eight hours every night working on the plan, with help from Dick and Ron. The little dot matrix printer I bought went through hundreds of pages of paper and a new ribbon almost every night as revised versions of the business plan spooled out just before I went to bed.

The three of us collaborated closely with two others who were working at Fairchild. Dr. John Dralla was a semiconductor fabrication manager with a Ph.D. in physics who knew the process well, and he was to head our sales efforts. Peter Fiekowsky was a brilliant young computer programmer who had helped to build the protoype and would help turn it into a real product. Ron introduced us to Mario Rosati, the famous Silicon Valley lawyer, who helped us plan our course of action.

Everyone was excited! The business plan was finally complete. We had a revolutionary product idea already prototyped and tested on real products, an obviously willing and ready market, a pretty good management team, and potential venture capital funds already lined up. In our first meeting at Wilson, Sonsini, Goodrich & Rosati, it was determined that everything was a "go" except for one possible hitch. Counsel wanted Fairchild's blessing before funding our start-up because it was clear that Fairchild had a potential claim on our invention (having funded development of the prototype). The question in our minds was whether Fairchild would let us run with it or demand a big piece of the action. We were not prepared for what happened.

We agreed that I would present the DVI business plan to the Schlumberger-Fairchild management with an open-ended offer for them to invest in the company the way they saw best. They could put up cash and own a good percentage of the business, they could license the technology to us, they could take future royalties, or they could write their own ticket. It seemed to us a more than reasonable and fair proposition for both sides.

What happened surprised us. Fairchild management was furious, accusing the DVI team of denying Fairchild a business opportunity. A call to Mario Rosati by Tony Ley, the top manager at the Fairchild Research Center, promised a lawsuit if anyone put another penny into the newly incorporated Digital Vision. Rosati replied that the last thing he wanted was a lawsuit, and Fairchild could keep its business opportunity.

We ended up having to set aside our entrepreneurial visions for DVI. I was asked to return to Fairchild for three months to rewrite the DVI plan for Schlumberger. Having no real option and a very large mortgage payment to make with a wife, two kids, and a dog (none of whom earned a second income for the family), I agreed. The DVI founding team dissolved. Three months turned to six, and the revised "EYESEE" (for Integrated Circuit) business plan was submitted to Schlumberger's top management. Schlumberger's worldwide operating management conducted extensive due diligence. Finally, they made me an offer to fund the plan with $2 million. Ten engineers were to be assigned to develop the product. The product would be designed in secret in a building at Fairchild's Automatic Test Equipment (ATE) Division in San Jose, CA.

I complained that the San Jose location was not very convenient for me and that I would need to do market research and expose the world outside Fairchild to our ideas if we were to build the best product. Also, I would need a motivated management team to build a business as we built the product. I personally would need motivation—if not outright equity ownership in the venture (we had proposed phantom-stock options), at least a substantial salary increase. In reply, it was explained to me that I was an employee, and I would be rewarded as all managers were: after the achievement of a success. Take it or leave it.

One day later I resigned to pursue backup plan B. Raul Brauner was an entrepreneur in Billerica, MA, who had earlier founded Contrex, Inc., to develop WaferVision™, which also would inspect semiconductor wafers optically. During the previous six months, Raul and I had grown quite close as he saw my invention as a key to growing his company. His repeated attempts to recruit me as an engineering vice president finally succeeded when Schlumberger's offer left me cold. We engaged our lawyers to draw up a resignation letter that would get me cleanly out of Fairchild and into working for Contrex. We agreed, for example, that I would not do any substantive engineering on a related product for six months. To prove our good intentions, I opened a West Coast Applications Development office in Santa Clara, CA, where I would work only on Contrex's existing product for the next six months. I had one salesman and I prepared to hire an applications programmer.

Fairchild was dismayed and asked me to attend four exit interviews. At each interview I was told that I had better keep my promise not to use Fairchild trade secrets. Although my contract with Contrex stipulated that they would pay for any legal fight, we hoped there would not be one. We stuck closely to our agreement, and I ended up commuting to Billerica, spending more time in motels around Boston's Route 128 than I did at home during the following six months.

Six months later, Contrex, Inc., with 65 employees and zero sales, found itself in a severe cash crunch. Because interest by East Coast venture capital sources dwindled, we headed to the West Coast. In the San Francisco Bay Area, we talked to a dozen venture capitalists, three of whom expressed keen interest. However, each also advised us to find a corporate partner if we wished to be funded by them, so we talked to General Signal, Intel, and a few others. Again there was lots of interest but no deal; at least not in the time we had left.

Then it hit me. Why not try Schlumberger? I called them, and a day later I found myself in the office of Dr. Marty Tenenbaum, the director of the Artificial Intelligence Laboratory, and my former boss. He had encouraged my entrepreneurial efforts in the past and saw great value in the EYESEE proposal, which was now nearing its end. After Marty complimented me on my boldness, I asked him to take the Contrex business plan upstairs to see if Schlumberger management still had an interest in the semiconductor optical inspection business.

Despite concern at Schlumberger about risk-taking, many saw a road to fame through investing a few million dollars in a highly leveraged start-up like Contrex, which essentially duplicated what DVI and EYESEE proposed to do a little while back. After a few months of due diligence, Schlumberger acquired a reported 51% interest in Contrex, Inc., for about $5 million. The original venture capitalists added a few million more, which equaled our accumulated debt. We paid all our creditors, and the company had a fresh start. While all this negotiation was going on, Mike Kaufman of Oak Investment Partners, our original venture capital investor, brought in a gunslinger to clean house. After the work force had been trimmed down from 65 to about 24 and Raul Brauner had been demoted, I was offered the key engineering vice presidency position for product design if I moved to Billerica. While this was an interesting proposition, I nevertheless declined due to overriding personal considerations in California at that time.

Schlumberger now owned the business opportunity they had earlier denied the entrepreneurial Digital Vision team and that was denied to them in their own backyard with my rejection of their offer to fund the EYESEE plan. It was too late, though. Their opportunity was lost because the entrepreneurial spirit had diminished, and Contrex faded away less than one year later.

20

Some Final Comments

> *"Nothing in the world can take the place of*
> *persistence. Talent will not; nothing is more*
> *common than unsuccessful men with talent.*
> *Genius will not; unrewarded genius is almost*
> *a proverb. Education will not; the world is*
> *full of educational derelicts. Persistence*
> *and determination alone are omnipotent."*
>
> — Calvin Coolidge

Starting your own company is going to be the most exciting and rewarding endeavor you will ever undertake. If you decide to engineer your own start-up, your life will be richer and fuller than you would have ever imagined. Your body and soul will come to life, and each of your days will be more fully lived. With this new life will come new pains as well as new pleasures; and because you will feel more alive, these pains and pleasures will be more intense.

Not everyone needs, wants, or can take such an intense lifestyle. Start-up entrepreneurs are often adrenaline freaks, driving in the fast lane. As the boss in the movie *Curly Sue* said to his aggressive female associate, "If you drive 190 miles an hour you're going to run into something." Start-up entrepreneurs thrive on metaphorical speed and do crash into things. Will you crash and burn? Will you stay in control? What is your comfortable cruising speed?

By this time, you probably know what you want to do: you want to start your own team-driven, high-growth, technology-based business. If you decide to launch your start-up, review the following summary of the most important points presented in this book:

- Build a strong management team that you would enjoy working with, can help you attract funds, and can help you grow a healthy, successful business.

- Create a strong board of directors that will provide your business with the experience and funding sources necessary for you to survive and prosper.

- Identify a growing market opportunity to which you can apply your engineering technology to develop a product for which there are known customers.

- Make sure you have a distinct and preferably unfair competitive advantage.

- Plan your business well in advance, and put your plan into writing.

- Make sure that high growth is one of your business objectives. Thoroughly understand why high growth is important to your success.

- Raise enough money to get started, and do not run out of money.

- Be profitable as early as possible.

- Do not produce a product that requires missionary sales.

- Let market- and customer-driven technology-fueled be your business model.

- Enjoy the process of building your new business, but try to balance your work and private life. "Like your work but love your spouse" is an applicable saying. However, prepare to be consumed by your new business, and plan to devote a significant part of your life and most of your energy to making your start-up successful.

- Use stock and stock option grants to motivate and reward those who will help to make your business a success.

- Beyond all else, persist and persevere until you win the start-up game.

This book has encouraged you to approach your start-up with extreme diligence in thinking things out and conducting extensive market research before attempting to launch your business. You are not expected to do everything suggested in this book, but you should focus on those areas that are unfamiliar to you where you stand to gain (or lose) a lot if you (do not) investigate first. Now, step into the fast lane and get on with what could be the most exciting event in your life!

I would be pleased to hear from you regarding this book.

Michael L. Baird
101 First Street, Suite 204
Los Altos, CA 94022

Professional Publications, Inc. ▪ Belmont, CA

Professional Resources

For your convenience, the following are pointers to various professional resources contributing to or otherwise cited in the manuscript.

Alpha Partners, 2200 Sand Hill Road, Suite 250, Menlo Park, CA 94025. Phone (415) 854-7024.
- venture capital seed financing

American Electronics Association, Surveys Department, 5201 Great America Parkway, P.O. Box 54990, Santa Clara, CA 95056-0990. Phone (408) 987-4200. Fax (408) 970-8565.
- salary surveys and compensation seminars

Brewer, Janet L., Law Offices of, 517 Byron St., P.O. Box 1299, Palo Alto, CA 94302. Phone (415) 321-4244. Fax (415) 326-0825.
- legal advice for start-up entrepreneurs

Bukstein, Roy, Bukstein CPA, 1301 Shoreway Road #126, Belmont, CA 94002. Phone (415) 637-1775.
- specialist in stock options

Entrepreneur, Bay Area, 1815-D Ygnacio Valley Road, Suite 360, Walnut Creek, CA 94598. Phone (415) 933-2934.
- newsletter for entrepreneurs

Institutional Venture Partners, 3000 Sand Hill Road, Building 2, Suite 290, Menlo Park, CA 94025.
- venture capital firm

Jenett, Bruce W., or Jacqueline A. Daunt, Fenwick & West, Two Palo Alto Square, Suite 800, Palo Alto, CA 94306. Phone (415) 494-0600.
- legal advice for start-up entrepreneurs

Mclean, William, Thoits Love Hershberger & Mclean, 525 University Ave., Palo Alto, CA 94301. Phone (415) 327-4200.
- legal advice for structuring employment contracts

Nelson, Dr. Philip B., Institute for Exceptional Performance, Three Embarcadero Center, Suite 1630, San Francisco, CA 94111. Phone (415) 433-7087. Fax (415) 989-6714.
- management candidate evaluation for executive recruiters

Plummer, Jim, Q.E.D. Research, Inc., 125 California Avenue, Palo Alto, CA 94306. Phone (415) 321-9827.
- consultant to venture capitalists and entrepreneurs

Software Success, P.O. Box 9006, San Jose, CA 95157-0006. Phone (408) 446-2504. Fax (408) 255-1098.
- newsletter for software entrepreneurs

Upside Magazine, P.O. Box 3804, Escondido, CA 92033-9905. Phone (619) 745-2809. Fax (415) 377-1961.
- $48 per year for a subscription

References and Suggested Readings

Ballas, George C., and David Hollas. *The Making of an Entrepreneur—Keys to Your Success*. Englewood Cliffs, NJ: Prentice-Hall, 1980.

Bartlett, Joseph W., *Venture Capital: Law, Business Strategies, and Investment Planning*. New York: John Wiley & Sons, 1988.

Baty, Gordon B. *Entrepreneurship for the Nineties*. Englewood Cliffs, NJ: Prentice-Hall, 1990.

Bell, C. Gordon, and John E. McNamara. *High-Tech Ventures: The Guide for Entrepreneurial Success*. Menlo Park, CA: Addison-Wesley, 1991.

Blanchard, Kenneth, and Spencer Johnson. *The One Minute Manager*. New York: Berkley Books, 1980.

Bolles, Richard Nelson. *The 1991 What Color Is Your Parachute?* Berkeley: Ten Speed Press, 1991.

Boston Consulting Group, Inc. *Perspectives on Experience*. Boston, MA: 1968.

Brandt, Steven C. *Entrepreneuring: The Ten Commandments for Building a Growth Company*. New York: A Mentor Book, New American Library, 1983.

Carlisle, Norman. *How to Make a Fortune from Your Invention*. New York: Warner Paperback Library, Warner Books, 1972.

Clifford, Donald K., Jr., and Richard E. Cavanagh. *The Winning Performance: How America's High-Growth Midsize Companies Succeed.* New York: Bantam Books, 1985–1988.

Davidow, William H. *Marketing High Technology.* New York: The Free Press, A Division of Macmillan, 1986.

Delaney, William A. *Why Small Businesses Fail—Don't Make the Same Mistake Once.* Englewood Cliffs, NJ: Prentice-Hall, 1984.

DeMente, Boyce. *The Japanese Way of Doing Business.* Englewood Cliffs, NJ: Prentice-Hall, 1981.

Dible, Donald M. *Up your Own Organization.* Reston, VA: Reston, A Prentice-Hall Company, 1974.

—, ed. *What Everybody Should Know About Patents, Trademarks and Copyrights.* Fairfield, CA: The Entrepreneur Press, 1978.

Drucker, Peter F. *Innovation and Entrepreneurship: Practice and Principles.* New York: Harper & Row, 1985.

Field, Drew. *Take Your Company Public—the Entrepreneur's Guide to Alternative Capital Sources.* New York: Simon & Schuster, 1991.

Fisher, Roger, and William Ury. *Getting to Yes.* New York: Penguin Books, 1985.

Gill, James O. *Understanding Financial Statements: A Guide for Non-Financial Readers.* Los Altos, CA: Crisp Publications, 1990.

Gosden, Freeman F., Jr. *Direct Marketing Success—What Works and Why.* New York: John Wiley & Sons, 1985.

Greene, Gardiner G. *How to Start and Manage Your Own Business.* New York: A Mentor Book, New American Library, 1975.

Grove, Andrew S. *High Output Management.* New York: Random House, 1983.

Hamilton, Robert W. *The Law of Corporations (in a Nutshell).* St. Paul: West Publishing, 1980.

—. *Corporations.* 2d ed. St Paul: Black Letter Series, West Publishing, 1986.

Hawken, Paul. *Growing a Business.* New York: Simon & Schuster, 1987.

Humphrey, Watts S. *Managing the Software Process.* Menlo Park, CA: Addison-Wesley, 1990.

Ichbiah, Daniel, and Susan L. Knepper. *The Making of Microsoft: How Bill Gates and His Team Created the World's Most Successful Software Company.* Rocklin, CA: Prima Publishing, 1991.

Jenkins, Michael D. *Starting and Operating a Business in California*. Alameda, CA: Oasis Press, 1980.

Jennings, Richard W., and Harold Marsh, Jr. *Securities Regulations—Case and Materials*. 5th ed. University Casework Series, Mineola, NY: The Foundation Press, 1982.

Karrass, Gary. *Negotiate to Close*. New York: Simon & Schuster, 1985.

Kawasaki, Guy. *Selling the Dream: How to Promote Your Product, Company, or Ideas—and Make a Difference Using Everyday Evangelism*. New York: Harper-Collins Publishers, 1991.

Kelly, Francis J., and Heather Mayfield Kelly. *What They Really Teach You at the Harvard Business School*. New York: Warner Books, 1986.

Kurtzig, Sandra L., and Tom Parker. *CEO: Building a $400 Million Company from the Ground Up*. New York: W. W. Norton & Company, 1991.

Lasser Institute, J. K. *How to Run a Small Business*. 4th ed. New York: McGraw-Hill, 1974.

Lewis, Stephen H. "Personal Stock Grants." *Venture* (May 1983): 34–35.

Lipper III, Arthur, and George Ryan. *Venture's Guide to Investing In Private Companies: A Financing Manual for the Entrepreneurial Investor*. Homewood, IL: Dow Jones-Irwin, 1984.

Lucht, John. *Rites of Passage at $100,000+ : The Insider's Guide to Absolutely Everything About Executive Job-Changing*. New York: The Viceroy Press, 1988.

Mackay, Harvey. *Beware the Naked Man Who Offers You His Shirt*. New York: Ivy Books, 1990.

Malone, Michael S. *Going Public—MIPS Computer and the Entrepreneurial Dream*. New York: Edward Burlingame Books, an Imprint of HarperCollins, 1991.

McQuown, Judith H. *INC. Yourself*. New York: Warner Books, 1981.

McVicker, Mary French. *Small Business Matters: Topics, Procedures, and Strategies*. Radnor, PA: Chilton Book Co., 1990.

Myer, John N. *Understanding Financial Statements*. New York: A Mentor Book, New American Library, 1964.

Nesheim, John. *Starting a High Tech Company and Securing Multi-Round Financing*. Saratoga, CA: Electronic Trend Publications, 1988.

—. *High Tech StartUp: The Complete How-To Handbook for Creating Successful New High Tech Companies*. Saratoga, CA: Electronic Trend Publications, 1992.

Nierenberg, Gerard I. *The Complete Negotiator*. New York: Berkley Books, 1986.

O'Donnell, Michael. *Writing Business Plans That Get Results*. Chicago: Contemporary Books, 1991.

Owen, Robert R., Daniel R. Garner, and Dennis S. Bunder. *The Arthur Young Guide to Financing for Growth*. New York: John Wiley & Sons, 1986.

Ozer, Jan L. "Going After the Gains on Restricted Stock." *Inc.* (April 1983): 113–14.

Plummer, James L., *Q.E.D. Report on Venture Capital Financial Analysis*. Palo Alto, CA: Q.E.D. Research, Inc., 1987.

Pooley, James. *Trade Secrets—How to Protect Your Ideas and Assets*. Berkeley: Osborne/McGraw-Hill, 1982.

Pratt, Stanley E. *How to Raise Venture Capital*. New York: Charles Scribner's Sons, 1982.

—, ed. *Pratt's Guide to Venture Capital Sources*, 14th ed. Wellesley Hills, MA: Capital Publishing, 1990.

Pressman, David. *Patent it Yourself*. Berkeley: Nolo Press, 1985.

Ribstein, Larry E. *Business Associations*. New York: Analysis and Skills Series, Matthew Bender & Co., 1983.

Rich, Stanley R., and David E. Gumpert. *Business Plans that Win $$$: Lessons from the MIT Enterprise Forum*. New York: Harper & Row, 1987.

Riggs, Henry, E. *Managing High-Technology Companies*. Belmont, CA: Lifetime Learning Publications, 1983.

Roberts, Edward B. *Entrepreneurs in High Technology: Lessons from MIT and Beyond*. New York: Oxford University Press, 1991.

Ronstadt, Robert, and Jeffrey Shuman. *Venture Feasibility Planning Guide: Your First Step Before Writing a Business Plan*. South Natick, MA: Lord Publishing, 1988.

Schöllhammer, Hans, and Arthur H. Kuriloff. *Entrepreneurship and Small Business Management*. New York: John Wiley & Sons, 1979.

Stalk, George Jr., and Thomas M. Hout. *Competing Against Time*. New York: The Free Press, A Division of Macmillan, Inc., 1990.

Tibbetts, Joseph S., Jr., and Edmund T. Donovan. "Compensation and Benefits for Startup Companies: How to Conserve Cash and Still Attract the Best Executives." *Harvard Business Review*. (January–February 1989): 140–47.

Tarrant, John. *Perks and Parachutes*. New York: Linden Press/Simon & Schuster, The Stonesong Press, 1985.

Trudel, John D. *High Tech with Low Risk (Venturing Safely into the 90s)*. La Grande, OR: Eastern Oregon State College, Regional Services Institute, 1990.

Von Gehr, George. "Valuation Assessment of Emerging Companies: A Universal Approach." Presentation at Von Gehr & Tan, 525 University Avenue, Suite 32, Palo Alto, CA 94301, Sept. 26, 1991.

Wasserstein, Bruce. *Corporate Finance Law—A Guide for the Executive*. New York: McGraw-Hill, 1978.

White, Richard, M. *The Entrepreneur's Manual*. Radnor, PA: Chilton Book Co., 1977.

Index

1933 Act, 198
3M, 37, 94
401(k) plan, 183, 252

A
Abraham, Dick, 266
accounting for risks, 245
accounts payable, 55
accounts receivable, 55
accredited investors, 162
acid test, 55–56
acquisition, 53, 139, 244
acquisition financing, 51
address of author, 273
adequate financing, 40, 65
adjusted net worth, 243
Adler & Company, 191
advantage, distinct competitive, 168
advertising, 87, 88, 121
advisory boards, 81
after-tax profit margins, 241
age discrimination, 77
Aldus, 193
Alpha Partners, 240, 241
Altman, E., Z-score, 56
American Electronics Association (AEA), 80, 183
angels, 160, 175
antidilution ratchet, 202
antidilution. *See* ratchet
Apple Computer, Inc., 30–31, 70, 237
applications of funds, 129
areas of opportunity, 4
Arthur Andersen & Company, 198

articles of incorporation, 194
Artificial Intelligence Research, 171
ASK Computer Systems, 158, 160, 174, 194
asset protection, 251
attire, 173
authorized shares, 194
award practices, 187

B
balance sheet, 54, 125
bankruptcy, 56, 57, 253
banks, 188
barriers to entry, 83, 86
Bartlett, Joseph W., 205
Bartlett's weighted-average method, 205–207
basic financial statements, 122
Bell, C. Gordon, 108
benefits, to customers, 84
Berry, Tim, 146
beta test site, 84
BizPlan*Builder*™, 141
board members and stock options, 215
board of directors, 69, 233, 272
    angels as members, 160
    diversity, 78
    election, 77
    power, 77
bonus payments, deferred, 254
Boston Consulting Group, 46
bottom up, design and development, 104
Bowen, David H., 8, 12, 63, 122, 260
brand name recognition, 89
Brandt, Steven, 66
Brauner, Raul, 268, 270

breach of fiduciary duty, 196
break-even point, 131, 156
Breeden, Richard, 161
bridge investments, 51
burnout financing, 205
business, 188, 260
business failure, 119
business growth milestones, 50
business model, 83, 272
business periodicals, general, 93
business plan, 112, 139, 239, 261, 272
    access, 111
    elements, 155
    importance, 65
    models, 111
    operational, 108
    outlines, 113–118
    planning and funding, 107–108
    process, 107
    purpose, 124
    samples, 111
    selling, 132
    shopworn, 169
    time required to write, 110
    types, 107
    unsolicited, 172
    written by management team, 208
Business Plan Toolkit™, 141
business valuations, 213
buying behavior, 97
buying cycle, 97

C

California Bar Association, 219
Callaway, Ely, 96
capital, 228, 260
capital asset pricing model (CAPM), 134
capital budgeting, 135
capital expenditure cycles, 97
capitalization, minimum level, 196
Carr, Robert, 214
carried interest, 164
cash conversion cycle, 129
cash flow, 226
cash flow analysis, discounted, 242
cash flow statement, 128–131
cash-on-cash returns (COC), 134, 139
cash, running out, 158

cash to finance growth, 156
Center for Venture Research, 160
CEO. *See* chief executive officer
chairman of the board, roles and
    responsibilities, 20
cheap stock, 195, 212
chief executive officer
    as the weak link, 76
    founder as, 72
    roles and responsibilities, 20, 43, 66,
        88, 110
    salaries, 183
chief financial officer, roles and
    responsibilities, 72
chief operating officer, roles and
    responsibilities, 21
chief technical officer, roles and
    responsibilities, 21
Christenson, Joe, 44–45
cofounder, 110
cold deals, 172
commissions, 88
commodity products, 94
common equity, 169
common shares, 233
common stock, 197. *See also* stock
common vision, 75
company identity, 83
company valuation, 241, 244, 245–246, 247
compensation, nonmonetary, 182–185
compensation, of board of directors, 79–80
competing companies, 170
competition, 7, 41
competitive advantage, 112, 272
competitive analysis, 91
competitive products, 93
competitor profiles, 85
compounded annual growth rate, 241
Computer Letter, 167
computer, personal, 111
concept development stage, 260
concept stage, 108, 110
confidential information, 174
confidentiality agreements, 111
conflicts of interest, 78
Consolidated Omnibus Budget
    Reconciliation Act of 1986 (COBRA),
        250–251

consultants, 10, 44, 215
consumer markets, problems for start-ups, 97
Contrex, Inc., 266
control, by investors, 78
control securities, 198
controlled-circulation publications, 93
controlling, 67–68
conversion formulas, 207
COO. *See* chief operating officer
co-owners, 188
copyright, 96, 261–262
corporate opportunity, 260
corporations, 190
cost
    advantage, 94
    analysis, 102
    and price, 89
    as a percent of total revenue, 120
    of capital, 135
    overruns, 102
CTO. *See* chief technical officer
cumulative preferred stock, 194
current assets, 55
current liabilities, 55
current ratio, 55
customer, 99, 272
    as source of capital, 159
    as source of help, 45
    as source of seed cash, 157
    importance, 65
    in *Fortune* 500 companies, 45
    knowing, 84
    loyalty, 83
customer list, 119
customer service, 83, 95

D

Data-Merge, 171
Davidow, William H., 30, 44, 92
dealer discounts, 88
deal size, average, 248
DEC, 120
decision makers, 88
deferred bonus payments, 254
deferred compensation, 181
deferred salary, 254
departure, terms, 254
dependent care reimbursement plans, 183

design methodology, 104
design reviews, 105
design superiority, 96
Digital Vision, Inc., 266
dilution, 188, 202, 226
    factor, 239
    for founder, 203
    of founders stock, 212
directing, 67–68
direct mail, 88
direct sales representative, 99
directors, 77
director's liability insurance, 80–81
disability insurance, 251
discounted cash flow analysis, 242
discount rate, 135
disposition of stock, 199
disqualifying stock disposition, 216
distinct competitive advantage, 41, 112, 168
distinctive competence, 85–86
distribution channel, 83, 99
distributor, independent, 99
diversification, of investments, 226
dividends, 194
    as form of profit sharing, 192
    declaring, 77
    payment, 129
    service, unreasonable, 194
documenting start-up meetings, 264
Donovan, Edmund, 181
down round, 204
Dralla, John, 267
due diligence, 63, 85, 168, 174, 214

E

early development, 50, 51
early stage financing, 49–51
early stage funds, 165
economy of scale, 46
Effland, Janet G., 79
Elder, William W. R., 153
elective deferral, 252
elements of success, 111
emotional distress payments, 253
employee stock purchase plan, 229–230
employees, key technical, 76
employment contract, 140, 252–253, 254, 260

engineering development activity, 72
engineers, product development, versus
    inventors, 104
entrepreneurs, would-be, 110
equitable compensation, 181–184
equity, 169, 247
    how much to give up, 136
    ownership, 26, 136, 182, 236
    paid-in, 234
    preferred, 259
    rewards, 179
equity insolvency, 57
Ernst & Young, 166
estate planner, 251
estimated future earnings, 243
executive advisory boards, 81
executive summary, 112
exercise price for options, 233
exercise schedules, 218
exit interview, 264
exit strategy, 53, 139
exit vehicle, 139
expanded voting rights, of preferred
    shareholders, 78
expansion financing, 49–51, 158
expense ratios, 120
experienced investors, 162
external specification document, 103

F

failed start-ups, founders from, 110
Fairchild Semiconductor, 266
family, 9, 28, 30, 170
fast growing. See high growth
fiduciary duty, breach, 196
Fiekowsky, Peter, 267
Field, Drew, 26
finance, 134
financial advisors, 175
financial controls, 124
financial independence, 12
financial performance, 182
financial position, 129
financial pro formas, 125
financial projections, 112, 124, 136
financials, definition of, 136
financial stages of growth, 108–109
financial statements, 80, 122

financing, 40, 49–51, 65, 156
financing rounds, 158, 169
Financing Sources Databook, The, 171
First Chicago Corporation, 245
First Chicago method, 244–245
first-stage early-development funds, 158
first-stage financing, 49–51
fitness, 264
fixed costs, 45, 131
Flexis Control Incorporated, 187
Fogelsong, Norman A., 114–115, 170
follow-on financing, 156
Ford, Henry, 46
forgivable interest loans, 197
formula value stock plan, 229
founder
    as investors, 195
    -employee, 188
    -owner, 187–188
    percentage of stock ownership, 193
    roles and responsibilities, 19
    shares, 196
founder's cash, 236
founder's stock, 188, 195, 254
    for key employees, 195
    paying, 236
    retaining after early termination, 196
    sold to distribute ownership, 196
    when available, 195
founding team, 109
four P's, of marketing, 87
fourth-stage financing, 51, 158,
franchises, 92
fringe benefits, 181, 182, 249
front-loading stock grants, 208
functional specification, 101–103
fundamental method, 245
funding sources, 97, 167
future earnings, estimated, 243
future percentage ownership, 239
future sources of capital, 228
future valuation, computing, 137
future value (FV), 134

G

Gates, Bill, 27, 29, 193, 267
Genentech, Inc., 202
general business periodicals, 93

general business plan, 139
General Electric, study on growth, 44
general partner, 163
Genμs, Inc., 112, 152
Gleba, David, 247, 248
global competition, 7
GO Corporation, 214
golden handcuffs, 254
golden parachute, 254
Golder, Stanley, 245
goodwill value, 244
grant, 187
Grossi, Brian J., 240, 241
gross margin, 98, 120
group insurance plan, 250
group term insurance conversion
    option, 250
growing market, 99, 112
growth, 43, 44, 46, 47, 92, 108
Gumpert, David E., 70

H

Hansens, Bob, 76
Harper, Jim, 187
Harvard Business Review, 181
Hayes, Ron, 266
health, 8, 264, 265
Hewlett-Packard, 7, 94, 120, 193
high gross margin, 98, 99
high growth, 9
high-growth market, 85
high return on investment, 98
Hillman Company, 266
hiring, 260
hurdle rate, investor's, 132, 135, 137

I

IBM, 7
IBM compatibility, 98
illiquid, 57
imputed interest, 197
Inc. magazine, 159, 171
incentive stock option (ISO), 215, 216, 217,
    219, 221, 253
income, 127–128
income statement, 125
income substitution, 159
income substitution business, 10, 47

incorporation service, 191
independent distributor, 99
independent sales representative, 99
individual retirement arrangement (IRA), 251
initial investment, 135
initial public offering (IPO), 50, 51 139, 191,
    192, 237, 243, 244, 247
    acquisition/buyout financing, 49–51
    market, 52–53
    MIPS Computer Systems, Inc., 23
    of the start-up, 47
    success rate, 26
inside director, 77
insolvency, 57
Institute for Electrical and Electronic
    Engineers (IEEE), 250
Institute for Exceptional Performance, 73
Institutional Venture Partners, 114–115,
    165, 170
insurance, 249–250
intellectual property asset, 227
intellectual property, in exchange for stock,
    202, 227
intellectual property protection, 261
interest, imputed, 197
interest rate, 196
internal rate of return (IRR), 135, 137,
    139, 240
internal specification, 103, 104
investing, without cash, 226
investment agreement, 175, 207
investment scenario, 240
investment. *See* stock purchase
investment term sheet, 207
investment turnover ratio, 56
investor
    amateur, 168
    determining how much to invest, 155
    expectations, 121
    hurdle rate, 132, 137
    private-individual, 160
    sophisticated, 120, 228
IPP. *See* intellectual property protection
invisible warrant, 202
issued shares, 195

J

JIAN, 130, 141
job security, 7–8

Jobs, Steve, 184
junior employee, percentage of stock
  ownership, 193
junk bond, 196

K

Kapor, Mitch, 98
Kaufman, Mike, 270
Kawasaki, Guy, 160
Kelley, Kenneth J., 114–115, 170
Kelly, Francis and Heather, 94
Keogh retirement plan, 252
key employee, 110, 225
key ratio, 54
Kurtzig, Sandra L., 84, 92, 98, 158, 164,
  174, 194

L

lawsuit, 196, 261, 264, 265
leadership challenge, 30
leadership style, 66
lead generation, 88
leveraged buyout, 51
Ley, Tony, 268
liability insurance, director's, 80–81
liability of board directors, 80
life insurance, 250
lifestyle venture, 11
limited liability company, 191
limited partner, 163
limited public offering, 162
liquidation preference, in investment
  agreements, 175
liquidity analysis, 54
liquidity date, 245
living dead, 26, 46
living documents, 103
LLC. *See* limited liability company
loan
    business, 259
    company, 198
    employee, 196
    forgivable interest, 197
    from company to purchase stock, 227
    guaranteed by entrepreneur, 259
    to company by founder, 228
    zero interest, 197

lost generation of funds, 139
Loyola University Graduate School of
  Business, 158

M

maintenance contract, 98
Malone, Michael S., 23, 26, 71
management buyout (MBO), 51, 244
management fee, 164
management, inexperienced, 70
management team, 69, 112, 159, 168,
  169, 272
    and old friends, 74
    completeness, 70
    dilution, 204
    emphasis in business plan, 112
    experience, 70
    importance, 65, 122
    inexperienced, 112
    nonperforming, 203, 207
    performing, 204
    top-performing, 73, 74
    well-balanced, 74–75
    writing the business plan, 109
manufacturing representative, 88
margin
    as a percent of total revenue, 120
    gross, 120
    high gross, 99
    net, 120
market
    competitors, 85
    development stage, 109
    exploitation, 70
    growing, 99
    high-growth, 85
    niche-oriented, 38
    opportunities, 85, 112, 172
    rapid time to, 40
    specialized, 84
market- and customer-driven technology
  fueled, 38, 93
market capitalization, 237
market gap, 88
market niche, 83, 85
market penetration, 87
market pull, 38
market research, 85

market share, 44, 87
market value, preferred stock versus
    common stock, 194
marketing, 86–87
marketing-driven, 93, 97
marketing goals, 87
marketing strategy, 87
Mclean, William, 253
Measurex Corporation, 38
medical insurance, 250
mentor, 81
methods of valuation, 237
mezzanine investment, 51
Microsoft Corporation, 29, 95, 193, 267
Minnesota Mining & Manufacturing. *See* 3M
missionary sales, 38, 91, 99, 272
money, running out, 272
money, time-value, 134
monopoly, 262
Morgan Stanley & Co., 164
Moritz, Michael, 150
mortgage, for seed funds, 259–260
multiple founders, 109

N

National Venture Capital Association
    (NVCA), 171
Nelson, Philip B., 73
net margin, 120
net present value (NPV), 135
net sales, 55
networking, 111, 172
NeXT Computer, Inc., 184
niche market, 38, 83, 84, 87
Nierenberg, Gerard I., 174
noncompete clause, 260
nondisclosure agreement, 173–175
nonemployees and stock options, 215
nonmonetary compensation, 182–185
nonperforming management team, 203, 207
nonqualified stock options (NQSO), 200,
    215, 216, 217–218, 219, 253
nonvested stock option, 254
North American Securities Administrators
    Association, 163
Northern California Venture Capital
    Association, 242
NQSOs. *See* nonqualified stock options

O

Oak Investment Management Co., 165
Oak Investment Partners, 270
obligations to employer, 260
O'Donnell, Michael, 110, 148–149
operating expense, 122, 123
operating statement, 125
operational business plan, 108
opportunity, areas, 4
opportunity, growing market, emphasis in
    business plan, 112
optimal capital structure (OCS), 134
option, 195, 213
    exercise price for, 233
    phantom-stock, 268
    practices, 214
    See also stock options
Oreffice, Paul, 37
organizing, 67–68
original equipment manufacturer (OEM), 88
Osborne, Adam, 95, 98
outplacement service, 253
outside directors, 77
outstanding shares, 195
ownership control, relinquishing, 11
ownership, future percentage, 239
ownership restricted stock, 198

P

packaging, 87, 88
Packard, David, 193
Palo Alto Software, 141
partnership, 190
patent, 96, 227, 261, 262
patent application, 262–263
patent engineering workbook, 263
payment of dividends, 129
pay to play provision, 175
penalties, in investment agreements, 175
penny stock, 193, 228
perceived differentiation of product, 95
percentage ownership, calculation, 195
percentage share ownership, 213
performance share plan, 229
performance specification, 102
performance target specification, 102
performance unit plan, 229
perquisites, 181

personal appearance, 173
personal capital, 260
personal computer, 111
personal financial risk, 265
personal-injury settlement, 253
phantom-stock option, 268
phantom-stock plan, 229
place, in marketing, 87
planning, 67–68
Plummer, James L., 50, 202, 242, 246
policy manual, 214
Pooley, James, 109, 261
Position Suitability Profile System™, 73
post-money valuation, 234, 235
Pratt, Stanley E., 50, 171
preferential tax rate, 218
preferred equity, 169, 259
preferred exit strategy, 139
preferred share, 202, 233
preferred stock, advantages, 194
preferred stockholder, 226
pre-money valuation, 234, 235, 247, 248
prenuptial agreement, 175
preparing financial projections, 124
pre-seed fund, 175
presentations to venture capitalists, 136
present value (PV), 134, 135, 243, 244
president, roles and responsibilities, 20, 21
price
    and cost, 89
    -earnings ratio (PE), 238, 241, 243
    in marketing, 87
    justified by value, 89
price wars, 88
Price Waterhouse, 200
pricing of shares, 193
private-individual investor, 160
private placement, 163
    exemption, 198
    memorandum, 140, 227
    service, 163
private stock offering, 161
problems, classic, leading to business
    failure, 119
producing your product, 99
product
    choosing a, 91, 92
    cost, 84

distribution, 87
family, 45, 46, 93, 99
identity, 83
importance, 65
marketing, 87
packaging, 88, 89
perceived differentiation, 95
positioning, 87, 94, 95
producing, 99
promotion, 89
source of idea, 47, 92–93
specialized, limitations for start-ups, 97
specification, 104
versus a business, 45, 93
versus a device, 92
product development engineers, 104
product development stage, 108
product ideas, avoiding elaborate, 97
product prototype, 104, 168, 261
profitability, early, 272
profitability, rapid, 38, 40, 119
profit and loss (P&L) statement, 125
profit margin (PM), 238, 241
profit participation, 164
promotion, 87
property in exchange for stock, 227
proprietary technology, 38, 168
proprietorship, 10
protection against ratchets, 208
proven distribution channel, 99
public offering, limited, 162
public relations, 87
public stock offering, 164
punitive financing, 204, 207

Q
QED Research, Inc., 242
quick ratio, 55–56

R
rapid profitability, 38, 40, 119
rapid prototyping methodology, 104–105
rapid time to market, 40
ratchet, 202, 204
    California, 205
    computing impact, 204–207
    example, 203
    full, 202, 205

protection against, 208
venture capital, 175, 202
ratchet down, 202, 207
ratchet factor, 205, 206
rate-of-return (ROR), 135, 244
rate on investment (ROI), 135
ratio, expense, 120
ratio, standard and expected, in business
    plan, 120–122
real property, in exchange for stock, 227–228
reasoning by extremes, 235, 247
recession, 52
Regulation A, 162
Regulation D, 198
remuneration, 179, 226
repurchase agreement, 198, 229
required return on investment, 135
research and development expense, 121
restart, 204
restricted securities, 197, 198
restricted shares of stock, 196
restricted shares, tax liability, 199
retirement plan, 251
return on equity, 241
return on investment (ROI), 132, 135, 155
    high, via rapid profitability, 98
    hurdle criterion, 136
    key to high, 119
    objectives, 112
    of company, 136–137
    of individual investor, 136, 137
    required, 135
revenue, 127–128, 246
revenue multiplier, 241, 242, 244–246
revenue per employee, 121
revenue ratio, 121
reverse-split, 193
rewarding employees, 184
Rich, Stanley R., 70
risk factors, 85
risk of forfeiture, 199
risks, accounting for, 245
Roberts, Edward B., 23, 26, 30, 31, 55, 78,
    92, 109, 158
Rock, Arthur, 69
Ronstadt, Robert, 11, 110
Ronstadt's Financials, 147, 149
Rosati, Mario, 267, 268

Rule 144, 197, 198, 199
Rule 504 private-placement
    memorandum, 161
Rule 706, 197
rule-of-thumb valuation, 136
rules of thumb for seed funding level, 157

S

salary, 179, 181, 182, 254
salary reduction arrangement, 252
sales, 86
sales and distribution, 87
sales appeal, 88
sales, missionary, 38, 272
sales per employee, 121
sales price, determining, 124
sales representative, independent, 99
San Jose Mercury News, 164, 165, 166
Schlumberger Ltd., 266
scientific advisory boards, 81
second-stage financing, 51, 158
Section 83(b), 199, 200, 218
Section 83(b) election form letter, 201
Section 125 cafeteria plans, 183
Securities and Exchange Commission, 161
securities laws, 163
seed capital, providing, 228
seed cash
    customers as source, 157
    how much needed, 156–157
    rules of thumb for amount needed, 157
seed deals, overpriced, 161
seed disbursement, 167
seed financing, 49–51
seed funds, provided by entrepreneur, 259
seed-level funding sources, in customers, 97
seed-level venture capital, 169
seed round financing, 158
seed stage, 108
seed-stage company valuation, 247
selling cycle, 88
SEP-IRA, 252
Sequoia Capital, 150
service, 87, 92, 95
severance agreement, 216
severance pay, 79, 253, 254
share ownership, percentage, 213
shareholder lawsuit, 196

shareholders, 190
shares
    pricing of, 193
    reselling, 197
    unregistered restricted, 197
shopping a business plan, 169
Shuman, Jeffrey, 110
Silicon Valley Entrepreneurs Club, 10, 76
simple cash flow statement, 129
simplified employee pension (SEP), 252
Skorina, Charles A., 74
skunk works, 105
slave wages, 183
small business, 9, 27, 188
small company offering registration
    (SCOR), 163
software companies, 166, 248
software, reusable, 105
Software Success, 8, 122
sole proprietorship, 227
solvency analysis, 54
sophisticated investor, 120, 226, 228
source code, copyrighting, 262
sources and applications of funds
    statement, 129
sources and uses of cash statement, 128–131
sources and uses of funds statement, 129
sources of funds, 129
specialized product, limitations for
    start-ups, 97
spreadsheet templates, 111
staffing, 67
stakeholders, 253
standard and expected ratios, in business
    plan, 120–122
Standard & Poor's Corporation, 237
start-up
    acquisition, 164
    capital, banks as source, 188
    definition, 50
    documenting meetings, 264
    failed, founders, 110
    financing, 49–51
    garage, 156
    joining someone else's, 110
    reasons to start, 5
    source of idea, 47
start-up round financing, 158

statement of condition, 125
statement of financial position, 125
statement of profit and loss, 125
statement of requirements document,
    99–100, 103
statistics
    unemployment, 7, 8
    vacation, 27
    venture capitalists investments,
        164–167
    working hours, 28–29
steady state stage, 109
stock, 182, 211, 212, 272
    and stock options, as bonuses, 188
    and stock options, summary table, 189
    cheap, 212
    representing ownership, 190
    restricted shares of, 196, 198
    reverse split, 193
    rule of thumb for value, 194
    selling in your company, 161
stock appreciation right (SAR), 222, 229
stock grant, 184, 208 212
stockholders, 190
stock option, 182, 211, 212, 214, 218,
    223, 254, 272
    as reward for performance, 184
    fair market value, 213
    nonvested, 254
    proportional to salary, 213
    rule of thumb for granting, 213
    vesting, 218
stock option plan, 223, 229–230
stock or stock option, as bonuses, 208
stock ownership, 187
    changes over time, 192
    founder's percentage, 193
    junior employees, 193
    percentages at various stages, 192
stock price appreciation, 164
stock purchase, 226–231
stock sales, rules against advertising, 163
stock transferability limitations, 199
strategic partner, 139
subchapter–S corporation, 191
success, elements of, 5, 20, 35, 38, 40, 66,
    69, 111
success, keys, 115

Success magazine, 159
success, measured by wealth generated, 187
Summit Ventures, 165
Sun Microsystems, 70, 120
superstars, hiring and paying, 183
sweat equity, 181, 183
Symantec, 95
systems integrators, 88

T

tax-free exchange, 227
tax-free incorporation, 227
tax liability, restricted shares, 199
tax rate, preferential, 218
Tax Reform Act of 1981, 216
Tax Reform Act of 1986, 199, 215, 218
team, management, 112
teamwork, 74
technical bankruptcy, 57
technical conferences, for identifying product
    ideas, 93
technology
    becoming too attached, 97
    focus on new, 38
    proprietary, 38
technology fuel, 94
technology leadership versus service
    leadership, 92
technology push, 37
telemarketing, 88
Tenenbaum, Marty, 269
term sheet, investment, 207
term sheet. *See also* investment agreement
third-stage financing, 51, 158
Tibbetts, Joseph Jr., 181
time analysis, 102
time-based competition, 98
time to market, 98
time-value of money, 134, 242
top down, design and development, 104
total assets, 55
trade press, image in, 81
trade secret, 96, 111, 174, 261, 263–264
trade shows, 88, 93
transferable share, 200, 202
transfer restricted stock, 197
trust fund, 251

turnaround, 204
turnover of cash ratio, 56

U

unemployment, estimates, 7–8
uniform limited offering registration
    (ULOR), 163
University of New Hampshire, 160
unreasonable dividend service, 194
unregistered restricted share, 197
Upside, 247
U.S. Department of Commerce's Patents and
    Trademark Office, 263
uses of funds, 129
U.S. Superintendent of Documents, 263

V

valuation
    calculation, 136
    future, computing, 137
    methods, 237, 243, 244, 246
    of business, optimizing, 131
    of company, 136, 233, 235,
        236, 237
    rule of thumb, 136
valuation study, 247
value-added reseller (VAR), 88
Value Line, 237
variable cost, 131
VenCap Data Quest, 171
venture capital
    availability, 3
    categories of investment, 168
    community, 169
    conflicts, 160, 168, 169
    directories, 170–171
    firms, 163
    funds, returns, 139
    investment guidelines, 71
    money tree, 164
    percentage of start-ups funded, 25
    ratchets, 175, 202
    seed financing, 240
    seed-level, 169
venture capitalist
    desired return, 41
    how to approach, 170

personal introduction, 170
versus angels, 160
Venture Capital Journal, 165, 166
Venture Economics, Inc., 165, 166, 171
VentureOne, 247, 248
vested in stock, 198
vesting, 208, 222, 227, 229, 253
    accelerated as a reward, 208
    in stock options, 213
vesting period, for stock, 200
vesting schedules, 218
vice president of engineering, 21, 72
vice president of manufacturing, 72
vice president of marketing and sales, 72
vice president of research and
    development, 21
vision, common, 75
volume discounts, 88
Von Gehr & Tan, 240
Von Gehr, George, 242
voting rights, expanded, of preferred
    shareholders, 78

W

Wall Street Journal, 139, 163, 164
Ward, John, 158

warranties, 87–88
warrants, 202, 228–229
wash out shares, 175
wealth building, 225, 228
wealth-building business, 10
wealth, limit as an employee, 240
wealth, rapid creation of, 73
weighted average, computing, 207
weighted average cost of capital (WACC), 134
weighted-average method, 204, 205
Werth, Larry, 58–60
Western Association of Venture
    Capitalists, 171
Wetzel, William E., 160
Wilson, Sonsini, Goodrich & Rosati,
    191, 267
word processing templates, 111
working capital, 55, 129

X

Xerox Corporation, 38

Z

zero interest loan, 197

About the Author

Mike Baird's vocation is founding, turning around, and restarting high-technology Silicon Valley start-ups. He is currently on a turnaround team as vice president of engineering of the $15 million venture capital-backed start-up Computer Aided Service, Inc., of San Jose, CA. Previously, he was the vice president of marketing, and earlier the vice president of engineering, during the turnaround of the now very successful venture capital-backed Flexis Control, Inc., start-up in Hayward, CA. Before that, he was the founder of Digital Vision, Inc. Baird has 20 years of technology and business management experience. Positions he has held include manager of several premier computer science research and development laboratories, product design manager for a *Fortune* 100 company, business consultant to 15 high-tech start-up companies, and due diligence consultant for various investors and underwriters. He has earned an M.S. and a Ph.D. in Information and Computer Science from Georgia Tech, an undergraduate degree in Industrial Engineering from the GMI Engineering and Management Institute, and an MBA from the University of Phoenix. He has published several dozen papers, written commercial copy, and delivered more than 100 presentations and lectures to domestic and international symposia and universities.

Professional Publications, Inc. ▪ Belmont, CA